Studies in Medieval Mysticism

Volume 4

THE ENGLISH PROSE TREATISES OF RICHARD ROLLE

Richard Rolle, the 'hermit of Hampole', wrote an extensive body of religious literature that was widely disseminated in late medieval England; but although many of his works have received substantial editorial attention, they have as yet attracted only limited detailed critical analysis, with scholarship largely focused on establishing facts about his life and striking character. This study aims to correct this imbalance by re-examining his English prose works – *Ego Dormio*, *The Commandment* and *The Form of Living* – in terms of their literary form, content and appeal rather than their relationship to Rolle's biography. The author argues that in these devotional works (which appealed to a broad readership in late medieval England) Rolle successfully refines traditional affective strategies to develop an implied reader-identity, the individual soul seeking the love of God, which empowers each and every reader in his or her own spiritual journey.

Dr CLAIRE ELIZABETH MCILROY teaches in the Faculty of Arts, Humanities and Social Sciences at the University of Western Australia.

Studies in Medieval Mysticism

ISSN 1465–5683

GENERAL EDITORS
Anne Clark Bartlett
Rosalynn Voaden

Studies in Medieval Mysticism offers a forum for works exploring the textures and traditions of western European mystical and visionary literature, from late Antiquity to the Reformation including both well- and lesser-known mystics and their texts. The series particularly welcomes publications which combine textual and manuscript study with current critical theories, to offer innovative approaches to medieval mystical literature.

Proposals or queries may be sent directly to the editors or publisher at the addresses given below; all submissions will recieve prompt and informed consideration.

Professor Anne Clark Bartlett, Department of English, DePaul University, 802 West Belden Avenue, Chicago, IL 60614–3214, USA

Professor Rosalynn Voaden, Department of English, Arizona State University, PO Box 870302, Tempe, AZ 85287–0302, USA

Caroline Palmer, Boydell & Brewer Limited, PO Box 9, Woodbridge, Suffolk, IP12 3DF, UK

THE ENGLISH PROSE TREATISES OF RICHARD ROLLE

Claire Elizabeth McIlroy

D. S. BREWER

First published 2004
D. S. Brewer, Cambridge

ISBN 1 84384 003 0

The Boydell Press is an imprint of Boydell & Brewer Ltd
PO Box 9, Woodbridge, Suffolk IP12 3DF, UK
and of Boydell & Brewer Inc.
PO Box 41026, Rochester, NY 14604–4126, USA
website: www.boydellandbrewer.com

A catalogue record for this book is available
from the British Library

Library of Congress Cataloging-in-Publication Data
McIlroy, Claire Elizabeth, 1970–
  The English prose treatises of Richard Rolle / Claire Elizabeth McIlroy.
    p. cm. – (Studies in medieval mysticism, ISSN 1465–5683 ; v. 4)
Includes bibliographical references (p.) and index.
  ISBN 1–84384–003–0 (Hardback : alk. paper)
1. Rolle, Richard, of Hampole, 1290?–1349 – Prose.   2. Christianity and
literature – England – History – To 1500.   3. Christian literature, English
(Middle) – History and criticism.   4. Mysticism – England – History –
Middle Ages, 600–1500.   5. English language – Middle English, 1100–1500
– Style.   6. Mysticism in literature.   I. Title. II. Series.
  PR2136.M35 2004
  248 – dc22   2003017981

This publication is printed on acid-free paper

Printed in Great Britain by
Antony Rowe Ltd, Chippenham, Wiltshire

CONTENTS

The author and publisher acknowledge the generous support of the Australian Academy of Humanities in providing a subsidy towards costs of publication.

ACKNOWLEDGEMENTS

I would like to begin these acknowledgements by expressing my sincere gratitude to the two scholars who first sparked my interest in medieval mysticism,
Andrew Lynch and Philippa Maddern of the University of Western Australia.
I would like to thank Andrew Lynch in particular firstly for introducing me to
the English writings of Richard Rolle and secondly for his unfailing patience,
wisdom and kindness throughout the long process of defining, constructing
and then refining my exploration of Rolle's English writings. I would also like
to acknowledge the support and the encouragement I have received from
other colleagues and friends at the University of Western Australia especially
Tony Barker, Toby Burrows, Philippa Christmass, Ernie Jones and Helen Vella
Bonavita.

To my family, especially my parents George and Mary Hilton, I owe a great
debt of gratitude for always believing in me and encouraging me to continue
with the labour of love that is the study of medieval literature and history.
Finally, I wish to thank my husband Andrew McIlroy for his inexhaustible
love and support, and for cheerfully sharing me with another man for so
many years without a hint of jealousy.

PREFACE

The Yorkshire hermit Richard Rolle of Hampole (c. 1290–1349) wrote an extensive body of religious literature that was widely disseminated in late medieval England. Today, while many of his works have received substantial editorial attention they have as yet attracted only limited detailed critical analysis. Instead, Rolle scholarship to date has been largely focused on explicating his popular reputation and offering psychological profiles of his striking personality. These are mainly drawn from autobiographical extracts in his Latin writings, and details of his life found in the hagio-biography composed in anticipation of his canonisation. Rolle's writings have thus been subsumed within a scholarship preoccupied with establishing facts about his life and character. His English works in particular, even though much of his modern fame rests with his status as a "Middle English Mystic", have received little critical attention due to their lack of personal content.

My book therefore aims to revisit the English prose works of this prolific writer in terms of their literary form, content and appeal rather than their relationship to Rolle's biography. In the introductory sections I look closely at what I consider to have been the major critical preoccupations with his biography so far: the construction of his own authority, the appraisal of his authenticity as a mystic, and the gendering of his English writings as male-authored works for a specifically female audience. In turn, Rolle's construction of audience in his English works is examined in relation to the tradition of affectivity, the rise of the devotional movement in the fourteenth century, and the development of reader-engaging strategies in late medieval devotional literature. I then present what is in effect the first detailed literary study of Rolle's three English prose treatises – *Ego Dormio*, *The Commandment* and *The Form of Living*. Examining these texts as individual reader-centred works of devotion, I suggest that they were favourably responded to by a broad readership in late medieval England because their implicit address to the reader avoids gender and socio-religious specificity. Rolle, I believe, successfully refines traditional affective strategies in his English works to develop an implied reader-identity, the individual soul seeking the love of God, which empowers every reader in his or her own spiritual journey.

The body of this work focuses on each individual text in the (presumed) chronological order of composition. *Ego Dormio*, Rolle's first English prose treatise, is discussed in terms of how the author engages the reader in an intimate journey towards the love of God, thus setting the tone for Rolle's vernacular corpus. To dispel the myth that it is merely an impassioned "epistle" written to a single female recipient, I have looked at *Ego Dormio* as a complex web of reader-writer relationships, carefully developed through a discourse of intimacy, which reveals the beginning of Rolle's exploitation of the individualisation of the reading experience. The fourth chapter discusses the short, didactic text *The Commandment* where it is suggested that although the practical instruction offered in *The Commandment* shows the influence of monastic devotion and seems uncharacteristically impersonal and distant, Rolle's careful construction of a specific reader-writer relationship, which both instructs and appeals to the reader's *affectus* within the constraints of homiletic discourse, permits the subtle emergence of the more personal and affective qualities found in Rolle's other vernacular treatises and is equally inviting to a wide variety of medieval readers. Finally, I discuss *The Form of Living*, which is the mostly widely read of Rolle's vernacular treatises, and, arguably, the most refined. This chapter outlines the development of a discourse of friendship in this work that invites the reader to adopt the subject position of Rolle's friend and disciple Margaret Kirkeby, and join with his authorial self in spiritual bliss in the contemplative life. It is suggested that the affectivity of Rolle's text enables it to address the work beyond the initial recipient. By way of subtle paths and directions, the implied reader is invited to take Margaret's place and become the individual addressee. Indeed, in each of Rolle's English prose treatises, the subtlety with which his discourse avoids gender-specificity and the creation in the text of an implied identity for the reader, the individual soul who seeks the love of God, is potentially inviting to a wide variety of medieval readers seeking guidance in their spiritual lives.

1

Richard Rolle, English Writer

Rolle's date, his style and his popularity give him a supreme place in the history of English prose. In English or in Latin he was, during the latter half of the fourteenth century and the whole of the fifteenth, probably the most widely read in England of all English writers.[1]

No literary study of Rolle has ever been written . . . moreover, except in the field of editing, Rolle scholarship has advanced with disappointing sluggishness.[2]

RICHARD ROLLE produced one of the most extensive bodies of religious literature of the early fourteenth century; the bulk of this literature is exegetical, but some works are based on Rolle's own mystical experiences, and others can be considered as didactic works, composed specifically with a view to exhorting others to turn to the love of God. Rolle wrote in both English and Latin, more prolifically in the latter, but his works in both languages were widely disseminated throughout the fourteenth and fifteenth centuries; this is shown by the large number of surviving manuscripts of his Latin and English writings. Genuine works by Rolle exist in over five hundred extant manuscripts from this period, more than fifty of which contain his English writings, making him a more widely disseminated author than even the celebrated later fourteenth-century English writer Geoffrey Chaucer.[3] It has been noted that in the fifteenth century alone a great many people must have dedicated their time to copying, translating and disseminating Rolle's output; presumably many more spent at least as much time reading him.[4] Indeed, if the volume of surviving manuscripts is any indication of contemporary popularity Richard

---

1 R. W. Chambers, "On the Continuity of English Prose from Alfred to More and His School". *Nicholas Harpsfield's Life and Death of Sir Thomas More*. Eds. E. V. Hitchcock and R. W. Chambers (London, 1932), ci.
2 N. Watson, *Richard Rolle and the Invention of Authority* (Cambridge, 1991), xi.
3 See M. A. Knowlton, *The Influence of Richard Rolle and Julian of Norwich on the Middle English Lyric* (The Hague, 1973), 12. Knowlton's investigation into medieval wills and documents bearing the ownership of books shows "a dozen owners of manuscripts of Rolle for one or two of *The Canterbury Tales*".
4 N. Watson, "Richard Rolle as Elitist and Populist: The Case of *Judica Me*". *De Cella in Seculum: Religious and Secular Life and Devotion in Late Medieval England*. Ed. M. G. Sargent (Cambridge, 1989), 124.

Rolle should be regarded, as R. W. Chambers suggests, as one of the most widely read English writers in fourteenth- and fifteenth-century England.

Today, Richard Rolle's influence on what is now described as the fourteenth-century English mystical tradition is well known and his writings have received considerable editorial attention. Many of his "popular"[5] Latin works, those widely disseminated in the fourteenth and fifteenth centuries such as *Incendium Amoris*, *Expositio Super Novem Lectiones Mortuorum* and *Emendatio Vitae*, are available to the modern reader in critical editions.[6] These Latin works have, for the most part, received modern critical attention both because they locate Rolle as a key figure in the English mystical tradition and because within them Rolle offers a wealth of autobiographical material which has provided an insight into his life as a fourteenth-century hermit and a profile of what is often described as his striking personality.[7] The autobiographical data provided by Rolle in his own works is supplemented by a fourteenth-century Latin *vita* which forms part of a work known as the *Officium et Miracula of Richard Rolle of Hampole*, composed by the nuns of Hampole in anticipation of his canonisation.[8] Such a profusion of biographical information, rare in connection with any fourteenth-century writer, has in many ways led to a modern preoccupation with establishing truths about Rolle's life and character. In short, scholarly interest in Rolle seems to have been aroused because: he is an English writer who produced a substantial body of literature that was

---

5   For a discussion of Rolle as a "popular" Latin writer in the medieval period see N. Watson, "Richard Rolle as Elitist and Popularist". Watson argues that there seems to have been a tension between one perception of Rolle as a "popular" writer and another of him as a "specialist" or "difficult" one. He concludes that within Rolle's Latin works themselves both "elitist" and "popularist" elements are present and that they are not altogether divergent, a feature which is possibly responsible for the wide dissemination of his writings.

6   M. Deanesly, ed. *The Incendium Amoris of Richard Rolle of Hampole* (Manchester, 1915) – hereafter cited as *Incendium Amoris*; M. Moyes, ed. *Richard Rolle's Expositio super Novem Lectiones Mortuorum: An Introduction and Contribution Towards a Critical Edition*. 2 vols. (Salzburg, 1988) – hereafter cited as *Richard Rolle's Expositio*; N. Watson, *Richard Rolle's Emendatio vitae; Orationes ad honorem nominis Ihesu edited from Cambridge University Library MSS. Dd.v.64 and Kk.vi.20* (Toronto, 1995). Rolle's *Incendium Amoris* has been translated into modern English on a number of occasions, most notably by Clifton Wolters in *Richard Rolle: The Fire of Love* (London, 1972). All translations of *Incendium Amoris* in this work are taken from this edition which is hereafter cited as *The Fire of Love*.

7   N. Watson, *Invention of Authority*, 34.

8   This document survives in three manuscripts, and of these only two contain the *Miracula*: Bodleian Library e Museo MS 193, Lincoln Cathedral MS C. 5. 2. and British Museum, Cotton Tiberias MS A. XV. I have used the edition by R. M. Woolley, *The Officium et Miracula of Richard Rolle of Hampole* (London, 1919) hereafter cited as *Officium et Miracula*. All translations are taken from F. M. M. Comper, *The Life of Richard Rolle, Together With an Edition of his English Lyrics* (London, 1928), 301–314 – hereafter cited as *The Life of Richard Rolle*.

widely read in the fourteenth and fifteenth centuries; he is a medieval English figure about whose life we have an unusual amount of (not always reliable) autobiographical and biographical information; and he is an English mystic in the English mystical tradition – a Yorkshire hermit writing about his own experiences as a contemplative in a period of English history that is now considered as dominated by interest in the interior spiritual life of the self and in the responsibilities of the individual.[9]

Once it was discovered that the name Richard Rolle was prominent in manuscripts containing vernacular devotional material, numerous vernacular works connected with him began to be edited by nineteenth-century scholars.[10] The rediscovery, to borrow the term first used by Malcolm Moyes, of the writings of Richard Rolle, in the latter part of the nineteenth century, occurred at a time of great resurgence in interest among scholars in the manuscripts of English writers from the medieval period. The foremost objects of this interest were writings by English authors in the vernacular. Manuscripts from the fourteenth and fifteenth centuries, as well as from earlier periods, long neglected in ancient libraries, were newly edited and presented to the modern reader as examples of the Middle English period in the history of English literature. Religious works were not as prominent as romance literature and secular poetry but a few notable works were taken up by editorial scholars.[11] But much of the early scholarly attention given to Rolle's vernac-

---

9 See J. Coleman, *English Literature in History, 1350–1400* (London, 1981), esp. 13–17. Coleman suggests that much fourteenth-century English literature focused on individual responsibility regarding salvation and institutional reform. She further argues that the increasing emphasis on private responsibility to bring the practice of Christian ethics more in line with ideals is also reflected in the increasing emphasis placed on authorial responsibility.

10 The first of these, a collection of several imperfect renderings of short prose treatises found in the Thornton Manuscript (now Lincoln Cathedral MS 91), was issued by the Reverend G. G. Perry in 1866 for the Early English Text Society. H. R. Bramley published an edition of Rolle's *English Psalter* in 1884 which remains today the only edition of that work. Bramley's work was closely followed by the Reverend R. Harvey's 1896 edition of the fifteenth-century vernacular translations of the *Incendium Amoris* and *Emendatio Vitae* by the Carmelite Richard Misyn, also for the Early English Text Society. See G. G. Perry, ed. *English Prose Treatises of Richard Rolle of Hampole* (London, 1866); R. Misyn, trans. *The Fire of Love and the Mending of Life or the Rule of Living of Richard Rolle*. Ed. R. Harvey (London, 1896); H. R. Bramley ed. *English Psalter. The Psalter Psalms of David and Certain Canticles, with a Translation and Exposition in English by Richard Rolle of Hampole* (Oxford, 1884).

11 The first ten years of the Early English Text Society produced editions of a number of Middle English religious works which included such texts as *Hali 'Meiðhad*, Dan Michel's *Ayenbite of Inwit*, and John Myrk's *Instructions for Parish Priests*. Prominent nineteenth-century editors such as Frederick Furnivall, James Morton and Frederic Madden also presented Middle English religious texts to the modern reader, newly edited from manuscript and early printed sources. See M. Moyes, *Richard Rolle's Expositio*, I, 1; James Morton, ed. *The Ancren Riwle; A Treatise on the Rules and Duties of Monastic Life, Edited and Translated from a Semi-Saxon MS of the Thirteenth Century*

ular works was limited to providing editions that aimed to display the English writer writing in the mother-tongue allowing him to take his place in the history of English prose without actually looking too closely at the works themselves.[12] Since the nineteenth century Rolle scholarship has been dominated by three main emphases – the preoccupation with his biography and his self-styled *auctoritas*, his status as a mystic, and his role as a friend and adviser of women. This preoccupation points to the contradictory nature of Rolle scholarship to date – in that although much of his modern fame as a four-teenth-century writer rests with his vernacular writings and his place in the history of English prose, scholarly interest has been in Rolle's biography as gleaned from his Latin works and from the Latin *Officium*. Consequently, although Rolle's English writings, most notably the three prose works *Ego Dormio*, *The Commandment* and *The Form of Living*, have received substantial editorial attention, they have as yet attracted only limited detailed critical analysis of their style, form and content because the emphasis on the figure of Rolle has continued in many modern views of his writings. In turn, interest in the ideological and theoretical structures underlying vernacular texts has only recently begun to allow works such as Rolle's to be considered literature, drawing the modern reader's attention away from the authorial and towards the literary.[13]

Rolle's writings in English certainly pose an interesting conundrum for modern scholars. In comparison to the large body of works he wrote in Latin,

(London, 1852); F. J. Furnivall, *Roberd of Brunnè's Handlyng synne (written A. D. 1303); with the French treatise on which it is founded, Le manuel des pechiez, by William of Wadington. Now first printed from mss. in the British-museum and Bodleian libraries* (London, 1862); F. Madden, *The New Testament in English according to the version by John Wycliffe about A. D. 1380, and revised by John Purvey, about A. D. 1388* (Oxford, 1879). The Early English Text Society began publication in 1864 and published a separate "blurb" in pamphlet form in which the editor, F. J. Furnivall, wrote: "This Society has been formed to print all that is most valuable of the yet unprinted manuscripts in English, and also to re-edit and reprint all that is most valuable in printed English books." See F. J. Furnivall, ed. *Publications: No. 1 – Original Series*. Early English Text Society (os) 1 (London, 1864).

12 See especially the German philologist Carl Horstmann in *Yorkshire Writers: Richard Rolle of Hampole, an English Father of the Church, and His Followers* (London, 1895–1896). In his extremely comprehensive, albeit eclectic, survey of vernacular prose and poetry attributed to Rolle, and other religious writers of fourteenth century Yorkshire, Horstmann was a pioneer in expressing the notion of Rolle as a medieval mystic and his volumes brought Rolle into notice at a time when mysticism was again beginning to be popular among readers of devotional texts. Hope Emily Allen later established a more accurate canon of Rolle's English works but even in her introduction of the English writings the focus is largely centred on providing biographical detail about the author. See H. E. Allen, *Writings Ascribed to Richard Rolle, Hermit of Hampole, and Materials for his Biography* (New York, 1927).

13 J. Wogan-Browne, N. Watson, A. Taylor and R. Evans eds. *The Idea of the Vernacular: An Anthology of Middle English Literary Theory 1280–1520* (Exeter, 1999), xv.

his vernacular works are relatively few in number and much shorter in length. In English Rolle composed the first vernacular translation of the Psalms of David, known as the *English Psalter*, three short prose works explicitly written for women religious, *Ego Dormio*, *The Commandment* and *The Form of Living* – as well as two prose Passion meditations and a number of religious lyrics. Yet, despite their comprising only a fraction of his substantial corpus it is these English works that have earned him his modern fame by offering him a place as one of the five "Middle English Mystics" in company with Walter Hilton, the anonymous author of *The Cloud of Unknowing*, Julian of Norwich and Margery Kempe. The vernacular prose works composed by this group are now considered as fundamental texts in the development of an English mystical literary tradition in the fourteenth century and are also the central works around which theories of the continuity of Middle English prose have been developed.[14] And despite the fact that their works generally concern a specialised religious vocation, the contemplative life, these English writers, in particular Rolle and Hilton,[15] are also frequently linked to the rise of vernacular devotional literature that attracted the growing literate lay audience in fourteenth- and fifteenth-century England.[16]

The fourteenth century itself has been described as the century during which, throughout Western Europe at least, the vernacular language was beginning to assert itself as the language of religious literature against Latin.[17] The major developments in the production of religious books in the period 1375 to 1475 appeared to be direct responses to, and catalysts of, the rapidly developing interest in and market for vernacular guides for godliness.[18]

---

14 A. K. Warren, *Anchorites and Their Patrons in Medieval England* (Berkeley, 1985), 103. Warren notes that as anchoritic "rules" Hilton's *Scale of Perfection* and Rolle's *The Form of Living* support theories for the continuity of a Middle English prose tradition that stems from the thirteenth century. See also H. E. Allen, *Writings Ascribed*, 430 and 517.

15 It is unlikely that Margery Kempe and Julian of Norwich were "widely read" authors like Rolle and Hilton. Kempe's book exists in a single manuscript copy and the long and short versions of Julian's revelations are extant in only four manuscript copies. *The Cloud of Unknowing* itself, as I discuss later, successfully discouraged readers who were not members of the spiritual elite but there are still many extant copies.

16 Elizabeth Robertson, assessing the circumstances affecting the production of English prose from the eleventh century onwards, writes: "The character of the extant works suggests that they were intended for lay audiences who had little schooling, and often for women. An audience that was relatively insignificant before the Conquest – those unlearned in Latin – became afterward the primary audience for English literature. This uneducated audience plays a crucial role in both the survival and the development of English prose". E. Robertson, *Early English Devotional Prose and the Female Audience* (Knoxville, 1990), 2.

17 R. M. Wilson, "Three Middle English Mystics". *Essays & Studies* 9 (1956), 88.

18 V. Gillespie, "Vernacular Books of Religion". *Book Production and Publishing in Britain, 1375–1475*. Eds. J. Griffiths and D. Pearsall (Cambridge, 1989), 317.

Citing W. A. Pantin, Anne Clark Bartlett notes that the ecclesiastical reforms of the thirteenth century mandated the production of pastoral manuals for parish priests and vernacular instructional treatises for both clerical and lay readers.[19] She argues that the subsequent proliferation of contemplative and mystical texts in the fourteenth and fifteenth centuries indicates that later generations of readers were unsatisfied with the basic teachings provided by primers and catechisms, or by tracts on the Ten Commandments and on confession. Records of book ownership, bequests, and patronage show that progressively more literate and sophisticated English female and lay audiences wanted guidance in an affective, even ecstatic, piety – a type of devotion that had formerly been available only to a demographically narrower group of readers. There is evidence to suggest that many medieval writers wrote on command and that many devotional works produced for lay readers were often translated or revised and copied by a patron's religious adviser, who would supervise the use of the book as well as its production.[20] Vernacular mystical writings, which were primarily intended for the use of unlearned clerics and religious, including nuns and anchoresses, were also read by devout lay people.[21] In this context, even works addressed exclusively to recluses, such as Walter Hilton's *Scale of Perfection*, achieved a wide readership.[22]

Medieval English taste for mystical literature may be represented at its most ambitious by the compendium in British Library, Additional MS 37790 (the Amherst manuscript) which draws together the legacy of Rolle's teachings on contemplation, some synthesis in the *Via ad Contemplationem* of teaching from Hilton and the *Cloud*-author's corpus, and Julian's "showings".[23] Lay readers, it seems, increasingly read eremitic literature, drawing from these treatises their own fulfillment according to the dimensions of their own interests and capabilities.[24] The proliferation of later Middle English devotional, sermon and mystical texts addressed to, or re-worked to address,

---

[19] A. Clark Bartlett, *Male Authors, Female Readers: Representation and Subjectivity in Middle English Devotional Literature* (Ithaca and London, 1995), 117. See also W. A. Pantin, *The English Church in the Fourteenth Century* (Cambridge, 1955), 190–191.

[20] J. Wogan-Browne et al., *The Idea of the Vernacular*, 13.

[21] W. A. Pantin, *The English Church*, 253.

[22] V. Gillespie, "Vernacular Books of Religion", 322.

[23] See B. Windeatt, *English Mystics of the Middle Ages* (Cambridge, 1994), 13 and n. 26, 275. The manuscript includes Misyn's Englishings of Rolle's *Emendatio Vitae* and *Incendium Amoris*; extracts from Rolle's *The Form of Living* arranged as a piece *De triplici genere amoris spiritualis*; extracts from *The Form of Living* (as *Tractatus de diligendo Deo*), and *Ego Dormio*; the only extant copies of the shorter version of Julian of Norwich's *Revelations* and *The Treatise of Perfection of the Sons of God*; *The Mirrour of Simple Souls*; an extract from the English version of Henry Suso's *Horologium Sapientiae*; a brief piece from an English version of the *Revelations* of St. Bridget of Sweden, together with some other brief pieces.

[24] A. K. Warren, *Anchorites and Their Patrons*, 122.

"good men and women . . ." also suggests that many authors and scribes further recognised the heterogeneity of their audience and began to address them accordingly.[25] The author of the early fourteenth-century *Northern Homily Cycle* claims to use English in order to make God's gifts accessible to "alle".[26] *The Abbey of the Holy Ghost*, a quasi-mystical work of religious instruction that addresses sympathetically a presumed audience of devout lay readers:

> A dere brethir and systirs, I see þat many walde be in religyone bot þay may noghte . . . and for-thi I make here a buke of the religeon of þe heart, that es, of þe abbaye of the holy goste, that all tho þat ne may noght be bodyly in religyone, þat may be gostely.[27]

Throughout this period, not only was primarily monastic and clerical material being made available to the laity, but texts written for the particular circumstances of female religious (which had achieved, somewhat earlier, extension of their audience into ranks of pious and noble gentlewomen) were being addressed to or compiled for laymen.[28] The vernacular writings Rolle composed for the initial edification of women religious, particularly his *English Psalter* and the three prose works, are an example of such a trend, for they survive in a number of manuscripts and compilations that show evidence of early lay ownership.[29] Rolle's English writings can duly be located in the context of an increasingly wide audience who demanded vernacular devotional literature. Yet, the evidence of wide readership does not

---

25 For examples see *John Myrk's Festial*. Ed. Theodor Erbe (New York, 1973). Almost every one of the sermons recorded in this collection begins by addressing the audience as "Good men and women . . . " See also A. Clark Bartlett, *Male Authors, Female Readers*, 119.

26 J. Wogan-Browne et al., *The Idea of the Vernacular*, 117. The authors note, however, that while the author of the *Northern Homily Cycle* presents a case for freeing God's word from exclusive clerical stewardship in order to give laypeople access to the Scriptures, the prologue does not advocate that laymen read for themselves.

27 *The Abbey of the Holy Ghost* cited in C. Horstmann, *Yorkshire Writers*, I, 321. *The Abbey of the Holy Ghost* is a translation of a French prose tract, *Abbaye du Saint Espirit*, extant in over twenty manuscripts and three early prints. The earliest version is in the Vernon manuscript, late fourteenth-century.

28 V. Gillespie, " 'Lukynge in haly bukes': *Lectio* in some Late Medieval Miscellanies". *Analecta Carthusiana* 106 (1984), 17.

29 See J. Hughes, *Pastors and Visionaries: Religion and Secular Life in Late-Medieval Yorkshire* (Woodbridge, 1988), 90–94. Hughes gives a comprehensive survey of the circulation of Rolle's works in the fourteenth and fifteenth centuries, especially in the diocese of York, claiming that many manuscripts of Rolle's *English Psalter* appear to have been owned or used by lay readers: Bodleian Library MS 953, Bodleian Library Tanner MS I, Bodleian Library Hutton MS 12 and Bodleian Library Laud. Misc. MS 448. The Longleat manuscript (Longleat MS 29) which contains all Rolle's English works also shows evidence of fifteenth-century lay ownership. See S. Ogilvie-Thomson, *Richard Rolle: Prose and Verse* (Oxford, 1988), xvii–xxi.

adequately account for the appeal of these works to medieval readers. We need to ask why this occurred.

The task of examining why Rolle's vernacular texts attracted a wide readership in the fourteenth and fifteenth centuries has been to some extent overshadowed by heavy interest in the historical figure of Rolle himself, and his contemporary reputation as a saint, a holy hermit and an *auctor*. A respected holy man during his lifetime, Rolle's medieval reputation as a saint began in earnest after his death. As tales of Rolle's exemplary life began to spread miracles were reported at the site of his tomb, and a cult emerged which honoured the sanctity of his eremitic life and the significance of his teachings. It was most likely in response to this interest in Rolle that the nuns of Hampole, sometime in the 1380s, were prompted to compile an *Officium et Miracula* in anticipation of his canonisation. The *Officium* details Rolle's life from his birth "in uilla de Thornton Eboracensis diocesis" to his death at Hampole in 1349.[30] Composed as nine lessons the document describes significant episodes in Rolle's life such as his placement at Oxford under the patronage of Thomas Neville, Archdeacon of Durham, his return to Yorkshire and conversion to the eremitic life, his accommodation by wealthy gentry patrons such as the Dalton family, and his lifelong spiritual trials and tribulations. It also provides details of miraculous events which were reported to have occurred both during his lifetime and at the site of his tomb. Of course, the credibility of the information supplied by the *Officium* is doubtful because it is an entirely hagiographical work.[31]

Since the purpose of the *Officium* is centred around elevating Rolle to the status of saint, the sanctity of his life and the holiness of his character are emphasised. His career as a writer is barely commented upon and any writings by him are referred to and quoted from only as a useful medium through which to discuss his piety and his spiritual development. The *Incendium Amoris*, described in this work as Rolle's first book, is the only one of Rolle's works that is named in the *Officium*. It is quoted only for its autobiographical content, such as the inclusion of the following passage where Rolle first recounts his experience of inner fire:

In libro siquidem [Incendium Amoris] predicto sic ait. admirabar amplius quam enuncio. quando sentiui cor meum primitus incalescere. et uere non ymaginarie. set quasi sensibili igne estuare.

---

[30] Numerous manuscripts fix the date of Rolle's death as occurring at Michelmas, September 30, 1349.

[31] The details of Rolle's life are depicted in the tradition of a saint's legend – a narrative with the double purpose of honouring the saint and instructing the audience in the significance of the saint for Christian faith. See T. Wolpers, *Die Englischen Heiligenlegenden des Mittelalters* (Tübingen, 1964) cited in *A Manual of the Writings in Middle English, 1050–1500*. Ed. A. E. Hartung (New Haven, 1970), Vol. 2, 410–411.

[For in the aforesaid book [The Fire of Love] he thus speaks: "I marvelled more than I can say when I first felt my heart grow warm and burn, truly, not in imagination but as it were with sensible fire".][32]

The inclusion of autobiographical passages such as this one in a hagiographical document allows the authors of the *Officium* to display their would-be saint celebrating his own mystical experience. In the *Officium*, Rolle's own utterance of his heavenly gifts in his Latin works is used as evidence of his sanctity and accordingly serves to validate the quest for his canonisation. Probably due to their lack of autobiographical material Rolle's English writings are not mentioned at all; only his personal friendship with, and miraculous healing of, his disciple Margaret Kirkeby are discussed in any detail; the works he supposedly composed specifically for her, the *English Psalter* and *The Form of Living*, are not remarked upon.[33]

It is the sixth lesson of the *Officium* alone that refers specifically to Rolle's career as a writer:

Admirande autem et utiles nimis erant huius occupaciones. in sanctis exhortacionibus quibus quam plurimos conuersit ad deum. in scriptis eciam suis mellifluis et tractatibus ac libellis ad edificacionem proximorum compositis que omnia in cordibus deuotorum dulcissimam resonent armoniam.

[Yet wonderful and beyond measure useful was the work of this saintly man in holy exhortations, whereby he converted many to God, and in his sweet writings, both treatises and little books composed for the edification of his neighbours, which all sound like sweetest music in the hearts of the devout.][34]

Even this acknowledgement of Rolle's skill as a writer of exhortatory devotional works functions primarily as an introductory passage to another anecdote regarding his blessedness. In this lesson Rolle is interrupted in his writing by the "domina domus" and a large company who ask him for some edifying words.[35] He obliges them on this account without ceasing in his writing on an entirely different subject which leads us to conclude that his writings are mentioned here only because they represent his divine gifts and are therefore useful in furthering the quest for his canonisation. For the compilers of the *Officium* the sanctity of Rolle's life validates his cult and the quest for his canonisation, not his works.

---

32 *Officium et Miracula*, 31; *The Life of Richard Rolle*, 304.
33 *Officium et Miracula*, 37–41; *The Life of Richard Rolle*, 306–308. These passages, and Rolle's relationship with Margaret Kirkeby, are discussed in detail in Chapter Five with particular reference to *The Form of Living*.
34 *Officium et Miracula*, 32; *The Life of Richard Rolle*, 304.
35 This is presumably Lady Dalton and her guests when Rolle was in residence in the Dalton house. See H. E. Allen, *Writings Ascribed*, 58.

Despite the efforts of the nuns of Hampole Rolle's canonisation was never realised but this did not appear to deter medieval scribes from depicting him as a holy author. His reputation as a saint, or at least as a holy hermit, is reflected in many of the rubrics that accompany fourteenth- and fifteenth-century manuscript copies of his works which often refer to him as "venerabilis" and "beatus". In most manuscripts he is rarely referred to as Richard Rolle and is instead referred to as simply "Richard the Hermit". The surname Rolle, which does appear in the *Officium*, is supplied only by eight manuscripts, one early edition and one will.[36] The title "Richard the Hermit" is, of course, used to highlight his eremitic vocation, a vocation that implies renunciation of worldly pleasures in favour of solitary devotion to God. Giving Rolle such a title empowers both his lifestyle and his character and presumably by association, his texts. The emphasis placed on sanctioning Rolle's vocation and his character reflects what Alistair Minnis argues is late-medieval concern for the integrity of the individual *auctor*, a need to validate texts in terms of the author as the cause of the text.[37] And as Nicholas Watson notes "the manuscripts leave the impression that affection and respect for Rolle as an individual and as a writer was at least as important a reason for the wide circulation he achieved as was the practical usefulness of what he wrote".[38] Even in later editions of Rolle's works it is his reputation as a man of holy character that is stressed by scribes in favour of commenting on the work at hand. An example of this is the *Remedy against the Troubles of Temptations* where, in both the printed editions by Wynkyn de Worde and in the manuscripts, a preface to an abridged version of *The Form of Living* sanctions the work by describing Rolle as "the dyscrete and vertuous Richard hampole".[39] It would appear that for medieval scribes of Rolle's works his reputation as a saint, or at least as a holy hermit, authorised the man more than the writings, and the writings more than their content.

Rolle's popular reputation as an authority is certainly attested by the amount of material that was falsely ascribed to him throughout the medieval period.[40] Numerous works in both Latin and English were wrongly ascribed

---

36 H. E. Allen, *Writings Ascribed*, 432. The manuscripts are Bodleian Library Oxford MS 66; British Museum e Museo MS 232; Bodleian Library Oxford, Rawlinson A. MS 389; University College Oxford MS 56; Cambridge University, Additional MS 3042; Trinity College Dublin MS 154; Longleat MS 32; Douai MS 396. The name Rolle is thought to be Norman in origin and tracing Rolle's ancestry has been difficult due to the rarity of the name in records from medieval Yorkshire.

37 A. J. Minnis, *Medieval Theory of Authorship: Scholastic Literary Attitudes in the Later Middle Ages* (Aldershot, 1988), 117.

38 N. Watson, "Richard Rolle as Elitist and Popularist", 123.

39 *Remedy against the Troubles of Temptations* cited in H. E. Allen, *Writings Ascribed*, 263. Allen does not provide any further bibliographical information for this quotation.

40 For a comprehensive survey of works falsely ascribed to Rolle see H. E. Allen, *Writings Ascribed*, 345–397.

to Rolle throughout the Middle Ages, but with more material in the vernacular bearing false ascription to him. These works included popular prose works such as the Latin mystical treatise *Stimulus Amoris*, Walter Hilton's *Scale of Perfection* (both Latin and English versions), the vernacular *Contemplations of the Dread and Love of God* and English translations of the *Speculum* of St. Edmund. A number of popular poems were also falsely ascribed to Rolle, the most prominent example being a didactic piece known as *The Prick of Conscience*. Hope Emily Allen, the first modern critic to reject Rolle's authorship of this work, notes that it is surprising that such a vast number of manuscripts ascribe this work to him because it bears so little resemblance to most other works by him and does not circulate often enough with his authentic works to give presumption of his authorship by association.[41] In general, the false ascription of popular devotional works to Rolle in manuscripts suggests that his medieval reputation as a spiritual director was considerable. The diversity and the proliferation of vernacular material ascribed to Rolle in the later Middle Ages further suggests that despite his vast Latin corpus, he had also gained a reputation as an author of English devotional works.

The attachment of Rolle's name to these popular works only furthers the idea that medieval scribes sought to emphasise his authorial reputation rather than promote the writings on their own merits. One of the very few manuscripts where commentary on Rolle's own writing style does occur is in the popular Latin mystical compilation *Speculum Spiritualium*. Here, alongside various sections quoted from the text of *The Form of Living*, is a passage where the style and quality of Rolle's vernacular prose are brought to the reader's attention as valuable – an incentive to consider this particular text as one of merit:

> Nonnulla preterea ad discretam abstinentiam pertinentia que prefatus Richardus hanpol scribendo direxit ad reclusam nomine margaretam reseruo pro finali huius tractatus capitulo. Et hoc ideo quia vt mihi videtur melius sonant eadem in lingua materna sicut idem richardus protulit quam si in linguam latinam transferentur.[42]

---

41 See H. E. Allen, *Writings Ascribed*, 397. See also H. E. Allen, *The Authorship of "The Prick of Conscience"* (Boston and New York, 1910). Allen points out that the medieval association of Rolle with this poem also influenced many modern scholars, such as Bernhard ten Brink who argued that "Richard's position in English literary history as an English poet rests chiefly on *The Prick of Conscience*". B. ten Brink, *The History of English Literature*. Trans. H. M. Kennedy (New York, 1889), I, 295.

42 *Speculum Spiritualium*. Syon Monastery MS M. 118, fol. xxxvii[v] cited in H. E. Allen, *Writings Ascribed*, 263 and 405–406. Allen describes the compendium *Speculum Spiritualium* as "mystical" rather than "popular". The author states in his preface that he withholds his name, and that he wishes to provide a compendium for those who cannot afford many books: it is composed with the contemplative specially in view, but the active will also find it useful. Other material by Rolle appears throughout, including an almost complete version of *Emendatio Vitae*.

[There are several matters besides, pertinent to separate abstinence, which the aforementioned Richard Hampole directed to a recluse by the name of Margaret in writing a chapter reserved to be the last of this tract. And [he did] this in such a way that, as it seems to me, those same [words] sound better in his maternal tongue just as that same Richard produced them, than if they were translated into Latin.][43]

The explanatory note, as well as the fact that extracts from one of Rolle's vernacular works were chosen to be included in this primarily Latin compilation, suggests that the scribe considered Rolle as an English writer of some worth, and the emphasis placed on the quality of his English prose supports the idea that Rolle had gained status as a writer in the vernacular. Vincent Gillespie's findings on the careful maintenance of the integrity of Rolle's English texts in manuscript compilations adds support to this notion. He argues that despite the widespread dissemination of the vernacular works of Rolle in miscellanies throughout the country, a large proportion of the extant copies of his vernacular works show an unusual respect for the structures in the texts which suggests that some care was taken in the presentation of his works, even when they were emended for the needs of a new audience.[44] Even though Latin works by Rolle such as *Incendium Amoris* and *Emendatio Vitae* were more widely disseminated in the Middle Ages, at least in terms of manuscript copies, it is now accepted that the Latin literate population of England was in decline in the fourteenth century and the only wider currency Latin works could have hoped to achieve would have been monastic, not general.[45] In all likelihood it was in response to such changes that Richard Misyn chose to execute the painstakingly literal translations of Rolle's *Incendium Amoris* and *Emendatio Vitae* into the vernacular in 1434–35, aiming to bring the English *auctor* to the forefront of the rapidly developing devotional tradition in English by offering his Latin works to an expanding vernacular audience: "þis wark has takyn to translacion of lattyn to englysch, for edificaycon of many saules".[46]

In the same way that evidence of the wide dissemination of Rolle's works reveals little about the specific appeal of his works to a wide audience, the *Officium*'s documentation of Rolle's biography, the rubrics supplied by scribes in medieval manuscripts and the efforts of early translators to confirm his reputation as a saint, an auto-hagiographer, a holy hermit, an *auctor*, a skilled and popular vernacular writer, also communicate hardly anything at all about

---

[43] All translations from the Latin are mine unless stated otherwise.
[44] V. Gillespie, "Vernacular Books of Religion", 328.
[45] See S. S. Hussey, "The Audience for The Middle English Mystics". *De Cella in Seculum: Religious and Secular Life and Devotion in Late Medieval England*. Ed. M. G. Sargent (Cambridge, 1989), 109–110.
[46] R. Misyn, trans. *The Fire of Love and the Mending of Life or The Rule of Living of Richard Rolle*. Ed. Ralph Harvey (London, 1896), 1.

his vernacular texts themselves or how their reading audience may have responded to them. In so many ways the figure of Rolle has overshadowed the text of Rolle and therefore, if we accept only the evidence above, we are limited to positioning Rolle's vernacular reading audience as recipients of his reputation only. But surely the texts themselves were written to be read – to offer something to a readership. Therefore, the question remains, if we limit interest in Rolle's vernacular writings to the autobiographical, hagiographical and biographical figure of Rolle himself, or discuss them only in terms of their initial audience of female religious, are we really reading the *texts* Richard Rolle wrote in English or appropriately assessing the wide appeal these works held in the fourteenth and fifteenth centuries?

Nicholas Watson acknowledges that Rolle's English works were probably foremost in the impetus behind the flood of prose works of instruction which began to appear in the fourteenth century, and found an ever increasing audience.[47] But he argues that in addressing a vernacular audience Rolle could only be reaching a narrower, not a wider, readership than in his Latin writings, and that he was not likely to have anticipated the scale of the English works' popularity, or to have realised that they would make so important a contribution to his reputation.[48] From this we are urged to assume that Rolle in no way anticipated textual trends or responded to audience demand, and although to suggest that he did would be almost impossible to establish, there is still no concrete credibility to the suggestion that he did not. When Rolle was writing his English treatises, sometime in the 1340s, the desire for English vernacular books of moral and spiritual guidance seems to have already begun in earnest among the laity.[49] Dan Michel of Northgate was possibly responding to that desire when in 1340 he prepared the *Ayenbite of Inwyt*, his prose translation of the popular devotional work *Somme le roi*, "uor lewed men/ vor uader/ and uor moder and uor oþer ken/ ham uor to berȝe uram alle manyer zen".[50] This fits in with W. A. Pantin's well-known axiom that "the devout and literate layman was one of the most important phenomena of this period; he represented an opportunity as well as a problem for the Church, and the opportunity was at any rate not ignored".[51] The prologue to Rolle's own *English Psalter*, said to have been written for Margaret Kirkeby, blatantly addresses a general readership of Latin illiterates:

> In this werk i seke na straunge ynglis, bot lyghtest and comonest. and swilk that is mast lyke til the latyn. swa that thai that knawes noght latyn. by the

47 N. Watson, *Invention of Authority*, 223.
48 N. Watson, *Invention of Authority*, 223.
49 G. Keiser, " 'Noght How Lang Man Lifs; Bot How Wele': The Laity and the Ladder of Perfection". *De Cella in Seculum: Religious and Secular Life and Devotion in Late Medieval England*. Ed. M. G. Sargent (Cambridge, 1989), 145.
50 *Ayenbit of Inwyt* cited in G. Keiser, "Noght How Lang Man Lifs", 145.
51 W. A. Pantin, *The English Church*, 262.

inglis may com til mony latyn wordis. In the translacioun i folow the lettere als mykyll as i may. And thare i fynd na propire ynglis i folow the wit of the worde, swa that thai that sall red it thaim thare noght dred errynge.[52]

Lay readers in the fourteenth and fifteenth century certainly appeared to respond favourably to Rolle's general address since manuscript numbers and the variety of manuscript dialects suggest that the *English Psalter* was his most widely disseminated vernacular work in the Middle Ages. For example, an early reference to the presence of the *English Psalter* in a gentry household is suggested in the will of Joan Walkyngham, made on her manor of Ravensthorpe in 1346 in the presence of Thomas Thweng, a relative of one of Rolle's patrons; Joan bequeathed "meum psalterium cum littera grossa et quendam librum scriptum littera anglicana".[53]

Examining the social significance of the eremitic movement in fourteenth-and fifteenth-century York, Jonathan Hughes discovered that throughout the fourteenth century recluses were prominent as counsellors of the laity, providing personal spiritual guidance to all levels of society. Their operations increased lay participation in the contemplative life, especially when, as Rolle did, they provided vernacular contemplative literature.[54] Hughes suggests that Rolle was probably the first hermit to establish himself as a leading confessor among the gentry of the East Riding and Richmondshire.[55] Similarly, Walter Hilton and the *Cloud*-author both served as confessors and advisers to recluses and religious communities, and to men in public life.[56] Some of the more expensive manuscript copies of Rolle's works suggest that the aristocracy, who were among Rolle's first patrons, were early readers of his works and followers of his teachings. By the end of the fourteenth and the beginning of the fifteenth centuries early copies of Rolle's vernacular works (and vernacular translations) were owned by prominent figures, both lay and clerical, such as the Minister of the Friars Minor, Lord Scrope of Masham, Henry FitzHugh, lord of Ravensworth and John Newton, treasurer of York Cathedral.[57] As noted above, one of the lessons in the *Officium* shows Rolle offering spiritual advice to his first gentry patron, Lady Dalton, and her

---

52 H. R. Bramley, *The Psalter Psalms of David and Certain Canticles, with a Translation and Exposition in English by Richard Rolle of Hampole* (Oxford, 1884). Prologue, 4.

53 J. Hughes, *Pastors and Visionaries*, 90. The full version of Joan's will appears in *Testamenta Eboracensia*. Ed. James Raine (Surtees Society, 1836), I, 17.

54 See J. Hughes, *Pastors and Visionaries*, esp. 77–78 and 109–126. Hughes argues that the career of Richard Rolle was of fundamental importance in elevating the status of the recluse as someone who was consulted on spiritual matters by laymen, and who therefore initiated changes in religious sensibility by influencing the development of lay participation in the contemplative life.

55 J. Hughes, *Pastors and Visionaries*, 109.

56 J. Hughes, *Pastors and Visionaries*, 109.

57 H. E. Allen, *Writings Ascribed*, 521–522.

company.[58] The *Officium*'s reference to Rolle's works as "little books composed for the edification of his neighbours" could suggest that Rolle wrote with his lay patrons and other lay readers in mind even when composing works that were explicitly addressed to female recluses, the surrounding monastic communities and the secular clergy.

Rolle's active involvement in lay devotional practices and the evidence that he was read widely by Christians in many different walks of life has prompted a number of modern critics to suggest that many of his works themselves possibly envisage a wider audience. According to W. A. Pantin mystics in fact "presuppose an audience thoroughly and severely drilled in the rudiments of faith and morals, and the widespread appeal of vernacular mystical literature in the later Middle Ages seems to argue that the program of religious instruction planned by the reforming bishops of the thirteenth century did succeed in reaching and indoctrinating certain sections of the laity".[59] R. M. Wilson, one of the first critics to compare Rolle's Latin and vernacular audience, argues that the elaborate, ornate style of Rolle's Latin works show that they "are intended to be read by highly literate readers" whilst Rolle's "plain" English works are "intended for devout lay people with little or no Latin" because they are "concerned only with giving, as lucidly as possible, advice on the attainment of the mystical life".[60] S. S. Hussey, examining the audience for the Middle English mystics, acknowledges that the dedications that occur with manuscript copies of Rolle's English prose works establish the early readers of these texts but argues that these should not be used to define the audience because "in these texts a wider audience is sometimes envisaged".[61] The suggestion that Rolle envisaged or sought a wider audience for his vernacular texts, coupled with his involvement in lay piety and the fact that we know a wide readership was eventually reached, poses an interesting question for the modern critic – what then did the vernacular works which Rolle wrote for an initial audience of female religious offer other medieval readers? Or, more precisely, what literary qualities within Rolle's English prose works might have appealed to lay as well as religious, male as well as female, readers and how, if at all, was this appeal generated within the text?

Referred to in modern scholarship as the "English epistles" (a title I shall dispute) Rolle's three vernacular prose works – *Ego Dormio, The Commandment* and *The Form of Living*[62] – were evidently written for a female audience, or as

---

58 *Officium et Miracula*, 32; *The Life of Richard Rolle*, 304. See also H. E. Allen, *Writings Ascribed*, 58.

59 W. A. Pantin, *The English Church*, 250.

60 R. M. Wilson, "Three Middle English Mystics", 90.

61 S. S. Hussey, "The Audience for the Middle English Mystics", 110–111.

62 I examine the three texts in what is now accepted as their chronological order of composition: *Ego Dormio, The Commandment* and *The Form of Living*. Their order of appearance in medieval manuscript collections varies considerably and they do not always appear as a group of three. I have used the collection of Rolle's English writ-

Sarah Ogilvie-Thomson has convincingly argued, for one woman, Rolle's friend and disciple Margaret Kirkeby.[63] They are also particularly interesting as works that were seemingly able to appeal to a much wider audience than the one for which they were explicitly composed. Utilising the terminology provided by modern reader-response criticism, I suggest that this is because the way in which Rolle's English prose works are written both invites and expects a wide variety of medieval readers. Such an analysis will therefore rely on the type of reader-oriented criticism that, as Robert Wright suggests, is less concerned with the literary text as an artifactual entity than with the process of reading, the interaction between text and reading audience.[64] The figure of the reader in Rolle's texts is transformed by the literary experience into what Wolfgang Iser describes as the implied reader, a term which incorporates both the prestructuring of the potential meaning by the text, and the reader's actualisation of this potential through the reading process.[65]

This is not to say that I seek to propose Rolle's intention in writing these works since, like most reader-oriented critics, I am conscious of the danger of making assumptions about the actual author and audience which are merely extrapolated from the narratorial construct.[66] Instead, the close examination of the three vernacular prose works looks to suggest ways in which Rolle's texts themselves are potentially inviting to a wide variety of medieval readers. In doing so I fully acknowledge that we cannot know exactly how readers responded to Rolle's texts or what it was they sought from them; still, as Janet Coleman succinctly points out, "we can never become a fourteenth-century audience, but we can read fourteenth-century literature with an eye and an ear better able to recognise the subtleties of stylistic experiments and realise the significance of its subject matter".[67] Rather than concentrating on Rolle as author, which has been the primary focus for critics in the past, I propose to look more to the textual effect of Rolle's vernacular prose. By closely examining the reader and writer constructions in his English prose works I seek to

ings found in Longleat MS 29, edited by Sarah Ogilvie-Thomson, because even though the texts appear in the order of longest to shortest in this collection it is considered that the copies of Rolle's works found here are closer to his autograph compositions than those found in other manuscripts. For the most accurate chronology of Rolle's works to date see N. Watson, *Invention of Authority*, 273–294. For more information about the Longleat collection see S. Ogilvie-Thomson, *Richard Rolle: Prose and Verse* (Oxford, 1988). Hereafter, page-and-line parenthetical references to Rolle's English works are to Ogilvie-Thomson's edition.

63 See S. Ogilvie-Thomson, *Prose and Verse, passim.*

64 R. E. Wright, "The 'Boke Performyd': Affective Technique and Reader Response in the *Showings* of Julian of Norwich". *Christianity and Literature* 36/4 (1987), 17.

65 W. Iser, *The Implied Reader: Patterns of Communication in Prose Fiction from Bunyan to Beckett* (Baltimore and London, 1974), xii.

66 R. Allen, "The Implied Author of Laȝamon's *Brut*". *The Text and Translation of Laȝamon's* Brut. Ed. Francoise Le Saux (Cambridge, 1994), 134.

67 J. Coleman, *English Literature in History, 1350–1400* (London, 1981), 17.

uncover the ways in which these texts become what Mikhail Bakhtin describes as the product of a reciprocal relationship:

> In point of fact, word is a two sided act. It is determined equally by whose word it is and for whom it is meant. As word, it is precisely the product of the reciprocal relationship between speaker and listener, addresser and addressee.[68]

Accordingly, my analyses of the individual works will rely on the notion that because of this reciprocity, the reader/writer relationship is of prime importance to the making of meaning within the text.

Rolle's English prose works are, I believe, particularly suited to reader-oriented criticism because each of these works suggests both an authorial self and a reader-identity, and leaves room for a reader agency with the potential to fulfil an affective objective: each and every reader can occupy the specially constructed space Rolle offers them in these works, as an individual addressee who seeks the love of God and union with God. Rolle constructs this implied reader in very general terms, as the individual soul – an ungendered reader-identity that was common in religious writings, and one that was even acceptable to contemporary detractors of Rolle such as the *Cloud*-author:

> Euermore where þou fyndest wreten þi-self in goostliness, þan it is vnderstonden þi soule, & not þi body.[69]

Rolle is able to appeal to *all* readers as the individual soul through the strategies of the separate affective discourses he employs in each text, which presuppose readers sufficiently schooled in, and consequently able to respond to, various medieval traditions of affectivity. In *Ego Dormio* the individual soul is wooed through a discourse of intimacy to become the bride of Christ of the *Song of Songs*; in *The Commandment* the individual soul's need to understand the love of God is appealed to through a discourse of plain instruction common to popular didactic literature; and in *The Form of Living* the individual soul is offered an idealised relationship with Rolle's authorial self – friendship in the contemplative life – reflecting medieval ideals of *amicitia* and *amicitia Dei*. Rolle draws the reader into these relationships through his skill as an affective writer: he carefully constructs his writings to direct the emotions of his audience toward a closer communion with God. The affective mysticism of his vernacular texts offers his readers the help and encouragement

---

68 M. Bakhtin, *Marxism and the Philosophy of Language* (London, 1973), 86. See D. Aers, *Community, Gender and Individual Identity: English Writing 1300–1430* (London, 1988), 3.
69 *The Cloud of Unknowing. The Cloud of Unknowing and The Book of Privy Counselling*. Ed. P. Hodgson (London, 1944), 115/4–5. Hereafter, page-and-line parenthetical references to *The Cloud of Unknowing* and *The Book of Privy Counselling* are to this edition.

they need to feel confident enough to approach God on their own. Indeed, it is largely Rolle's preoccupation with the *affectus* of his reader and his skill as an affective writer that in many ways permit the opening of his works to a wider audience. Through his focus on the interior life and on the emotional spiritual responses of the reader a universal appeal is achieved that offers each and every reader the opportunity to occupy the special place within the text as the individual soul seeking to love God.

Rolle's construction of the implied reader as the individual soul further suggests that his vernacular texts transcend the gender of their initial audience. Explicit gendered directives found in these texts are, in a way, exploited as feminine, but in an altered context that does not restrict them to a literally female audience. When the soul (hence, the implied reader) is always feminised, the gender of the reading subject is of no real consequence to the accessibility of the texts themselves. Caroline Walker Bynum and Joan Ferrante have both noted that the twelfth century shows an increase in the personification of key concepts as female and it is often found that the soul is usually pictured as female by both female and male writers.[70] And while it can be argued that this is in part because the gender of *anima* is feminine in Latin, the feminisation of the soul in later devotional literature would appear to serve other purposes.

The idea that Rolle's ultimate reading subject in each English treatise is the feminised soul rather than an actual woman partly opposes some recent scholarship that has seen Rolle's vernacular works as devotional texts written for the specific spiritual edification of female religious.[71] While it need not be disputed that Rolle was writing for an initial audience of women, here again modern critics of Rolle have turned to the man, not the texts themselves or their reception, to portray him as a writer of gendered literature – a male author offering gendered advice to a specifically female readership. Rolle's prose works, particularly *The Form of Living*, have been labelled as specifically female-audience texts that strive to continue the tradition of vernacular male-authored works for anchoritic women begun by the author of *Ancrene Wisse*. In an attempt to augment the concept of Rolle as a gendered writer, his Latin works have also been searched for evidence of misogyny. Similarly, the use of gendered imagery and language within his English prose works has been discussed as evidence of Rolle's acceptance of the misogynistic stereo-

---

[70] C. Walker Bynum, *Jesus as Mother* (Berkeley, 1982), 138. See also J. Ferrante, *Woman as Image in Medieval Literature from the Twelfth Century to Dante* (Columbia, 1975).

[71] For example, Nicholas Watson resolutely refers to Rolle's vernacular audience as female at all times. He is particularly concerned with Margaret Kirkeby as a catalyst for Rolle's decision to write in the vernacular and uses information that suggests Rolle wrote *The Form of Living* and the *English Psalter* specifically for her to claim Margaret as a key figure in the development of English spirituality as well as English prose. See N. Watson, *The Invention of Authority*, 91.

type that it is a male author's duty to instruct female recipients in devotional matters. Rolle's acknowledged friendship with one woman, Margaret Kirkeby, the only details of which are found in the hagiographical *Officium*, has been used to explain his decision to write in English. Once again, assessment of Rolle's character, drawn from his reputed personal relationships with women and his Latin utterances against them, has clouded discussion of the texts themselves. Even when some modern scholars concede that Rolle's English prose works were expected to reach a wider audience than the women, or woman, for whom they were originally composed, his vernacular audience is rarely discussed as other than female. Rolle is seen writing to a specifically female religious audience, without acknowledgement of the textual content that suggests that a wider audience is sought in these works, or recognition that manuscript reception of these works suggests that they appealed to a variety of readers who were not always female or professional religious.

This is not to say that the gender of Rolle's initial audience is without consequence in these works – gendered language and gendered tropes are apparent throughout – but it would appear that gender-specific discourse features throughout the writings in order to feminise both the reader and Rolle's own authorial self in acknowledgement of the soul as conceptually feminine. The feminised soul unites with God without necessarily demanding a gender-specific reader. The argument that this type of audience construction is not gender-specific both explores and expands on ideas developed by Anne Clark Bartlett and Kathleen Garay. Bartlett's notion that a "rhetoric of sexual equality" pervades many male-authored Middle English texts for a female audience is compatible with Rolle's vernacular address; this rhetoric emerges in the English treatises not because the initial audience is female but because the implied audience lacks gender-specificity.[72] Suggesting that the figure of the individual soul (the implied reader) is feminised in Rolle's English prose works and that Rolle himself adopts feminised authorial roles throughout these texts also supports Kathleen Garay's assertion that Rolle, like many of the mystical writers of this period, employs what can best be described as an ungendered discourse in his works – an "essentially undifferentiated voice that may be identified as a female one".[73] In line with Garay's argument that the mystical discourse (male- and female-authored) may be seen as representing a shared mode, grounded in the feminine, Rolle's texts, it would seem, also envisage an audience that both expects and accepts this feminised role for the soul/reader. Accordingly, the proposal that Rolle constructs an ungendered implied reader in his vernacular prose writings calls for a

---

72 A. Clark Bartlett, *Male Authors, Female Readers*, 101. Bartlett argues that these Middle English texts "refuse to validate conventional misogynistic stereotypes".

73 K. Garay, " 'A Naked Intent Unto God': Ungendered Discourse in Some Late Medieval Mystical Texts". *Mystics Quarterly* 23:2 (1997), 37.

re-assessment of them as works that envisage a wider readership, beyond the initial female recipient(s), thus offering a greater understanding of how and why Rolle's few, short English prose works were able to appeal to a wider readership in late medieval England.

Before examining the individual texts it is necessary to look more closely at Rolle as a writer of affective literature in the vernacular and to examine ways in which his texts could have been read and responded to by a varied medieval audience – lay as well as religious readers who increasingly turned to affective devotional works initially composed for women recluses as guides to their own spiritual lives. Discussing medieval English mysticism in terms of the cultural moment, Marion Glasscoe suggests that lay demand for teaching about contemplative spirituality together with the particular emphases of individual mystics who met and also stimulated it in fourteenth-century England both represents, and engages with, a complex web of theological and socio-historical development.[74] The following chapter seeks to locate Rolle's English prose works more broadly within their own cultural moment – the fourteenth-century affective tradition – in order to assess how these English texts reflect Rolle's authorial commitment to common affective devotional practice, and how his skill as an affective writer in the vernacular may have influenced the appeal of the texts. Within this discussion Rolle's theological inheritance and the influences of the Latin affective tradition on his vernacular affective literature are explored and literature similar to Rolle's, literature that focuses on the personal and the emotional within devotional practice, is shown to be not only widespread in medieval England but responded to by a wide variety of medieval readers.

---

[74] M. Glasscoe, *English Medieval Mystics*, 37.

2

"Ihesu louynge, Ihesu thynkynge, Ihesu desyrynge":[1] Affectivity, the Devotional Movement and Rolle's Implied Reader

To þe I writ þis speciali, for I hope in þe more goodnes þan in anoþer, þat þou wil gif þi þoght to fulfil in dede þat þou seest is profitable for þi soule, and þat lif gif þe to in þe whoch þou may holyest offre þi [hert] to Ihesu Criste, and lest be in besynesse of þis world. For if þou stabilly loue God and brennyngly whils þou lyvest here, withouten dout þi sete is ordeyned for þe ful hegh and ioiful bifore þe face of God amonge [his] holy angels.[2]

The counterpart of the implied author is the implied reader – not the flesh and bones you or I sitting in our living rooms reading the book, but the audience presupposed by the narrative itself.[3]

I

ROLLE'S DISTINCTION as a writer of devotional literature derives mainly from his affective method. Briefly stated, affective language in devotional literature excites and directs the emotions of the audience so that readers are drawn first to holiness and then to union with God. The recognition of the need for affective devotion in Christianity ultimately derives from the Apostle Paul who states in his epistle to the Roman Christians that the problem for the believer is not so much in knowing how to behave, but in knowing how to drive his or her emotions and passions into such an intimate relationship with the divine that obedience and worship become instinctive (Rom. 7:15–25).[4] In the Christian scheme, such a task is not easy, for the unholy

---

1 *The Form of Living*, 17/557.
2 *Ego Dormio*, 26/33–39.
3 S. Chatman, *Story and Discourse: Narrative Structure in Fiction and Film* (Ithaca and London, 1978), 149.
4 See the first chapter of W. Netherton, " 'Joy Gars Me Jangell': Affective Devotion in the English Writings of Richard Rolle" (Texas, 1997). Netherton's dissertation exten-

trinity – the World, the Flesh, and the Devil – constantly tempt the believer away from commitment. Moreover, because humans are fallen, the will is corrupt and the natural inclination of the affections (*affectus*) leads them away from what they know to be good. The Christian must be drawn, seduced even, to spirituality and righteousness. The stirring of the emotions to draw the believer to piety, to a closer union with God, to make the believer indeed the "bride of Christ" or the "lover of God", is the goal of affective devotion. As Vincent Gillespie points out, the role of affective literature is to regain the attention of the *affectus*, by winning it away from the proximate things to which it has become attached and focusing it firmly on absolute good, to enable the intellect to penetrate more deeply into its understanding of absolute truth, which it knows to be desirable but from which it is constantly distracted by the dissipation of the will.[5] Rolle is an affective writer in both Latin and English, but his English prose treatises appear both to exploit and expand traditional affective methods by closely involving readers in the devotional narratives he supplies for them. In his vernacular works he takes one step further the traditional strategy of inviting a personal relation with God by constructing not only a space for the reader to occupy but also a network of intimate reader/writer relationships within the texts, relationships which encourage specific affective responses in the reader, all designed to draw him/her closer to the goal of spiritual perfection.

Rolle's textual relationship with his vernacular audience is complex and intricate. One the one hand there is the impression that the three vernacular tracts he composed were probably initially directed to one woman on the different occasions of her spiritual development and that this woman, presumably Rolle's friend and disciple Margaret Kirkeby, was the inspiration for the English works. Through this relationship Rolle declares his views on spiritual *amicitia*, the role of the *sponsa Christi* and the love of God. Yet, while Margaret's spiritual development may well have been the original issue in the English treatises, the way in which he addresses and constructs his initial reading subject has many interesting implications for further readers. On the other hand, as close examination of each text will reveal, Margaret may well be the catalyst for the English treatises but neither she nor any specific person is addressed exclusively in these works. Instead Rolle relies on strategies of affective language to construct a separate discourse in each work that appeals to each reader as an individual soul, and so potentially invites a wider audience. Capitalising on tropes of spiritual friendship, Rolle employs a language of love and intimacy in his English works to develop the reader/writer rela-

---

sively references biblical texts commonly drawn upon in affective literature of the later medieval period.

[5] V. Gillespie, "Mystic's Foot: Rolle and Affectivity". *The Medieval Mystical Tradition in England: Papers Read at Dartington Hall, July, 1982*. Ed. Marion Glasscoe (Exeter, 1982), 203.

tionship and his invitation to the unitive state. But though he employed this language to great effect, he did not have to invent it. He redeployed materials and teaching clearly present in the traditional sources of affective literature. His apparent success in gaining a broader readership must in part be due to the familiarity and intelligibility of other affective works made for the growing vernacular audience of his period. There was emerging a type of literature that promoted reader-engagement in the text, in much the same way as Rolle's English works did, and sought similarly to individualise Christocentric devotional experience.

Rolle's deployment of affective strategies to engage and direct his audience shows marked influence of elements of the twelfth-century affective tradition, particularly the development of concepts surrounding the affective, intellective and imaginative faculties in the ascent to perfection and mystic union, and their influence on Rolle's exhortation to achieve the unitive state can be seen clearly in his English prose works. In turn, the vernacular devotional movement in England, begun in the late thirteenth century, drew on earlier affective literature and further developed traditional themes and images, such as Christ's life and Passion, to encourage intimate and individual devotional practices. The construction of audience in this type of literature, where the reader is often invited to adopt the subject position, the "I" figure, within the narrative, shows striking similarities to Rolle's construction of reader-identity, his positioning of the reader as an individual soul, found throughout his English works. Evidence of the popularity of this type of literature amongst a variety of medieval readers, both male and female, lay and religious, is substantial and this, alongside Rolle's skill as an affective writer, may have influenced the wide dissemination of his English writings. In the three separate prose treatises written by Rolle the construction of reader-identity certainly shows the influence of traditional affective methods but it is also a more subtle construction than the explicit "I" figure found in much of the affective literature of the period. Rolle's reader is more an implied reader, a reader presupposed by the narrative itself, extending beyond the initial audience of female religious, and able to appeal to a variety of readers of the vernacular in late medieval England.

II

Before he wrote the English treatises Rolle engaged in a commentary on what is perhaps the most affective text in Christocentric religion, the *Song of Songs*. Despite the idiosyncrasy of this commentary, he reverts to, and shows dependence on, commentary techniques already long established. His interpretation of the "oleum effusum" verse closely follows that of Bernard of Clairvaux in his fifth sermon on the *Song of Songs*, and partakes in the spreading of the devotional cult of the Holy Name in England.[6] Denis Renevey notes that an interesting aspect of Rolle's reliance on feminine imagery is also exposed in this commentary.[7] Besides the Christocentric interpretation, Rolle reverts to mariological interpretations of the *Song of Songs* at important moments. Hence, some of the most imaginative associations in *Super Canticum Canticorum* are created to define the relationship between the Virgin Mary and her son. From this, nuptial and filial imagery emerges which highlights Rolle's recognition of spiritual union as the goal of affective devotion. Furthermore, the presence of devotions to the humanity of Christ and the Holy Name at the heart of his commentary prefigures the use of the same devotions in the treatises alongside love imagery, to encourage readers to participate in the devotional practices suggested. When Rolle came to write his English works he had already established a connection with forms of mysticism that function by engaging the reader.

In writing the English treatises Rolle combined two long-standing religious traditions: that of biblical exegesis, which he practised in both Latin and English; and that of liturgy, both as a source for some of his imagery, and as model for the arrangement of the different voices present in the treatises. *The Form of Living* is also replete with devotional material for the spiritual well-being of solitaries and therefore participates in the anchoritic tradition of *Ancrene Wisse* and the "Wooing Group".[8] This is a tradition which also derives largely from the *Song of Songs* and its commentary tradition for the most affective and spiritual sections. Together, these three traditions not only allow Rolle to position himself as a sophisticated spiritual adviser, they also appear to influence him to consider a particular strategy which draws on the *Song of Songs* tradition while addressing a primary audience of those who are about to enter,

---

6   H. E. Allen, *English Writings*, 66–67 and 39–43. For further information on Rolle and the cult of the Holy Name see D. Renevey, "Name above Names: the Devotion to the Name of Jesus from Richard Rolle to Walter Hilton's *Scale of Perfection I*". *The Medieval Mystical Tradition: England, Ireland and Wales*. Ed. Marion Glasscoe (Cambridge 1999), 103–121.

7   D. Renevey, "The Moving of the Soul: The Functions of Metaphors of Love in the Writings of Richard Rolle and Antecedent Texts of the Medieval Mystical Tradition" (Oxford University, 1993), 188–189. The following paragraphs develop ideas posited by Renevey on the significance of the *Song of Songs* and its commentary tradition on Rolle's English works and earlier texts such as *Ancrene Wisse* and the "Wooing Group". I have referred to Renevey's doctoral thesis throughout but much of this material has recently been reworked by Renevey and published as *Language, Self and Love: Hermeneutics in the Writings of Richard Rolle and the Commentaries of the Song of Songs* (Cardiff, 2001).

8   The four texts that make up the "Wooing Group" are *Þe Wohunge of Ure Lauerd, On wel Swuðe God Ureisun of God Almihti, On Lofsong of Ure Louerde* and *On Lofsong of Ure Lefdi*. For versions of these works see *Þe Wohunge of Ure Lauerde*. Ed. W. M. Thompson (London, 1958); *Old English Homilies*. Ed. R. Morris (London, 1868); *Middle English Religious Prose*. Ed. N. F. Blake (London, 1972).

or already belong to, the solitary life as advocated by the anchoritic tradition.[9] Rolle's intimacy with his audience, emphasised in the treatises because each is implicitly addressed to an individual reader, is therefore most apparent in the language of love he uses, drawn from traditional affective sources. To come to understand how Rolle achieves this intimacy with his audience, and how the specific roles he assigns the reader in his texts promote individualised reader response, we should first look at traditional forms of affective mysticism and how they operate in terms of reader engagement.

Rolle's construction of audience, his employment of love imagery, and the intimate tone of his language in the English treatises draws our attention to what could be termed the sensuous dimension of the mystical and theological schema he presents. Within this sensuous dimension the desire for mystic union is almost always at the forefront because, in general terms, union, the culmination of the redirection of the *affectus*, is the ultimate goal of affective devotion. Rolle's perception of mystic union and his employment of the language associated with it of course raises the question of his theological inheritance. He appears to have drawn his literary inspiration from the great monastic writers of the twelfth century and many of his works can be read as popularisations of the traditions he inherited. Bernard McGinn argues for the relative unimportance of union with God as a mystical concept in the early western church. He suggests that Augustine, who despite his dependence on Plotinus for whom union understood as fusion with the One was crucial, seems to know nothing of it. Similarly, Cassian, although interested in forms of contemplation leading to pure prayer, does not mention union and Gregory the Great disregards union altogether in his mystical thought.[10] In effect, in the Latin West at least, union was not the basic category for the description of the immediate experience of God before the twelfth century, but during the course of the twelfth century consideration of the nature of union with God and its relation to love and knowledge became widespread.[11]

Following re-readings of Pseudo-Dionysius, in what McGinn describes as the explosion of systematic expositions of mystical theology in the twelfth century, notions of union were comparatively harmonious in the new orders of Cistercians and Victorines.[12] Bernard of Clairvaux, William of St. Thierry, and Hugh and Richard of St. Victor, amongst others, established a fountain-

---

9   D. Renevey, *The Moving of the Soul*, 189. See also S. S. Hussey, "The Audience for the Middle English Mystics", 110.

10   B. McGinn, "Love, Knowledge, and Mystical Union in Western Christianity: Twelfth to Sixteenth Centuries". *Church History* 56 (1987) 8. Of Augustine, McGinn states that he speaks of "*touching* Eternal Wisdom" or "*beholding* Eternal Wisdom" in this life in his *Confessions* and *Contra Faustrum* respectively, but does not mention union. Many of the following examples are derived from this excellent overview of mystic union throughout five successive centuries.

11   B. McGinn, "Love, Knowledge and Mystical Union", 8.

12   B. McGinn, "Love, Knowledge and Mystical Union", 8.

head of affective mysticism, dominated by intense devotion to the person of Christ and the longing for mystic union, which would dominate the praxis of experiential religion for many centuries.[13] Bernard outlines love as central to mystical ascent when he describes the four degrees of ascent of charity in *De diligendo Deo*, basing his theological assumptions on the Pauline doctrine from 1 Corinthians 6:17, "Qui autem adhaerat Domino, unus spiritus est" [But he who cleaves to our Lord is one spirit], and using three familiar metaphors to express the union – the drop of water in a vat of wine, the iron in the fire, and the air transformed into sunshine – each suggesting some sort of fusion of substance between human and God.[14] He also draws extensively on bridal metaphor in his *Sermones in cantica*, insisting that marital love is the highest form, the love that expresses union, which adds weight to the assessment of his system as one of purely affective mysticism.[15] Douglas Gray argues that the devotional movement of the fourteenth century which sought to draw Christians into more personal, loving relationships with God drew strength from the affective force of Bernard's emphasis on the urgent personal meditation on the humanity of Christ and especially on the details of the Nativity and the Passion.[16] In Bernard, then, we can begin to see the emergence of affective literature that promotes a type of reader-engagement with the traditional themes and images associated with mystic union. Later medieval English authors of religious literature certainly appeared actively to encourage knowing and affectively internalising aspects of Christ's life and death as an important part of devotional practice for their readers.

Other twelfth-century writers who may have influenced Rolle's promotion of union as the goal of affective devotion include Richard of St. Victor, in his brief treatise *De Quattuor Gradibus Violentae Caritatis*, and William of St. Thierry, Bernard's contemporary and friend; both stress the role of love in the process of ascent.[17] Perhaps the writer most influential on the English mystics

---

13 See Giles Constable, "Twelfth-Century Spirituality and the Late Middle Ages". *Medieval and Renaissance Studies* 5 (1969), 27–60.

14 Throughout this study I use the Vulgate Bible (Madrid, 1977) and the Douay-Rheims translation (London, 1975). I have modernised some of the spelling from the Douay-Rheims edition. For further discussion of the unitive metaphors noted above see Robert E. Lerner, "The Image of Mixed Liquids in Late Medieval Mystical Thought". *Church History* 40 (1971), 397–441.

15 McGinn suggests as an example *Sermones in Cantica* 83.4–6 with comparisons to *Sermones super Cantica* 45.1 and 6, 52.2–6, 59.2, and 69.7. In *Sermones in Cantica* 82.8 Bernard identifies *caritas* with *visio Dei* and *similtudo Dei*.

16 D. Gray, *Themes and Images in the Medieval English Religious Lyric* (London and Boston, 1972), 20.

17 For more information on the theological perspective of Richard of St. Victor's writings on contemplation see the introduction to *Richard of St. Victor: Selected Writings on Contemplation*. Trans. and intro. C. Kirchberger (London, 1957). On the mystical doctrine of William of St. Thierry see O. Brooke, "William of St. Thierry's Doctrine of the Ascent to God by Faith". *Studies in Monastic Theology* (Kalamazoo, 1980), 134–207.

of the fourteenth century was the Franciscan Bonaventure who concerns himself intimately with union and the path to it. In his *Itinerarium Mentis in Deum*, Bonaventure's complex outline of the six stages in the ascent to God discusses spiritual ascent under the rubric of *raptus* in this life and *beatitudo* in the next, drawing on Chapter One of Pseudo-Dionysius's *De mystica theologia*.[18] In short, in Bonaventure's mystical schema all powers of the soul are brought to bear in the ascent, but affectivity goes beyond intellect. Bonaventure writes:

> In this passing over, if it is to be perfect, all intellectual activities must be left behind and the height of our affection must be totally transferred and transformed into God.[19]

While primarily affective, Bonaventure's mysticism has been considered by Etienne Gilson as a kind of "intellectualised affectivity".[20] However, drawing a line between intellectual and affective mysticism and placing different writers on each side is of little use in determining relations between love and knowledge in the path to union. McGinn notes that Christian mystical theology is based upon the twin premises of the unknowability of God on the one hand and God's accessibility to love on the other, and that it is therefore extremely difficult to find any Christian theology of mysticism which is not affective in the sense of giving love a crucial role in the striving toward God.[21] Indeed, this is clearly seen in the twelfth-century emphasis on the personal relationship with Christ, where love is almost always constructed in terms of simple human emotion. This notion was expressed in its most exaggerated (and arguably heretical) form by Peter Abelard, who maintained that the sole efficacy of the Redemption lay in Christ's demonstration of his love to man, thereby winning man's love in return.[22] It can therefore be argued that much twelfth-century affective literature promoted individual human love for God as the means to achieving the goal of affective devotion, union. Subsequently, when Rolle came to write his own affective works he had behind him a wide range of theologians who considered love and knowledge in the ascent to union as central to their doctrine, and could draw on their reading to form his own conception of how the unitive state, and the pathways to it, could be formulated for his vernacular audience. Throughout the English treatises Rolle guides his readers on their own journey to perfection through a language of love carefully drawn from elements of the affective tradition that

---

[18] B. McGinn, "Love, Knowledge, and Mystical Union", 10.

[19] Bonaventure, "The Soul's Journey into God", *Bonaventure: The Soul's Journey into God; The Tree of Life; The Life of St. Francis*. Trans. E. Cousins (New York, 1978), 113.

[20] E. Gilson, *The Philosophy of St. Bonaventure* (Peterson, 1965), 420.

[21] B. McGinn, "Love, Knowledge, and Mystical Union", 12.

[22] R. Woolf, *Art and Doctrine: Essays on Medieval Literature*. Ed. H. O'Donoghue (London, 1986), 100.

are designed to appeal to and inflame the human senses in order to achieve the goal of union.

To assess the full impact of the influence of traditional notions of love and knowledge in Rolle's English works, particularly his use of conventional mystical terminology as well as the ways in which this differs from his exemplars and antecedents, it is necessary to examine the role of the sensuous in the language of mystical texts. This essentially hinges upon medieval interpretations of the three human faculties most often referred to in theological discussions of the ascent to perfection: the intellect (*intellectus*), the affections (*affectus*) and the imagination (*imaginatio*). Rolle's interpretations of these faculties are crucial to our understanding of his construction of audience in the English works because within them we can begin to observe his extended use of elements marking the role of the reader as pivotal to the making of meaning within a devotional text.

Amongst the vernacular writings of fourteenth-century devotional authors, as well as many scholastic authors, there is little unanimity over whether the soul's union with God was achieved through the *intellectus* or the *affectus*, or about the role of *imaginatio* within the quest to perfection. To illustrate the diversity of interpretations, as well as outline Rolle's use of sensuous language in devotional works, we can compare him to two later fourteenth-century English mystics who, in many ways, followed his lead as a mystical writer without necessarily concurring with his conception of the roles of the intellective and affective faculties – Walter Hilton and the anonymous author of *The Cloud of Unknowing*. For Hilton, although both the intellective and the affective faculties of the soul play a role within the mystical quest, ultimately it is through its intellectual capacities that the soul achieves union. The *Cloud*-author, on the other hand, maintains that once the intellect has been engaged it is through the *affectus* alone that the soul is able to penetrate the cloud of unknowing "wiþ a sharpe darte of longing loue".[23] Rolle also maintains that it is through the *affectus* that the soul experiences union with God, yet his approach differs radically from that of the *Cloud*-author. Rolle permits imagination a fairly crucial role in the soul's journey in traversing from the second to the third degree of love, while the *Cloud*-author limits the function of this practice to that of moral correction and denounces all use of imagination above this preliminary level. He is so vehement that many have come to regard this aspect of *The Cloud of Unknowing* as a polemical attack on Rolle's devotion.[24]

The Cloud of Unknowing was written for a monastic elite, and perhaps because of this an elevated use of *imaginatio* is negated and denigrated, its carnality seen to distort the spiritual truths toward which the disciple aspired:

23 *The Cloud of Unknowing*, 26/11–12.
24 See D. Knowles, *The English Mystical Tradition*, 54.

Þerfore bewar in þis werk þat þou take none ensaumple at þe bodely assencion of Criste, for to streyne in ymaginacion in þe tyme of þi preier bodely upwardes, as þou woldest clymbe abouen þe mone. For it schulde on no wise be so goostly.[25]

Alastair Minnis asserts that the *Cloud*-author, having emphasised that one cannot attain the height of perfection by intellectual means in *The Cloud of Unknowing*, concedes in *The Book of Privy Counselling* that meditations are still the best way for the beginner in the mystical journey to come to an awareness of both the self and God:

Neuerþeles 3it ben þees faire meditacions þe trewest wey þat a synner may haue in his begynnyng to þe goostly felyng of himself & of God . . . & who-so comeþ not in þis weye, he comeþ not trewly . . .[26]

Walter Hilton holds a fairly similar attitude towards imagination. Within his spiritual scheme it is indispensable, the key for lifting the soul from "bodily" to "ghostly" understanding, without which it becomes subject to the rule of sensuality. An example of how later writers (and presumably audiences) responded to this perception of the soul can be seen in the fifteenth-century morality play *Wisdom* where Anima enters, "most horrybull wyse, fowlere þan a fende".[27] This powerful image of the fallen soul, drawn directly from Hilton's *Scale of Perfection*, rests upon the Augustinian division of the soul into sensual and rational faculties. It further serves to demonstrate Hilton's atti- tude towards the senses. Corporeal meditations, while serving a purpose in the second level of contemplation, that of lifting the gaze of the soul from the mutable in which it so easily becomes enmeshed, must be left behind in order to reach the third and final stage of the contemplative journey. Bluntly stated:

Alle gostly þinges ere seen & knowen by vndrestandynge of þe soule, not bi ymaginacioun.[28]

Imagination is merely the handmaiden of reason, "for þe vnderstandynge is ladi, & þe ymaginacioun is a mayden servende to þe vnderstandynge when nede is".[29] According to Minnis, no matter how much fervour of devotion and fire of love the soul may feel, as long as its conception of God is largely or wholly dependent on imagination rather than intellection, it has not yet

---

25 *The Cloud of Unknowing*, 111/5–9.
26 *The Book of Privy Counselling*, 158/17–25 cited in A. Minnis, "Affection and Imagina- tion in *The Cloud of Unknowing* and Hilton's *Scale of Perfection*". *Traditio* 39 (1983), 350–351.
27 *Wisdom*, Ed. M. Eccles (London, 1969), 143/904.
28 W. Hilton, *The Scale of Perfection* cited in A. Minnis, "Affection and Imagination", 355.
29 W. Hilton, *The Scale of Perfection* cited in A. Minnis, "Affection and Imagination", 355.

attained perfect love or contemplation.[30] For Hilton and the *Cloud*-author it seems that whilst imaginative meditation, essentially a heightened form of reader-engagement with the text, is good and worthy, it can only ever achieve the lower levels of the mystical journey.

The Augustinian and Pseudo-Dionysian traditions that emphasise the unknowability of God, to which Hilton and the *Cloud*-author respectively owe such debts, have tended to dominate research into fourteenth-century texts categorised as mystical. The type of affectivity and carnality found in the writings of Rolle, such as the Franciscan harnessing of *imaginatio*, have been over-shadowed. Rolle himself has been regarded as an eccentric enthusiast, who while attempting to direct the spiritual lives of others knew little of mystical experience himself.[31] Yet, it would seem that any argument about Rolle's actual experience with mysticism pales into insignificance against the well-attested popularity of both his cult and his writings. The fact that the *Cloud*-author deemed Rolle worthy of comment at all suggests that his influence was important enough to dispute. Moreover, experimental as it may have been, Rolle's commitment to recording and assimilating his own mystical experience in his Latin works at least speaks volumes about his own understanding of the spiritual journey towards the ultimate goal he prescribes for his readers in the vernacular – the unitive state.

By offering a prominent position to imagination within his mystical schema, Rolle, while developing Bernardine affectivity, demonstrates affinities with Franciscan devotion.[32] Whether affinities with other traditions release Rolle from the somewhat disparaging criticisms which he has received for not being definable within Augustinian, Pseudo-Dionysian or Dominican models of mysticism needs further investigation. Franciscan devotion, with its determined Christocentricity, is regarded by Ewert Cousins as "the mysticism of the historical event" which appears to enable the individual to realise absolute truth by means of *imaginatio* on the life and Passion of Christ.[33] Rolle, who

---

[30] A. Minnis, "Affection and Imagination", 355.

[31] The preoccupation with establishing an accurate biography for Rolle and offering psychological assessments of his character in earlier scholarship also helped to arouse debate over his status in the history of English mysticism and, subsequently, the authenticity of his own mystical experiences. One his most vituperative detractors was D. Knowles, *The English Mystical Tradition* (New York, 1961), 48–66. Knowles originally expressed reservations about the authenticity of Rolle's mystical experiences in an earlier work, *The English Mystics* (London, 1927). See also R. M. Wilson, "Three Middle English Mystics". *Essays & Studies* 9 (1956); M. Jennings, "Richard Rolle and the Three Degrees of Love". *Downside Review* 93 (1975); K. C. Russell, "Reading Richard Rolle". *Spirituality Today* 30:2 (1978); B. Windeatt, *English Mystics of the Middle Ages*. (Cambridge, 1994).

[32] H. E. Allen, *English Writings*, xlv. Allen notes that "Franciscans are the religious with whose ideal he [Rolle] shows the greatest sympathy through his works".

[33] E. H. Cousins, "Francis of Assisi: Christian Mysticism at the Crossroads". *Mysticism and Religious Traditions*. Ed. S. T. Katz (New York, 1983), 166.

may well have been influenced by Franciscan spirituality during his time as a student at Oxford, shows a remarkable affinity for the Franciscan mystical tradition. This may have contributed to the ease with which Rolle established himself in Hampole where the confessors to the nuns were Franciscans.[34] Like the Francis of Assisi seen in medieval biographies, Rolle experiences a super-natural sweetness, warmth and song in the course of his mystical journey. Both Thomas of Celano and Bonaventure record how Francis tasted the sweet-ness of divinity,[35] burned with the fire of love,[36] and heard heavenly melodies which far surpassed anything of earthly origin.[37] Thomas of Celano, in his *Second Life of St. Francis*, records how Francis responded to his reception of heavenly music:

> Some times Francis would act in the following way. When the sweetest melody would bubble up in him, he would give exterior expression to it in French, and the breath of the divine whisper which his ear perceived in secret would burst forth in French in a song of joy. . . . This whole ecstasy of joy would often end in tears and his song of gladness would dissolve in compassion for the Passion of Christ.[38]

Bonaventure himself particularly influenced Rolle's concept of *canor* which is quite distinctly Franciscan – and specifically Bonaventuran – in content and tone; and Bonaventure's influence on Rolle is clear when we consider Rolle's contemplation of the life and Passion of Christ.[39] Psalm 56, the Easter Psalm, is the perfect example of Rolle's dependence on Franciscan spirituality because when Bonaventure explicates this Psalm in his *Vitis mystica*, he discusses the "sweet harmony" of Christ's work, the "burning love" of grace, and the *canor* of the song of penance begun on the cross; this mystical schema could certainly be seen as prefiguring Rolle's *calor*, *dulcor* and *canor*. According to William Pollard, only the anonymous English *Meditation on the Life and Passion of Christ* (wrongly attributed to Bonaventure) and the *Vitis mystica* of

---

34 H. E. Allen, *English Writings*, xlv.
35 Thomas of Celano, "Second Life of St. Francis". Trans. P. Hermann. *St. Francis of Assisi, Writing and Earlier Biographies: English Omnibus of the Sources for the Life of St. Francis*. Ed. M. A. Habig (London, 1979), II Celano LXI, 94, 440. "The world was tasteless to him who was fed with heavenly sweetness."
36 Bonaventure, "The Major Life of St. Francis". Trans. B. Fahy. *St. Francis of Assisi, Writing and Earlier Biographies*, IX, 1, 698. "No human tongue could describe the pas-sionate love with which Francis burned for Christ, his Spouse; he seemed to be com-pletely absorbed by the fire of divine love like a glowing coal."
37 Thomas of Celano, "Second Life of St. Francis", II Celano LXXXIX, 126, 467.
38 Thomas of Celano, "Second Life of St. Francis", II Celano XC, 127, 467.
39 See W. F. Pollard, "The 'Tone of Heaven': Bonaventuran Melody and the Easter Psalm in Richard Rolle". *The Popular Literature of Medieval England*. Ed. T. J. Heffernan (Knoxville, 1985), 252–276. See also W. Netherton, "Joy Gars Me Jangell", ch. 3.

Bonaventure can compare with Rolle's tone and specificity of image.[40] William Hodapp further suggests that Rolle follows the Bonaventuran conception, found in his systematic treatment of the *via mystica* in *De triplici via*, that attending to Christ's life and his Passion through meditation, prayer and contemplation is central to the mystical journey itself.[41]

The Franciscan tradition bears another connection to Rollean thought in that both Rolle and Francis sustained a deep devotion to the Holy Name. Thomas of Celano records that Francis

> was filled with love that surpassed all human understanding when he pro-
> nounced your holy name, O holy Lord; and carried away with joy and
> purest gladness, he seemed like a new man, one from another world.[42]

His devotion to the incarnate Word and the Passion subsumed and encapsulated everything else; "he was always occupied with Jesus; Jesus he bore in his heart, Jesus in his mouth, Jesus in his ears, Jesus in his eyes, Jesus in his hands, Jesus in the rest of his members".[43] In Rolle's English treatises and his earlier Latin works the devotion to the Holy Name, and his emphasis on the humanity and Passion of Christ, both permeate and focus his mysticism. In *The Form of Living* Rolle's emphasis on the salvific features of the name of Jesus is quite explicit:

> If þou wil be wel with God, and haue grace to reue þi lif right, and cum to þe
> ioy of loue, þis name Iesus, fest hit in þi herte þat hit cum neuer out of þi
> þoght. And when þou spekest to hym, and seist "Ihesu" þrogh custume, hit
> shal be in þyn ere ioy, in þy mouth hony, and in þyn hert melody . . . If þou
> þynke Ihesu continuely, and hold it stably . . . hit openeth heuyn and maketh
> a contemplatif man. (18/610–620)

For Rolle, Christ is both the bridegroom with whom he desires the soul of the recipient of *Ego Dormio* to be wed, and the cause and inspiration of his own love, which frequently makes him burst forth in lyrical song. These features in Rolle may not be direct borrowings from writings by or about Francis of Assisi but they are certainly Franciscan in flavour, perhaps similarities or nuances picked up from his Franciscan education at Oxford. The figure of Francis seemed to appeal to Rolle's followers also, as is evidenced by the description of his conversion in the *Officium*, which mirrors that of Francis. Indeed, the spread of Franciscan affective spirituality to a broader vernacular reading public must have assisted the assimilation of Rolle's similar ideas, wherever he derived them from.

---

[40] W. Pollard, "The 'Tone of Heaven' ", 270.
[41] W. F. Hodapp, "Sacred Time and Space Within: Drama and Ritual in Late Medieval Affective Passion Meditations". *Downside Review* 115 (1997), 237–238.
[42] Thomas of Celano, "First Life of St. Francis", I Celano XXIX, 82, 297.
[43] Thomas of Celano, "First Life of St. Francis", I Celano IX, 115, 329.

When we look closely at the three English treatises, the link with Franciscan spirituality lies mostly in shared attitudes and tone, which Rolle probably acquired through his debt to Bernardine affectivity and his concern with the redirection of the *affectus* of his readers. Vincent Gillespie, in his discussion of Rolle's assertions about the nature of mystical union, notes the emphasis which is placed on restoring the fallen *affectus* or will. Following Robert Grosseteste, Gillespie outlines the functions performed by the intellective and affective faculties of the soul, the former in recognising and understanding a given sensory perception or possibility and the latter in adjudicating the nature of the situation or object, whether it is good and spiritual, or evil and carnal.[44] He maintains that Rolle accepted the view that the soul's natural orientation towards the good and spiritual was distorted by the Fall, giving it a tendency toward carnal pleasure. In order to prevent such debauchery the *affectus* needed to be governed by the aspirations of the *intellectus*. The corporeal imagery used to denote this idea, regarding each faculty as a foot of the soul, led to the notion that while the *intellectus* kept in step with the spirit, the *affectus*, without proper guidance, tended to lag behind.[45] Its carnal orientation resulted in the will's inability to focus on spiritual entities. Part of the soteriological power of the Incarnation lay in Christ's ability to provide a mirror of the divine into which the will could gaze. The nativity and Passion became especially potent symbols of this function of Christ's human nature, and so became the focus for much devotional literature and affective meditation. Gillespie concludes that the affectivity of both Rolle and the Franciscan movement was born out of a desire to correct the nature of the *affectus*, so that it conformed to the will of God. Throughout his English works, as we shall see later, Rolle frequently exploits the problem of the wilful *affectus* by constructing negative/positive positions which allow the reader agency in self-reflection.

Imaginatio centred on the figure of Christ thus aided the correction of the *affectus* by enabling its desires to become focused on the Divine. By feeling compassion for the human and carnal nature of Christ, the *affectus'* desire was redirected away from temporal pleasures. However, as noted above, this process was only regarded by most espousers of mysticism as useful at a relatively lowly stage of the mystical journey. Once the *affectus* became re-orientated, such meditations on Christ's humanity should be left behind as

---

44 D. A. Callus, "Robert Grosseteste as Scholar". *Robert Grosseteste, Scholar and Bishop: Commemorative Essays*. Ed. D. A. Callus (Oxford, 1955), 16 cited in V. Gillespie, "Mystic's Foot", 203. Paraphrasing Robert Grosseteste, Callus writes that once the intellect has verified the data by reference to what it knows of the true, the *affectus* yearns towards the good or away from the bad. Gillespie then suggests that this is how it would have been if man had not been a fallen creature, because, as a result of the fall, the will has been corrupted, and it runs after the joys of the world instead of resolutely fixing itself on the good.

45 See V. Gillespie, "Mystic's Foot", *passim*.

the devotee became aware of the nature of the Godhead. In *The Cloud of Unknowing*, devotees are to employ the intellective faculty, and only when the ineffability of God is realised should they employ the transformed *affectus*, which is able to beat at the cloud of unknowing with the longing dart of love:

> & þou schalt step abouen it stalworþly, bot listely, wiþ a deuoute & a plesing stering of loue, & fonde for to peerse þat derknes abouen þee. & smyte apon þat þicke cloude of vnknowyng wiþ a scharpe darte of longing loue, & go not þens for þing þat befalleþ.[46]

In Rolle, the *intellectus* does not perform this warning and transforming function. Instead, the entire process is affective. In this Rolle clearly reveals his relationship to Bernardine spirituality, especially in the central role Bernard assigned to the principle of affective love; for Bernard the internal, individual perception of God, the process of learning by experience, becomes at once intellectual and deeply affective. In suggesting the importance of *imaginatio* for the correction of the *affectus*, Rolle does not propose anything extraordinary to which Hilton or the *Cloud*-author would not give consent. This problem arises when Rolle suggests *imaginatio* as a useful practice at the climactic stages of the mystical journey. It is here that he appears to exceed the limitations placed on *imaginatio* by both the *Cloud*-author and Hilton, for which, as already stated, both possibly polemicised against him.

Despite the criticism which Rolle appears to receive from his contemporaries for precisely this aspect of his mystical schema, Watson argues that such a use of *imaginatio* is not present in Rolle's more sophisticated writings. He suggests that Rolle's Passion lyrics and meditations were written to fulfill a relatively lowly function in the lives of spiritual beginners, while his more sophisticated English and Latin works make fairly few references to the Passion.[47] Watson also disputes the extent to which Rolle should be aligned with Cistercian spirituality, and in doing so holds that it would be a mistake to regard him [Rolle] as mainly a Christocentric writer because his debts to Cistercian spirituality are those of mood and imagery more than Christology.[48] Yet this down-playing of the Christocentricity of Rolle's mysticism seems to rest on the assumption that Rolle's devotion to the Holy Name is not found at the height of his mystical experience – his reception of *canor* – and that it is a concept empty of any real theological content.[49] This appears an odd assumption, given the power traditionally ascribed to the name of God

---

[46] *The Cloud of Unknowing*, 26/8–12.
[47] N. Watson, *Invention of Authority*, 55.
[48] N. Watson, *Invention of Authority*, 55.
[49] N. Watson, *Invention of Authority*, 55. Watson writes "it is true that he associates devotion to the Holy Name with more advanced spiritual states; but his invocations of Jesus are almost devoid of any theological content, and their structural importance . . . is in their connection with his experience of *dulcor*".

within Christian religion, as demonstrated in *The Form of Living* where Rolle charges his reader to keep Christ continually in his/her thoughts and speaks of the intense love which he/she will feel for Christ in the third degree of love, the height of mystical experience. It is also worth noting that in *Emendatio Vitae* Rolle pointedly mentions the importance of Christ to a soul at the climax of mystical ecstasy:

> In illo gradu anima constituta, illum vnum diligit, solum Christum sitit, Christum concupiscit, in solo illius desiderio anelat, ad ipsum suspirat, ex ipso inardescit, in ipso feruens requiescit. Nichil igitur dulcescit, nichil sapit nisi Ihesu indulcoretur, cuius memoria quasi musicum melos in conuiuio uini.

> [The soul set in this degree loves him alone; she yearns only for Christ, and Christ desires; only in Him she abides, and after him she sighs; in Him she burns; she rests in His warmth. Nothing is sweet to her, nothing she savours, except it be made sweet in Jesus; whose memory is as a song of music in a feast of wine.][50]

Furthermore, the argument rests upon the belief that Rolle presents a mystical schema which is always systematic. Such an assumption seems difficult to substantiate when the diversity of approach within his English pieces is considered. In describing the central tenets of his approach to God, the three degrees of love, Rolle draws upon his sources in different ways. In *The Form of Living* he develops ideas found in *De Quattuor Gradibus Violentiae Caritatis* of Richard of St. Victor, while in *Ego Dormio* the degrees of love are borrowed from this text but his delineation of them is more moralistic, and does not rely upon Richard of St. Victor's analysis. In *The Commandment*, the three degrees of love are named briefly in the early part of the work but do not appear to have the same significance as they do in Rolle's other vernacular treatises.

In *De Quattuor Gradibus Violentiae Caritatis*, the mystical ascent progresses through four degrees of love – *insuperabilis*, *inseparabilis*, *singularis* and *insatiabilis* – but their definitions are imprecise. Watson suggests that Richard of St. Victor's treatise demonstrates ordered measureless love in its very form (four orders which are continually changing), and in its elaborately patterned but violently exciting language.[51] Rolle perhaps used this text as a main source for his definitions of the three degrees of love because of this imprecision; as I noted above, he is certainly flexible with the definitions in the English treatises. Similarly, the practice of *imaginatio* has differing functions in different Rolle's texts. *Emendatio Vitae* recommends Passion meditation for beginners,

---

50 *Emendatio Vitae. Richard Rolle: Emendatio Vitae; Orationes ad honorem nominis Ihesu*. Ed. N. Watson (Toronto, 1995), 59/71–76; *The Mending of Life*, 231.
51 N. Watson, *Invention of Authority*, 20.

"Est autem meditacio bona de passione Christi et morte . . . Estimo quod hec meditacio utilior est omnibus aliis hiis qui iam nouiter ad Christum conuertuntur" [the meditation of Christ's passion and His death is good . . . I trow this meditation is most profitable of all others to them that are newly turned to Christ.][52] *Ego Dormio* portrays it as preparatory material for aiding the transition between the second and third degree of love:

> And thynke oft þis of his passione . . . if þou wil thynke þis euery day, þou shalt fynd gret swetnesse . . . And þan entres þou in to þe þrid degree of loue. (30–31/174–217)

This again has overtones of the Cistercian approach. For Bernard, rapture is a supremely intense delight felt by the soul for the sweetness of God and that rapture assumes prominence in Bernard's mysticism because feeling is prominent; for rapture is, presumably, a supremely *felt* experience.[53] Rolle appears to employ *imaginatio* throughout his mystical schema because of its ability to increase the soul's compassion for the divine, and thus continually develop the desire for the beloved.

It would seem that the key to Rolle's understanding of *imaginatio* lies in his regard for the *affectus* and how it can be aligned to accept the role of the bride of Christ and then progress to the unitive state. In this, Rolle's debt to Bernardine affectivity is of central importance. In opposition to Cuthbert Butler, Andrew Louth argues that the mysticism of Bernard is highly distinctive and differs both from that found in the writings of Gregory and of Augustine. The latter both offer the intellective faculty a position of some prominence within their mystical schema. Louth argues that Bernard makes the mystical journey through the affective faculty alone; Bernard, while regarding knowledge and love as complementary, holds them as distinct in his outline of mysticism. He divorces his mysticism from his theology, and concentrates on the *affectus* which is able to tap the deepest depths of man's being. This anthropomorphic response centres on imagery drawn from the *Song of Songs*. At its highest level, the soul becomes wed to the bridegroom, Christ, to whom He then offers the secret whispering of his heart. Bernard emphasises, against the intellectual tradition, the uniqueness of each unitive encounter, "For indeed there is not one queen but several, and many concubines, and young women without number. And each finds for herself with the Bridegroom, and says: My secret is mine, my secret is mine (Isaiah 24:16)."[54] The soul does not share in a universal knowledge of the divine, but in a

---

52 *Emendatio Vitae*, 51/1 and 52/14–15; *The Mending of Life*, 221.
53 A. Louth, "Bernard and Affective Mysticism". *The Influence of Saint Bernard: Anglican Essays with an Introduction by Jean Leclerq O. S. B.* Ed. B. Ward (Oxford, 1976), 3.
54 Bernard of Clairvaux, *Sermo* 23. iv. 9; I, 29–31/114 cited in A. Louth, "Bernard and Affective Mysticism", 5.

private erotic coupling of itself and Christ. It is this imagery which Rolle so seductively deploys in *Ego Dormio* when he woos the reader to the bed of his Lord:

> Forþi þat I loue þe, I wowe þe, þat I myght haue þe as I wold, nat to me, bot to my Lord. I wil becum a messager to brynge þe to hys bed . . . (26/6–8)

The terminological similarities between Bernard, Augustine and Gregory would appear to disguise deeper conceptual differences: with Bernard there is a sharp contrast between knowledge and love, for love is not primarily a desire for possession and delight in possessing, as with Augustine, but a feeling: "Amor est affectio naturalis" . . .[55] Such assumptions rest upon analysis of Bernard's use of *sapientia* as being equivalent to *sapor boni* (a taste for the good),[56] rather than the intellectual activity which it represents within the Augustinian tradition. Bernard, it would seem, represents a completely new tradition of mysticism which stands apart from both its Augustinian and Pseudo-Dionysian counterparts.[57] Furthermore, it is recognised that the Victorines, whose influence is clearly seen in Rolle, systematised Bernard's affectivity and drew upon other traditions in the formulation of their mystical schemas. Further research into Rolle's relationship to Cistercian spirituality is needed to determine whether Rolle fits into the purely affective tradition of mysticism generally associated with Bernard. Against this proposition, Watson asserts that Rolle lays claims to continuous ecstasy, and therefore stands apart from his Bernardine heritage; he cites a passage from *Super Canticum Canticorum* as evidence.[58] However, numerous passages in Rolle's English and Latin works appear to make the meaning of this text more ambiguous, as the following examples demonstrate. In *Incendium Amoris*, Rolle's refusal to sing the liturgy because of the resultant disturbance of mystical ecstasy indicates the unstable nature of such experiences. He states:

> Porro, ut potui in scripturis perscrutari, inueni et cognoui quidem summus amor Christi in tribus consistit: in feruore, in canore, et in dulcore; et hec tria ego expertus sum in mente non posse diu persistere sine magna quiete.

---

55 Bernard of Clairvaux, *De Diligendo Deo*, VIII. 23; III, 6/138 cited in A. Louth "Bernard and Affective Mysticism", 3.

56 Bernard of Clairvaux, *De Diligendo Deo*, X. 27; III, 15/143 cited in A. Louth "Bernard and Affective Mysticism", 3.

57 A. Louth, "Bernard and Affective Mysticism", 7. God is not loved because he cannot be known . . . God is to be loved because it is only love that involves the whole man at his deepest. God is not to be sought as an object of knowledge, for knowledge does not affect man at all deeply.

58 N. Watson, *Invention of Authority*, 152. The passage reads "and because this song of eternal love is not with us *non raptim* (hurriedly) and *non momentanae* (momentarily), but *set continue adest nobis* (continually)".

[As far as my study of Scripture goes, I have found that to love Christ above all else will involve three things: warmth and song and sweetness. And these three, as I know from personal experience, cannot exist for long without there being great quiet.][59]

In any case the duration of warmth, sweetness and song still did not amount to perfection. Perhaps the clearest example of this is Rolle's desire for death, as the short prose work *Ghostly Gladness* potently illustrates:

> Gostly gladnesse in Ihesu, and ioy in hert, with swetnesse in soule of þe sauour of heuyn in hope, is helth in to hele, and my lyf lendeth in loue, and lightsomnes vmlappeth my thoght. I dred nat þat me may wirch wo, so myche I wot of wele. Hit ware no wonder if dethe ware dere, þat I myght se hym þat I seke; bot now hit lengthes fro me, and me behoueth to lyve here til he wil me lese. List and lere of þis lare, and þe shal nat myslike. Loue maketh me to melle, and ioy maketh me jangle. Loke þou lede þi life in lightsomnes; and heuynesse, hold hit away. Sorynesse let nat sit with the, bot in gladnes in God euermore make þou þi glee. (41)

It would be hard to deny that this short prose work describes anything less than the heights of the mystical journey on earth, "þi life in lightsomnes", before longed for death opens the gateway to the ultimate spiritual reward. This desire for death is present in both *Ego Dormio* and *The Form of Living*. Rolle clearly states that while the role of the bride, effectively the unitive state, can be accepted on earth, true and everlasting perfection is not possible in this life:

> Bot þou shalt witte þat no man hath perfite sight of heuyn whils þei ben in body lyvynge here, bot as sone as þai dey, þai ben broght bifor God, and seth hym face to face . . . and wonneth with hym withouten end . . . (25/889–893)

This admission demonstrates that Rolle does not claim to be one of the *perfectissimi*, as Watson claims. What he does claim is the power of affectivity to bring the soul as near to perfect union as possible on earth.

The progressive and imprecise development of the *affectus* causes Rolle sometimes to offer an account of mysticism that did not sit well with others. The notion that love is a feeling, which appears to be carried over into Rolle's understanding of *calor*, *dulcor*, and *canor*, caused the *Cloud*-author to remonstrate on the dangers of confusing spiritual and physical sensations:

> Þei reden & heren wel sey þat þei schuld leue vtward worching wiþ þeire wittes, & worche inwardes . . . as þei wolde see inwardes wiþ þeire bodily iȝen, & heren inwardes wiþ þeire eren, & so forþe of alle þeire wittes, smellen, taasten, & felyn inwardes . . . & wiþ þis coriouste þei trauayle þeire

---

59 *Incendium Amoris*, 184–185; *The Fire of Love*, 88–89.

ymaginacion so vndiscreetly, þat at þe laste þei turne here brayne in herer hedes.[60]

A passage in *Ego Dormio* that follows the second lyric details the function of *imaginatio* in the second degree of love. Rolle writes:

> If þou wil þynke þis euery day, þou shalt fynd gret swetnesse, þat shal draw þi hert vp, and mak þe fal in wepynge and in grete langynge to Ihesu; and þi þoght shal be reft abouen al erthly þynges, abouen þe sky and þe sterres, so þat þe eigh of þi hert may loke in to heuen. (31/212–215)

The *Cloud*-author responds to such assertions with aghast mockery:

> For ȝif it so be þat þei ouþer rede, or here redde or spoken hou þat men schuld lift up here hertes vnto God, as fast þei stare in þe sterres as þei wolde be abouen þe mone . . . Þees men willen sumtyme wiþ þe coriouste of here ymaginacion peerce þe planetes, & make an hole in þe firmament to loke in þerate. Þees men wil make a God as hem lyst, & cloþen hym ful richely in cloþes, & set hym in a trone . . .[61]

The emotional response to imaginative meditation demanded by Rolle's text is certainly in stark contrast to the *Cloud*-author's damning account of those who would dare to use imagination to "loke in to heuen". Here, Rolle's promotion of reader-engagement in the text is clearly highlighted whereas the *Cloud*-author can be observed explicitly warning against it.

There was a continuous debate about whether the *intellectus* or the *affectus* was pre-eminent; medieval writers demonstrate no consensus of opinion on this point. The accusations of the *Cloud*-author against the sensuousness of Rolle's experience betray his own debt to the Pseudo-Dionysian tradition – a tradition which harnesses the intellect in order to realise the ineffability of God before returning to the *affectus*. For Rolle, like Bernard, love is both feeling and knowledge. While Rolle may not in fact stand firmly in this tradition of Bernardine spirituality and many modern scholars may reject Rolle's affective mysticism, just as the *Cloud*-author did, numerous medieval devotees, as manuscript evidence attests, held him in high regard. The complexity of the mystical spirituality of fourteenth-century England should not be underestimated. It would be rash to assume that there was some kind of consensus that marginalised Rolle simply because both the *Cloud*-author and Hilton present mystical schemas which are hostile to his. The limited circulation of the *Cloud*-author, compared with Rolle's popular mysticism, meant that a later fourteenth-century and fifteenth-century audience would be far more likely to have access to the works of Rolle. As Gillespie points out, the author of *The*

---

60 *The Cloud of Unknowing*, 96/14–24.
61 *The Cloud of Unknowing*, 105/6–13.

Cloud of Unknowing and its related treatises seems to have attempted to prevent widespread distribution of his texts by warning off inexpert readers and, to judge by the surviving evidence of manuscript ownership, to have been largely successful.[62] Bearing this in mind, it seems clear that Rolle's brand of affectivity and his extended use of reader-engaging elements (such as *imaginatio*), not the *Cloud*-author's elitist doctrine, had more far-reaching implications for medieval devotional reading tastes and habits in fourteenth- and fifteenth-century England. Indeed, Rolle was certainly not writing his affective vernacular devotional works in a vacuum. Affective literature very much like Rolle's, that appealed to the human senses through a language of love, that focused on the humanity of Christ, and that often invited the general reader to reach the heights of mystical devotion, was widely available and, if the evidence of the proliferation and diverse ownership of manuscripts is accepted, was favourably responded to by a wide variety of medieval readers.

III

Modern scholars have struggled to define satisfactorily the vast body of affective material that sprang up in fourteenth- and fifteenth-century England. W. A. Pantin describes it as a particular line or process of devotional and mystical development which had been going on since the eleventh century that increasingly focused devotion on intense personal feeling and tenderness towards the person of Christ.[63] Yet, as Pantin points out, it is difficult to find a satisfactory name for this development: one might call it Christocentric piety, or affective piety, or simply the devotional movement. Needless to say, this devotional movement continued to flourish and spread in the fourteenth century, and in one way or another has profoundly affected Christian spirituality ever since.[64] Michael Sargent further notes that the description "devotional" can refer inclusively to the entire range of piety from simple, affective prayer to works describing, or inciting to, contemplative union.[65] What does

---

[62] V. Gillespie, "Vernacular Books of Religion", 322.

[63] W. A. Pantin, *The English Church*, 190.

[64] W. A. Pantin, *The English Church*, 190. See also D. Gray, *Themes and Images*, 18–19. Gray suggests that " 'the devotional movement' is perhaps the most convenient title, provided that we do not think of it as a single, unified, organised 'movement' but rather as a general drift underlying a series of separate, though related, movements and expressions of it".

[65] M. G. Sargent, "Minor Devotional Writings". *Middle English Prose: A Critical Guide to Major Authors and Genres*. Ed. A. S. G. Edwards (New Brunswick, New Jersey, 1984), 147. See also V. Lagorio, "Problems in Middle English Mystical Prose". *Middle English Prose: Essays on Bibliographical Problems*. Eds. A. S. G. Edwards and D. Pearsall (New York, 1981), 129–148.

seem clear is that the personal/emotional aspect, particularly the responses of the individual to themes and images associated with the humanity of Christ, is the key to defining this type of devotion and the literature associated with it. For Caroline Walker Bynum the affective piety of the Middle Ages is based on an increasing sense of, first, humankind's creation in the image and likeness of God and, second, the humanity of Christ as guarantee that what we are is inextricably joined with divinity.[66] Christ is seen as the mediator who joins human substance to divinity and as the object of a profound experiential union; God is emphasised as creating and creative; the cooperation of the Trinity in the work of creation is stressed and the dominant note of piety is optimism and a sense of momentum toward a loving God. Devotion to, and the promotion of *imaginatio* on, the person of Christ, drawn from the traditional sources noted above, became prominent in vernacular affective texts from the later thirteenth century onwards. Often in this type of literature the reader (or hearer, as the case frequently was) was not only expected to focus his/her attention on Christ, but was also encouraged to participate as an individual in the discourse of the text. In short, many texts gave readers a model for constructing themselves as individual souls.

By the later thirteenth century much of this affective material was written in the vernacular. English was the language of the homily in the mass and it was increasingly used in the literature of moral theology which focused on providing religious instruction on the basics of Christianity for the laity as well as the for the less educated clergy.[67] *Speculum Vitae*, a later fourteenth-century Northern compendium of spiritual instruction which participates in three medieval traditions of catechetical and devotional writings – the *summa*, the *speculum* of vices and virtues, and *Pater noster* schematisations – illustrates both the linguistic shift occurring in the fourteenth century and the opening of texts to as wide an audience as possible:

> Na latyne wil I speke ne wast
> Bot inglische þat men uses mast
> For þat es yhour kynde langage
> Þat ȝhe have mast here of vsage . . .

---

66 C. Walker Bynum, *Jesus as Mother*, 130.
67 W. A. Pantin, *The English Church*, 191. Pantin notes that one of the most important developments came from the *De informatione simplicum* section of Archbishop Pecham's legislation, beginning *Ignorantia sacerdotum*, which gives a program of religious instruction: the fourteen articles of faith, the ten commandments of the Law and the two commandments of the Gospel, the seven works of mercy, the seven virtues, the seven vices, and the seven sacraments are to be expounded to the people in the vernacular four times a year. See also J. Frankis, "The Social Context of Vernacular Writing in Thirteenth-Century England: the Evidence of the Manuscripts". *Thirteenth Century England*. Eds. P. R. Cross and S. D. Lloyd (Woodbridge, 1986), 175–184.

> For þat langage es mast schewed
> Als wele amonge lered als lewed.[68]

As the devotional movement developed in the fourteenth century, in lay as well as religious contexts, and Latin literacy further declined, the vernacular became the primary medium through which popular affective devotion was promoted. A popular didactic poem widely attributed to Rolle in the medieval period, *The Prick of Conscience*, explicitly acknowledges the expected linguistic limitations of its audience:

> Now haf I here als I first undirtoke,
> Fulfilled þe seven partes of þis boke . . .
> Namly til lewed men of England,
> Þat can noght bot Inglise undirstand;
> Þarfor þis tretice drawe I wald
> In Inglise tung þat may be cald
> Prik of Conscience als men may fele . . .[69]

Increasingly, it would seem, medieval writers responded to the need for vernacular devotional material that could satisfy, as *Speculum Vitae* suggests, "lered" as well as "lewed". As one version of St. Edmund's *Speculum* in the Vernon manuscript puts it: "Þis may be 30r halyday werk,/ Hit wol avayle boþe lewed and clerk".[70]

Prominent amongst the literature of this vernacular devotional movement are the numerous religious lyrics and Passion meditations written in English which, according to Rosemary Woolf, had grown directly and unself-consciously from the Latin devotional movement noted above.[71] One of the outstanding aspects of many of these poems and meditations is that, from the thirteenth century onwards, we are able to see the development of the role of the individual, and the practice of *imaginatio*, in vernacular religious literature, particularly in the construction of the reader as the "I" figure in the text, the meditator. Influenced by works such as the *Speculum* and the *Meditationes vitae Christi* ascribed to Bonaventure, writers of late medieval

---

68 *English Metrical Homilies from Manuscripts of the Fourteenth Century.* Ed. J. Small (Edinburgh, 1862), 4 cited in V. Gillespie, " 'Lukynge in haly bukes' ", 7. See also *A Manual of the Writings in Middle English*, Vol. 7, 7; W. A. Pantin, *The English Church*, 229–230. Manuscript evidence suggests that the *Speculum Vitae* was in circulation before 1384 and while no definite source has been found it was attributed to both Rolle and William of Nassington during the medieval period.

69 *The Prick of Conscience.* Ed. R. Morris (Berlin, 1863), l. 9533 f. cited in H. E. Allen, *The Authorship of "The Prick of Conscience"*, 127.

70 C. Horstmann and F. J. Furnivall, eds. *Minor Poems of the Vernon MS* (London, 1892), 269 cited in A. Taylor, "Into his Secret Chamber: Reading and Privacy in Late Medieval England". *The Practice and Representation of Reading in England*. Eds. J. Raven, H. Small and N. Tadmar (Cambridge, 1996), n. 26, 48.

71 R. Woolf, *The English Religious Lyric in the Middle Ages* (Oxford, 1968), 2.

devotional literature increasingly recognised the importance of individual participation in the narrative of Christ's life and Passion to devotional practice.[72] One of the earliest vernacular lyrics to offer such a reader-identity is the thirteenth-century "Nou goth sonne under wod":

> Nou goth sonne under wod,
> Me reweth, Marie, thi faire rode,
> Nou goth sonne under tre,
> Me reweth, Marie, thi sone and the.[73]

William Hodapp cites J. A. W. Bennett's description of the poem as an instance of "one of the greatest revolutions in feeling that Europe has ever witnessed ... Nothing in Anglo-Saxon verse and little in Latin hymnody prepares us for such presentations of sacred scenes and emotions as these."[74] The dramatic, meditative impact of the poem lies in its immediacy, evoked in its present-tense verbs "goth" and "reweth", and in the action and attitude of the persona, who becomes intimately involved in the scene and attempts to ease Mary's sorrow. The invitation to the reader to participate in the text, to inhabit the persona's subject position and address Mary directly at the foot of the cross, points to an interesting facet of late medieval devotional practice – authors encouraging their audience not only to commemorate Jesus' sacrificial act but also, in a sense, to recover it through an imaginatively dramatic engagement with the Passion narrative itself.[75] The poem was widely read in fourteenth- and fifteenth-century England, surviving in a large number of manuscripts, which further suggests the favourable reception of the practice of imaginative meditation in late medieval England.[76]

It is now generally accepted that Rolle himself, who is most often thought of as a mystical writer, also wrote a number of vernacular lyrics and two prose Passion meditations.[77] This reveals not only his acceptance of, and commit-

---

72 The Latin *Meditationes vitae Christi* can be found in Bonaventure, *Opera Omnia Sanctae Bonaventurae*. Ed. A. C. Peltier (Paris, 1864–1871) vol. 12, 509–630; For Edmund's *Speculum* see Edmund of Abingdon, *Speculum Religiosorum* and *Speculum Ecclesie*. Ed. H. P. Forshaw (London, 1973).

73 D. Gray, *A Selection of Religious Lyrics* (Oxford, 1975), Poem 21, 17.

74 See W. Hodapp, "Sacred Time and Space Within: Drama and Ritual in Late Medieval Affective Passion Meditations". *Downside Review* 115:4 (1997), 235–248. See also J. A. W. Bennett, *Poetry of the Passion: Studies in Twelve Centuries of English Verse* (Oxford, 1982).

75 W. Hodapp, "Sacred Time and Space Within", 235–236.

76 See D. Gray, *A Selection of Religious Lyrics*, 109–110. Gray notes "this quatrain is found in the extremely popular and influential *Merure de Saint Eglise* by Edmund of Canterbury (d. 1240) . . . Over sixty manuscripts in three languages are extant."

77 There has been some debate over Rolle's authorship of these works, particularly the two Passion meditations, but it seems that they are now generally accepted as Rollean texts. See H. E. Allen, *Writings Ascribed*, 281; M. F. Madigan, *The Passio Domini Theme in the Works of Richard Rolle: His Personal Contribution in its Religious,*

ment to, mediums of religious instruction generally associated with popular devotional literature, but also his active participation in the tradition of religious literature that invites the reader to adopt the principal subject position within the text. As Vincent Gillespie points out, throughout the whole body of his English works Rolle emphasises the value of reflection on particular actions and images from scriptural narrative (especially on the Passion of Christ as elaborated by tradition and from the liturgy), focusing on the affective potential of such activities for kindling devotion.[78] The shorter of Rolle's Passion meditations, *Meditation A*, is the less affective of the two but nonetheless encourages readers to focus their devotion through meditative practice. Recognisable as a brief paraphrase of the Pseudo-Bonaventuran *Meditationes vitae Christi*, *Meditation A* provides instruction for the reader, the "wreched kaytif" in need of spiritual guidance, on how to meditate.[79] As a meditative exercise it has a similar function to the Passion lyric in *Ego Dormio* that exhorts the reader to "thynk oft þis of his passione" (30/174) in order to move from the second to the third degree of love.

The longer text, *Meditation B*, is exclusively focused on the Passion and is more concerned with the position of the reader in the text. Throughout this work the reader is explicitly constructed as the "I" figure who at times actively participates as a spectator at the scene of Christ's suffering on the cross:

> Þan was hit reuth to se þy body al stremed on blode. A, lord, swete Ihesu, me þynketh I se þe rede blode ren doun by þy chekes, stremes aftyr euche stroke of þy coronynge and scorgynge. (76/287–289)

Close, personal contact, not only with Christ but also with all those present at the Passion scene, is generated for the reader when the meditator first describes the Virgin Mary's lamentations in the present tense and then addresses her directly:

> Now she wronge hir hondes, wepynge and seighynge; now she cast hir armes [abrode]; þe watyr of hir eyghne dropped at hir fete . . . Now, lady, þat peyne and passioun shold haue be myne, for I had deserued hitte and was cause þerof. (77/333–351)

Anne Clark Bartlett notes that Passion narratives commonly use the figure of a grieving Virgin Mary as a reader in the text to guide the audience's contemplation of Christ's suffering and death.[80] Moreover, by recounting the story in the

---

    Cultural, and Literary Context (Salzburg, 1978), 278–291; and S. Ogilvie-Thomson, *Prose and Verse*, xcii–xciv.

[78] V. Gillespie, " 'Lukynge in haly bukes' ", 9.

[79] The text appears in S. Ogilvie-Thomson, *Prose and Verse*, 64–68. For a more detailed description of the contents of *Meditation A* and *Meditation B* see N. Watson, *Invention of Authority*, 241–242.

[80] A. Clark Bartlett, *Male Authors, Female Readers*, 125. Bartlett cites the *Tretyse of Loue* as

present tense (using the "I/thou" grammatical relationship) Rolle presents an exercise in which, through the process of reading, the engaged meditator directly recovers the sacred space and time of the Passion.[81] In Rolle, individual sensibility is married with traditional forms of meditation in order to encourage readers to participate more directly and imaginatively in their faith.

Even in the writings of Walter Hilton and the *Cloud*-author, where the role of meditating on the Passion is assigned to the lower rungs of mystical experience, the power of imaginative meditation on the person of Christ is not entirely discounted. As an example Vincent Gillespie looks to Hilton's assertion that "we shall live under the shadow of his manhood as long as we are here" and argues that even the *Cloud*-author recognises that meditation on the Passion forms the bridge between the active and contemplative life and even carries with it some potential for significant contemplative experiences:

Þus hiȝe may actyue come to contemplacion, and no hiȝer: bot ȝif it be ful seeldom and by specyal grace.[82]

Julian of Norwich's writings on the Passion serve as an example of how an individual living a religious life could, and did, actively participate in imaginative meditation on the person of Christ. In the second chapter of her revelations Julian tells us that she desires to be present at the Passion so that she can experience a "bodily sight" of Christ's suffering:

Me thought I woulde haue ben that tyme with Magdaleyne and with other that were Cristus louers, that I might haue seen bodilie the passion that our lord suffered for me . . . And therefore I desyred a bodely sight, wher in I might haue more knowledge of the bodily paynes of our sauiour, and of the compassion of our lady and of all his true louers that were lyuynge that tyme and saw his paynes, for I would haue be one of them and haue suffered with them.[83]

---

an especially noteworthy example: "Then she rose up on her feet and with very great pain faced the cross, where she might best embrace the blessed body of Jesus Christ, whom she had formerly suckled with her own sweet breasts, but she could not reach him . . ." See *Tretyse of Loue*. Ed. J. H. Fisher (London, 1951), 70–71.

81 W. Hodapp, "Sacred Time and Space Within", 240.

82 W. Hilton, *The Scale of Perfection*. Ed. E. Underhill (London, 1923), 362; *The Cloud of Unknowing*, 53/21–23 cited in V. Gillespie, "Strange Images of Death: The Passion in Later Medieval English Devotional and Mystical Writings". *Analecta Cartusiana* 117 (1987), 123.

83 Julian of Norwich, *A Book of Showings to the Anchoress Julian of Norwich*. 2 vols. Eds. E. Colledge and J. Walsh (Toronto, 1978), Chapter 2 [The Long Text], 285/8–286/16. See W. Hodapp, "Sacred Time and Space Within", 241. Hodapp suggests that this passage echoes, albeit indirectly, pseudo-Bonaventure's instruction to be present at sacred scenes thus emphasising the importance of immediacy in medieval devotional practice. See also A. Clark Bartlett, *Male Authors, Female Readers*, 115–117.

Robert Wright argues that, in stressing the poignancy of Christ's Passion and subjective identification with the crucified Lord through "com-passion", Julian's work reveals its distinct relation to the spirituality of her own age.[84] In short, her desire to see Christ suffer, and then suffer with him, emphasises the importance of individual participation in Christocentric devotion and highlights the need for the individual to adopt an imaginative role within the devotional narrative as a means to her own spiritual fulfillment.

Margery Kempe is perhaps the most outstanding example of how those living in the world could also form the intense, intimate devotion to the person of Christ, and particularly his Passion, advocated by meditative literature.[85] Throughout her book, Kempe tells us that her spiritual life has been influenced by the writings of Rolle, Hilton, and Bridget of Sweden, and by works such as James of Milan's *Stimulus Amoris*, all of which discuss intimate devotion to Christ. On many occasions she role-plays scenes with Christ, and with other figures such as Mary Magdalen and the Virgin Mary, and describes her relationship with them as immediate and personal.[86] She tells us that she sees Christ coming to his Passion, and Mary falling at his feet in sorrow, in "þe syght of hir sowle":

> Than sche beheld in þe syght of hir sowle owr blisful Lord Crist Ihesu comyng to-hys-Passyon-ward, &, er he went, he knelyd down & toke hys Moderys blissyng. Þan sche saw hys Moder fallyng down in swownyng befor hir Sone . . .[87]

Like Julian, she refers to her experience of the Passion vision as if it were a "bodily syght", as if she had been there:

> And þerfor þe sayd creatur must nedys wepyn & cryin whan sche sey swech gostly sy3tys in hir sowle as freschly & as verily as 3yf it had ben don in dede in hir bodily syght, and hir thowt þat owr Lady & sche wer al-wey to-gedyr to se owr Lordys peynes.[88]

Margery Kempe's participatory visionary experiences support Hodapp's argument that meditation creates a "real" space for the meditator to occupy in

---

Bartlett writes that Julian exhibits a "thirst for a deeper, more participatory understanding of the divine".

[84] R. E. Wright, "The 'Boke Performyd' ", 14.

[85] W. A. Pantin, *The English Church*, 256.

[86] For a discussion and examples of Kempe's role-playing see S. Beckwith, *Christ's Body: Identity, Culture and Society in Late Medieval Writings* (London and New York, 1993), esp. 83–88.

[87] *The Book of Margery Kempe. The Book of Margery Kempe: The Text from the Unique MS. owned by Colonel W. Butler-Bowden.* Eds. Stanford B. Meech and Hope Emily Allen (London, 1940), 187/25–29.

[88] *The Book of Margery Kempe*, 190/26–30.

the narrative itself.[89] Furthermore, she clearly illustrates that a medieval person, in a lay as well as religious context, could embrace devotional material that encouraged her to adopt imaginative roles as a part of her spiritual life.

In a similar vein to the Passion meditations, many of the short religious poems, often called lyrics, of the late medieval period supply the reader with an imaginative space to occupy. According to Rosemary Woolf the medieval lyric sought to evoke feeling and emotion in the reader by personally involving him/her in the narrative of the poem.[90] In the majority of medieval Passion lyrics, as a well-known fourteenth-century lyric that echoes the *Jesu Dulcis Memoria* potently illustrates, the relationship of both the poet and the pious reader to Christ is one of intense and intimate devotion:

> Jesu, for love thou steigh on roode,
> For love thou yaf thin herte blode;
> Love thee made my soules foode,
> Thi love us bought til al goode . . .
>
> Jesu my God, Jesu my kyng,
> Thou axist me noon othir thing,
> But trewe love and herte yernyng,
> And love-teeris with swete mornynge . . .[91]

Douglas Gray suggests that individual response is the prime objective of this meditative poem because Christ's Passion is the supreme expression of his love and demands a reciprocal love from the individual soul.[92] Another fourteenth-century lyric, "Whanne ic se on Rode", encourages an intimate experience of the Passion by inviting the reader to become the figure in the text who witnesses in person, along with the Virgin Mary and John, Christ crucified on the cross:

> Whanne ic se on Rode
> Jesu, my lemman,
> And besiden him stonden
> Mayre and Johan,

---

89 See W. Hodapp, "Sacred Time and Space Within", 243.

90 R. Woolf, *The English Religious Lyric in the Middle Ages* (Oxford, 1968), 19. The main subjects of the medieval religious lyric are those central to medieval meditation, the Passion, and the Last Things, especially death, with the emotions proper to them, love and fear. In order that the reader may feel these emotions personally and keenly, he/she is persuaded to imagine himself/herself in a scene which will provoke them, and which is often described in minute visual detail.

91 C. Brown, *Religious Lyrics of the XIVth Century* (Oxford, 1957), Poem 89, 111–112 cited in D. Gray, *Themes and Images*, 122. See also R. Woolf, *The English Religious Lyric*, 174. Woolf notes that in many of the translations of this Latin poem there exists a "moving, simple directness, possible only in English".

92 D. Gray, *Themes and Images*, 123.

> And his rig iswongan,
> And his side istungen,
> For the luve of man;
> Well ou ic to wepen,
> And sinnes for to leten,
> Yif ic of luve can . . .[93]

The long meditative poem "Jesu, that hast me dere iboght", a poem deriving from the vernacular translation of the *Philomena* of John of Hoveden, constructs the "I" figure as the reader of the prayer inviting Christ to write in his/her heart of the Passion:

> Write thou gostly in my thoght,
> That I mow with devocion
> Thinke on thy dere Passion.
> For thogh my hert be hard as stone
> Yit maist thou gostly write theron
> With nail and with spere kene,
> And so shullen the lettres be sene.[94]

Like being "present" at the crucifixion, the image of writing the Passion on the heart, a common image in medieval devotional literature, etches Christ's suffering and his sacrifice for the love of man into the memory of the reader. In adopting the subject position offered by these poems, the reader not only becomes an individual participant in the narrative of the text; he/she comes to play a very important imaginative role in Christocentric religion and he/she becomes the direct recipient of Christ's love for mankind. The affective force of such a powerful, intimate image touches the reader at the core of all emotions, the heart, and, in the resultant exclusive bond of love that is formed between the reader and Christ the goal of affective devotion is fulfilled – the reader's *affectus* is turned to accept the love of Christ. The large number of devotional manuscripts and compilations that include these affective pieces suggests that they enjoyed widespread popularity in the medieval period. Poems such as "Jesu, that hast me dere iboght" remained popular well into the fifteenth century and survive in a large number of manuscripts.[95]

Similarly, many of the lyrics attributed to Rolle employ devotional religious themes that offer some sort of imaginative role for the reader.[96] For example,

---

[93] R. T. Davies, *Medieval English Lyrics: A Critical Anthology* (London, 1963), Poem 30, 99.
[94] R. T. Davies, *Medieval English Lyrics*, Poem 45, 120.
[95] See R. Woolf, *The English Religious Lyric*, 163–164.
[96] Many lyrics were attributed to Rolle in the medieval period but those that are now considered to be genuine Rolle works are essentially the group of lyrics found in Longleat MS 29 and Cambridge University Library MS Dd.v.64. I refer exclusively to the Longleat collection edited by S. Ogilvie-Thomson.

in "Love is lif þat lesteth ay" the reader is invited to become the "I" figure who expresses the personal bond, the burning love, between Christ and man:

> Ihesu, þat me lif hath lent, in to þi loue me brynge;
> Tak to þe al myn entent, þat þou be my desyrynge.
> Wo fro me away ware went, and comyn my coueitynge,
> If þat my soul had herd and hent þe songe of þi praysynge.
>
> Thi loue is euer lestynge, fro þat we may hit fele;
> Therin me make brennynge, þat no þynge may me kele.
> My þoght take in þi hand and stabil hit euery dele,
> That I be nat holdynge to loue þis worldis wele. (42/21–28)

In "Ihesu, Goddis son, Lord of mageste" the voice of the reader calls out to Christ:

> Ihesu, Goddis son, Lord of mageste,
> Send wil in to my hert only to couait þe;
> . . . .
> Ihesu, þe Maiden son, þat with þi blode me boghte,
> Thirle my soule with þi spere, þat loue in me hath wroght.
> . . . .
> Ihesu, my God, my Kynge, forsake nat my desyre;
> My thoght make hit be meke, I haue bothe pride and ire.
>
> (44/1–2, 5–4, 9–10)

An emotionally charged poem, "Ihesu, Goddis son" echoes the popular theme of Love writing a meditation of the Passion on the heart of the meditator, found in poems such as "Jesu, that hast me dere iboght", by referring to the experience of Christ's suffering as a spiritual wound.[97] The reader does not only desire a vision of the Passion but a corporeal sign; he/she wishes Christ to "wound my hert within, and weld hit at þy wille/ . . . Root hit in my hert, þe memorie of þy pyne" (44/13–17). Rolle similarly incorporates individualising affective strategies into his prose treatises in order to complement the devotional narrative. Nicholas Watson argues that this similarity exists exclusively because Rolle wrote all his English works for a singular audience, female religious, but while I agree that this material would have almost certainly appealed to his initial female religious audience,[98] I further suggest that the traditional, or, more precisely, the popular elements within these vernacular works, such as intimacy with the person of Christ and devotion to the Passion and the Holy Name, also explain their appeal to many other readers in the medieval period. The implied reader-identity in the prose treatises, the individual soul, is a subtle extension of the common construction of the "I" figure

---

97 R. Woolf, *The English Religious Lyric*, 164–166.
98 See N. Watson, *Invention of Authority*, 232–236.

that is found in many popular fourteenth- and fifteenth-century English devotional texts. Rolle's construction of audience in his vernacular prose treatises must have been an important factor in their appeal to a wider readership.

Records of late medieval book ownership in England show us that in both lay and religious households vernacular books were more likely to be sacred than secular.[99] Moreover, even though there are not nearly as many English as Latin books of religion in circulation – the largest group of book owners, the clergy, mainly kept Latin works – many vernacular religious texts enjoyed wide dissemination. Copies of Rolle's and Hilton's English works proliferated in devotional manuscripts, and Nicholas Love's *Mirrour of the Blessed Lyf of Iesu Crist*, an English translation of the *Meditationes vitae Christi*, was arguably the most popular book of the fifteenth century; not only was it available in a vast number of manuscripts, it was twice printed before 1500.[100] Evidence of specific medieval readers, lay and religious, actively embracing this type of literature can also be gleaned from a number of sources, most notably texts written by medieval readers that describe their experiences and documentation of the ownership of devotional works. The books by Margery Kempe and Julian of Norwich provide an invaluable insight into the uses and influences of affective texts in late medieval devotional practices for lay and religious alike.

There are a considerable number of recorded female readers of vernacular devotional literature in late medieval England. Josephine Koster Tarvers cites the two nuns of Syon, Anne Colyvylle and Clemencia Thasburght, who owned Bodleian Library, Laud Misc. MS 416, a miscellany of devotional materials and Middle English poetry. Amongst the English manuscripts that show evidence of lay female ownership is Bodleian Library, Ex museo MS 232, a compilation made by John Flemmyng of Rolle's meditation on the Passion, Gregory on humility, the *Mirror of St. Edmund*, and a number of prayers, bearing the ownership marks of two women, "Anne Helperby" and "Elyzabethe Stoughton".[101] Similarly, Bodleian Library, Rawlinson MS C. 882,

---

[99] M. Deanesly, "Vernacular Books in England in the Fourteenth and Fifteenth Centuries". *Modern Language Review* xv (1920), 350. See also M. Exon, "The Production and Ownership of Manuscript Books in Late Medieval England" (Western Australia, 1994), esp. 92–99.

[100] M. Deanesly, "Vernacular Books in England", 354. Caxton printed Love's translation in 1488, and Pynson in 1495. It was later printed by Wynkyn de Worde in 1517 and 1523. For a modern edition of the text see Nicholas Love, *The Mirror of the Blessed Lyf of Jesu Christ*. Eds. J. Hogg and L. F. Powell, 2 vols. (Salzburg, 1989) or *Nicholas Love's Mirror of the Blessed Life of Jesus Christ: A Critical Edition Based on Cambridge University Library Additional MSS 6578 and 6686*. Ed. M. G. Sargent (New York, 1992).

[101] J. Koster Tarvers, " 'Thys ys my mystrys boke': English Women as Readers and Writers in Late Medieval England". *The Uses of Manuscripts in Literary Studies: Essays in Memory of Judson Boyce Allen*. Eds. C. Cook Morse, P. Reed Doob and M. Curry Woods (Kalamazoo, 1992), 317.

a copy of the fourteenth-century English manual of popular religious instruction known as *The Pore Caitif*, bears two ownership inscriptions by women, the slightly awkward "Iste liber constat Domina Margarete Erloy, cum magno gaudio et honore Ihesu Christi", and the more pragmatic "iste liber constat Domina Agnese Lyell; hoo thys boke stelyth, schall have cryst curse and myne".[102] These last two inscriptions are particularly interesting in the context of individualised religious devotion because they reflect each reader's personal involvement with both the book itself and with the primary subject of the book, Christ; in Lady Margaret's case the book provides her with an experience of "great delight and honour" in Jesus Christ whereas for Agnes, her ownership of a religious work about Christ gives her agency to join with Him in cursing any who dare to come between her and her devotions.

An unparalleled example of a female reader's engagement with a single devotional text is given by Cicely, Duchess of York, who, in a copy of Rolle's *The Form of Living*, scratches out the name Margaret, the name of the apparent original recipient, and replaces it with her own.[103] Cicely, the mother of Edward IV and Richard III, is a well-known archetype of a woman living a life of extreme piety within the secular world.[104] Her life consisted of a daily ritual of hearing matins in the morning, masses in her private chapel before and after breakfast, readings from pious works during dinner, retirement to private devotions, and, finally, a supper where she repeated to those around her what she had heard at dinner.[105] Reading and listening to reading played a vital role in these devotions. Furthermore, Cicely's appropriation of the role of the reader in *The Form of Living* shows how literature that constructed distinct reader-identities, or offered readers an imaginative role, could be favourably responded to by someone beyond the original addressee of the text. Rolle's construction of the reader-identity Cicely adopts for herself in this text is discussed in detail in relation to *The Form of Living*. Other manuscripts provide

---

102 J. Koster Tarvers, " 'Thys ys my mystrys boke' ", 317–318. Tarvers includes other examples of religious works owned, and bequeathed in wills, by women such as Bodleian Library, Misc. Liturg. MS 104, made around 1340, that contains a Latin Psalter with late fourteenth- and early fifteenth-century prayers added in Latin, English and French. For more examples see S. G. Bell, "Medieval Women Book Owners: Arbiters of Lay Piety and Ambassadors of Culture". *Women and Power in the Middle Ages*. Eds. M. Erler and M. Kowaleski (Athens, 1988), 149–187.

103 The copy of *The Form of Living* in which Cicely's name appears is the second booklet in a four-booklet collection found in Bodleian Library, Rawlinson MS C. 285. See V. Gillespie, "Vernacular Books of Religion", 327–328.

104 For more information on Cicely's pious life see C. A. J. Armstrong, "The Piety of Cicely Duchess of York: A Study in Late Medieval Culture". *England, Burgundy and France on the Fifteenth Century*. C. A. J. Armstrong (London, 1983), 135–156.

105 See A. Taylor, "Into his Secret Chamber", 46–47. The description of Cicely's daily ritual is drawn from "Orders and Rules of the House of the Princess Cecill, Mother of King Edward IV". *A Collection of Ordinances and Regulations for the Government of the Royal Household* (London, 1790), 37.

similar examples of lay female engagement with mystical and devotional works. In late medieval Yorkshire a number of "pious dowagers", who appeared to regard widowhood as a release from the rigours of active life which enabled them to pursue a more intense form of worship, sought advice from texts such as Rolle's Passion meditations and Hilton's *Scale of Perfection*.[106] Clearly, many of the lay women who owned devotional texts willingly embraced the religious rhetoric within.

Examples of male readers and owners of vernacular devotional literature are also widespread in late fourteenth- and early fifteenth-century England. In the fourteenth-century *Meditations on the Passion of Christ* by John Whiterig, the Monk-Solitary of Farne, the image of Christ as an open book for the reader's use – "his body, hanging on the cross, is a book open for your perusal"[107] – may well be drawn from Rolle's *Meditation B*:

> More yit, swet Ihesu, þy body is lyke a boke written al rede ynke: so is þy body al written with rede woundes. (75/236–237)

A number of male owners of English devotional works have also been identified: William Thorp who bequeathed an English book composed by "Richard the hermit" in 1391, John Staynis, a monk of Thetford, who bequeathed *The Prick of Conscience* to Margaret Salis of Sherwood between 1380–1400, and John Dygoun, a recluse at Sheen about 1438, who owned a copy of the *Pore Caitif* (later bequeathed by the same Dame Margaret Erloy who is noted above).[108] In a lay context, a number of wealthy Yorkshiremen, such as the Scropes of Masham, and John Newton, treasurer of York Cathedral, were known to be both patrons and early adherents of the teachings of Rolle as well as early owners of his vernacular devotional works.[109] Jonathon Hughes suggests that Richard Scrope's interest in Rolle may explain the compilation at Lichfield of one of the finest collections of Rolle's writings; between 1386 and 1398 *Ego Dormio*, *The Commandment*, *The Form of Living* and the *Incendium Amoris*, all in northern dialect, and other northern works such as *The Prick of Conscience* and John of Hoveden's *Philomena*, were copied into a single volume.[110] Further-

---

106 J. Hughes, *Pastors and Visionaries*, 292–293. As examples Hughes uses Joan Beaufort, who was personally advised by Margery Kempe, and Eleanor Roos, who owned books by Rolle and Hilton as well as a copy of the *Revelations of St. Maud*, which she eventually left to another woman Joan Courtenay.

107 John Whiterig, the Monk-Solitary of Farne, cited in V. Gillespie, " 'Lukynge in haly bukes' ", 10. See also W. A. Pantin, "The Monk-Solitary of Farne: A Fourteenth-century English Mystic". *English Historical Review* 59 (1944), 162–186; H. Farmer, "The Meditations of the Monk of Farne". *Analecta Monastica* 4 (1957), 141–245.

108 M. Deanesly, "Vernacular Books in England", 352 and 356.

109 H. E. Allen, *Writings Ascribed*, 521–522.

110 J. Hughes, *Pastors and Visionaries*, 203. The manuscript in question is Bodleian Library, Rawlinson MS A. 389. Hughes notes that the quality of the English texts

more, testamentary records show that other members of the Scrope family – Richard's uncle Geoffrey Scrope, his nephew Henry Lord Scrope, and a kinsman Henry Lord Fitzhugh – all showed interest in vernacular devotional material at some times in their lives.[111] Such interest reveals that male as well as female, lay as well as religious, readers in late medieval England responded favourably to a wide variety of vernacular devotional material that sought to inflame the senses through imaginative role-playing, to awaken the emotions and pull at the heart, and to engage the reader in intimate devotion to the person of Christ.

IV

Andrew Taylor's discussion of private reading in late medieval England points to the fact that we have yet to recognise fully the potential of vernacular religious literature to offer insight into late medieval English reading practices and that the lack of scholarly attention to this material derives mainly from its non-literary status.[112] But this situation is slowly changing. In the following chapters Rolle's construction of audience in his English prose treatises is examined in the context of the influence of the three areas discussed above: the reader-engaging elements found in the affective tradition; the proliferation of fourteenth- and fifteenth-century vernacular devotional material that drew from and extended this tradition; and the favourable reception, by lay and religious readers, such material enjoyed in the late medieval period. By the end of the thirteenth century there had already begun a movement towards vernacular devotional literature that deployed traditional affective themes and images – such as the life and Passion of Christ, nuptial imagery, and the grieving Virgin Mary – in order to engage the reader in the text by inviting him/her to occupy a specific space within the narrative itself. When Rolle came to write his own vernacular works it is likely that he was influenced by such literature and by the apparent demand for it, an influence that is most clearly seen in the reader-oriented nature of his English writings. Whereas his lyrics and Passion meditations show explicit similarities to the literature discussed, Rolle's prose treatises develop the genre further in that they are more flexible in offering a wider variety of subject positions; while they show

bespeaks good sources, and the attribution of the unified text of *The Form of Living* and *Ego Dormio* to "quodam notabile Ricardi Rolle heremite", one of the few manuscripts to use Rolle's surname, suggests an informed ancestry within the region where Rolle lived.

111 See J. Hughes, *Pastors and Visionaries*, esp. 201–205.
112 A. Taylor, *"Into his Secret Chamber"*, 48.

the influence of traditional methods they develop a uniquely subtle and refined approach to audience construction.

In the anthology *The Idea of the Vernacular: An Anthology of Middle English Literary Theory 1280–1520*, a work that comprises "a wide selection of Middle English discussions of writing: its composition, cultural position, real and imagined audience, and reception",[113] the recovery of actual medieval audiences is seen as fundamental to the volume's insistence on historicity, but there is an important sense in which "audiences" do not preexist the texts that are addressed to them but are called into being by them.[114] The vernacular audience is here discussed not only as a construction of the reading and writing process, but also as a prior determining factor in the production of the text:

> Those who are explicitly addressed are not always those whose interests are at stake in the production of the text . . . "audiences" are born (and reborn) somewhere between authorial desire, the desires of actual historical audiences, and the cultural and linguistic possibilities that shape acts of reading.[115]

Vernacular translation is discussed as employing a topos of openness that posits a mythical world in which social difference and division is swept away by universal access to English.[116] It is suggested that while many texts address the laity and women – the classic *illiterati* – as those for whom English translation is most necessary, this audience can sometimes be little more than a pretext for the production of the text in English, a production that may serve other interests.[117] Vernacular texts, it would seem, need not always be considered as productions solely directed to the linguistic constraints of the *illiterati*, because use of the vernacular itself implies an openness that permits, and indeed encourages, a kind of universal readerly appeal.

Rolle's English treatises do not conform to the traditional audience-based approaches to his work: they do not comply with many of the tenets of epistolary literature; they do not explicitly address specific persons; nor do they appear to be exclusively gendered directives that solicit only a female audience. Instead, in each work Rolle offers a guide to the spiritual life, drawn from both the traditional sources and methods noted above, as well as from his own experiences in the mystical journey, and offers the reader an identity potentially appealing to a male or female, lay or religious, audience in late medieval England – the individual soul. To describe the emergence of this

---

113 J. Wogan-Browne, N. Watson, A. Taylor and R. Evans, eds. *The Idea of the Vernacular: An Anthology of Middle English Literary Theory 1280–1520* (Exeter, 1999), xiii.
114 J. Wogan-Browne, et al. *The Idea of the Vernacular*, 110.
115 J. Wogan-Browne, et al. *The Idea of the Vernacular*, 111.
116 J. Wogan-Browne, et al. *The Idea of the Vernacular*, 120.
117 J. Wogan-Browne, et al. *The Idea of the Vernacular*, 120.

type of reader construction in Rolle's medieval texts I have relied on elements of modern reader-response criticism that discuss the reader as "implied", a construction that comes from within the text rather than as a direct result of a specific audience, or "real" reader. As I stressed earlier, this does not mean that I am determined to presuppose Rolle's intentions or to offer his English works as a medieval example of a modern theoretical model in practice. Instead, I suggest that one of the ways we may come to understand how Rolle's texts were able to appeal to a wide variety of medieval readers is by examining the subtleties of audience construction in his works, and the potential reader-responses generated from this, by using the terminology and ideological structures provided by modern reader-response theory.[118]

In Rolle's English treatises an implied reader-identity is apparent because the messages within the texts implicitly define the reader's role as that of the individual soul seeking guidance in the spiritual life. This implied construction, the reader as the individual soul, is crucial to how the text is responded to within the reading process. In conjunction with the implicit reader construction potential reader/writer relationships are constructed within the texts, relationships between the implied reader and the fictionalised author, which are instrumental in both generating meaning and directing the reader's responses. In each text the implied reader is appealed to through a distinct affective discourse designed to promote agency in his/her own spiritual life. In Rolle's first vernacular treatise, *Ego Dormio*, the reader is addressed through a discourse of intimacy as the untried soul facing a liminal crisis in his/her spiritual life – whether to dedicate the self to God as the eternal bride or return to the comforts of the world and the bosom of the family. To ease this dilemma the reader is engaged in intimate role-playing, with Rolle's authorial self acting as the "messager" of God who is to woo the reader to the marriage bed, in a manner that virtually demands an acceptance of the role of the bride. In *The Commandment*, an instructional discourse offers the reader a short but comprehensive guide to turning the soul to the love of God. The world he/she has chosen to leave in favour of the spiritual bridal chamber is brutally contrasted with the glorious choice, almost as an affirmation of the decision itself. In his last vernacular work, *The Form of Living*, Rolle develops a discourse of friendship to encourage the reader to adopt the role of his disciple and companion in the final stages of the spiritual journey as he/she enters the

---

118 Most notable amongst the texts on reader-response criticism are E. Wolff, "Der intendierte Leser". *Poetica* 4 (1971), 141–166; W. Iser, *The Act of Reading: A Theory of Aesthetic Response* (Baltimore and London, 1978) and *The Implied Reader: Patterns of Communication in Prose Fiction from Bunyan to Beckett* (Baltimore and London, 1974); W. Ong, "The Writer's Audience is Always a Fiction". *PMLA: Publications of the Modern Language Association of America* (1975): 9–21. An excellent selection of reader-response criticism is found in Jane P. Tompkins, *Reader-Response Criticism: From Formalism to Post-Structuralism* (Baltimore and London, 1980).

exalted world of contemplation. Rolle locates this text on the eve of the reader's spiritual enclosure, reminding the recipient that the dangers of the world are ever apparent and that he/she is not immune despite their exalted position in the eyes of God. Truly turned to God, the reader feels the warm embrace of the implied friendship that permeates the work as a whole; the final affirmation of spiritual *amicitia*, alluded to in both *Incendium Amoris* and *Melos Amoris*, and so often read by modern critics as genuine proof of Rolle's misogyny, confirms instead his love and respect for what is potentially a wide and enduring vernacular audience.

Rolle's texts constantly look beyond the apparent original readers, beyond Margaret Kirkeby, or the nuns of Hampole, to anyone who will "hold þyn ere and hyre of loue" (26/1-2). The intimate, affective and ecstatic language, drawn from a wide range of traditional sources, and addressed to the implicit individual soul in Rolle's English texts, far from narrowing the scope of the works, instead succeeds in opening them to a broader audience because the invitation to self-definition which is their hallmark permits an individual response from every potential recipient: to each and every reader Rolle writes "speciali".

3

"I wil becum a messager to bring þe to his bed":[1]
Ego Dormio

Ihesu, Goddis son, Lord of mageste,
Send wil in to my hert only to couait þe;
Ref me likynge of þis world, my loue þat þou may be;
Take my hert in to þi way; set me in stabilite.[2]

I

*E*GO DORMIO is the first of the English prose treatises composed by Richard Rolle on the subject of the journey towards spiritual perfection. According to the chronology set out by Nicholas Watson, which divides Rolle's writings into stages based largely on the evidence of self-borrowing throughout his texts, *Ego Dormio* falls into the category of "late works" in which, along with *Melos Amoris*, it pre-dates *Super Lectiones Mortuorum*, *Emendatio Vitae*, *The Commandment*, *The Form of Living* and, in all likelihood, the *English Psalter* and the shorter vernacular prose pieces.[3] Because it is Rolle's first vernacular prose work of any length, *Ego Dormio* is of particular interest as the beginning point of his vernacular utterance and his address to a vernacular audience. Throughout this work Rolle relies on both his own Latin works and other writings from the Latin affective tradition to provide the form, theme and content of the text. However, this should not be discounted as mere

---

1   *Ego Dormio*, 26/7–8.
2   *Lyrics* (ii) 44/1–4.
3   See N. Watson, *Invention of Authority*, 273–294. Watson's chronology argues that *The Commandment* and *The Form of Living* both derive material from the Latin epistle *Emendatio Vitae* whereas *Ego Dormio* does not. *Emendatio Vitae* borrows from four Latin works, the *Latin Psalter*, *Super Psalmum Vicesimum*, *Super Canticum Canticorum* and *Contra Amatores Mundi*. *Melos Amoris* also uses material from the last two of these works but is not recognisable as a source for *Ego Dormio*. Thus, *Ego Dormio* and the short English prose works appear to post-date at least *Super Canticum Canticorum* but are earlier than *The Commandment* and *The Form of Living*. It is unclear whether the *English Psalter* was composed before or after *Ego Dormio*, hence the difficulty in assigning it the place of Rolle's first vernacular work. However, it seems clear that it is the first English prose treatise.

borrowing and, as the following detailed discussion reveals, Rolle's first vernacular treatise can instead be considered as an illustration of his willingness and ability to adapt, and further develop, his ideas and his method both to a new language and a new audience.

Ego Dormio is a relatively short but detailed explication of the three degrees of love, themselves ultimately derived from Richard of St. Victor's *De Quattuor Gradibus Violentae Caritatis*, where love is described as "insuperable", "inseparable", "singular", and "insatiable"; Rolle omits the fourth degree "insatiable".[4] The argument for *Ego Dormio*'s early composition in the Rolle canon relies heavily on the occurrence of the three grades of love appearing here without their titles. The text opens with an erotic invitation, wooing the reader to become the lover of Christ by using language and imagery that relies heavily on traditional exegesis of the *Song of Songs* (26/1–15). The nine orders of angels are then described (26/16–32) as a prelude to Rolle's explication of the three degrees of love which provides the reader with an affective ladder of perfection (27/65–264). Hence, after the amatory prologue much of the early part of the work maintains a didactic tone and is concerned with more humble concerns, such as the keeping of the ten commandments, being mindful of the seven deadly sins and remaining "stabil in þe trouth of holy chirch" (27/69–70). As the work progresses through the degrees of love Rolle's persuasive language becomes more intense. Each degree of love is carefully outlined for the reader and accompanied by a lyric designed to engage the reader's *affectus* and arouse love in the heart. The first lyric, "Al perisshethe and passeth þat we with eigh see" (28/84–91), signals the reader's dismissal of the world and its false lure. The second lyric, "My kynge þe watyre grete" (30–31/175–211), urges the reader to focus on Christ's Passion so that "þe egh of þi hert may loke into heuyn" (31/215). The third lyric, which closes the work, "My songe is in seghynge" (32–33/266–313), is described by Rolle as "a songe of loue" (32/265) which will be fastened in the heart of the reader once the third degree of love is embraced and the pinnacle of the ladder is reached.

As Rolle's first English treatise, *Ego Dormio* is also his first vernacular work in prose that is not exegetical. All the same, biblical translation and commentary are never entirely absent from Rolle's works, as the opening lines of *Ego Dormio* attest:

> Ego dormio et cor meum vigilat. The þat lust loue, hold þyn ere and hyre of loue. In þe songe of loue I fynd hit written þat I haue set at þe begennynge of my writynge: "I slepe and my hert waketh". (26/1–3)

The carnal and sensuous imagery of the *Song of Songs* had long been part of the metaphorical discourse of love in medieval religious writing and used as a

---

4   Richard of St. Victor, *De Quattuor Gradibus Violentae Caritatis. Richard of Saint-Victor: Selected Writings on Contemplation.* Trans. C. Kirchberger (London, 1957).

means of religious instruction.[5] In the opening lines of *Ego Dormio* Rolle's exegetical commentary establishes this short prose work as didactic, and introduces love as the central theme of the work. In turn, the quotation from the *Song of Songs* at once positions the work as a more lyrical piece, quite different from Rolle's other English prose texts or the Latin work to which they are related, *Emendatio Vitae*. Comparatively, his first English treatise contains less specialised mystical content than the later works; it is not offered as a guide to the contemplative life like *The Form of Living*, nor does it contain as many distinctive didactic elements as *The Commandment*. Instead, *Ego Dormio* is more a message of love sent by Rolle's authorial self, the self-appointed "messager" of God in this text, to the reader. Indeed, what is particularly interesting about this work is not so much its basic composition or its didactic and exegetical content, but the developing reader/writer relationships that draw the reader into a tri-partite intimacy with Rolle's authorial self and with God; an invitation to intimacy that is not directed to a pointed or defined audience but transcends the initial reading subject, a young female religious, and opens the work to a wider readership. In *Ego Dormio*, and in each of Rolle's English treatises, the choice of language and metaphor shows the influence of the gender of the explicit audience but this does not necessarily gender the text itself. Instead Rolle's employment of gendered tropes throughout *Ego Dormio* speaks more for his construction of the soul as feminine than it does for his assumption that the work will reach a female audience only; in this way the potentially anti-feminist sentiment in the work becomes diffused.[6]

There is much in *Ego Dormio* to suggest that Rolle actually sought to appeal to a mixed audience in that the reader is constructed not as generically male or female but simply as the young lover of God being wooed to the spiritual marriage bed. In this sense his composition of an affective and passionate work that embodies the *contemptus mundi* theme and the theme of the love of God, the latter being central to all Rolle's vernacular treatises, implies that he is not concerned with the exterior life of the reader but is primarily focused on the interior spiritual life. The reader is positioned very much in the manner of the lover of the *Song of Songs*, as medieval commentators understood it, who represents every individual soul seeking the intimate love of Christ. Describing the mystical experience in sensual and sexual terms, using the

5 B. McGinn, "The Language of Love in Christian and Jewish Mystics". *Mysticism and Language*. Ed. S. T. Katz (Oxford, 1992), 202–235.
6 See A. Clark Bartlett, *Male Authors, Female Readers*, 145. Bartlett writes that *Ego Dormio* is "simultaneously a letter of friendship, a narrative of nuptial contemplation, and a courtly romance. On its own, each of these three 'counterdiscourses' offers an alternative to ascetic misogyny and a vocabulary for articulating more appealing feminine identities. But in combination, these discourses constitute an even more powerful destabilisation of a given text's antifeminism, multiplying the opportunities for the construction and reconstruction of identities."

marriage bed as a trope for divine union, has the effect of drawing the reader into a relationship of love with Christ, rather than one of servitude or gain, a feature perhaps drawn from Bernard's seventh sermon on the *Song of Songs*:

> If someone is a slave, he fears his master's face. If he is a hireling, he hopes for payment from his master's hand. If he is a pupil, he bends his ear to his master. If he is a son, he honours his father. But she who asks for a kiss feels love. This affection of love excels among the gifts of nature, especially when it returns to its source, which is God.[7]

The outcome is that the reader of *Ego Dormio*, male or female, is wooed by the author/text (each of whom is Christ's "sonde" – message and messenger) to accept the role of bride to the ultimate spouse; such a marriage is thus opened to all those who read this text aright. The openness of the invitation implies that the mystical marriage, with its promise of everlasting love and salvation, can be sought not just by religious and solitaries, but by a wide variety of readers "þat lust loue".

II

Though labelled as an epistle by modern scholars, *Ego Dormio* does not conform to the conventions of medieval letter writing. Giles Constable, drawing on the *artes dictaminis* of the late Middle Ages, argues that a letter was supposed to be constructed along certain very definite lines.[8] He cites C. H. Haskins's break-down of the accepted theory of medieval letter writing, which is worth quoting in full to do justice to the complexity of the ideal medieval epistle:

> There should be five parts arranged in logical sequence. After the salutation – as to which the etiquette of the medieval scribe was very exacting, each class in society having its own terms of address and reply – came the exordium, consisting of some commonplace generality, a proverb, or a scriptural quotation, and designed to put the reader in the proper frame of mind for granting the request to follow. Then came the statement of the particular purpose of the letter (the narration), ending in a petition which commonly has the form of a deduction from the major and minor premises laid down in the exordium and narration, and finally the phrases of the conclusion.[9]

---

[7] Bernard of Clairvaux, *Sermons on the 'Song of Songs'. Selected Works.* Trans. G. R. Evans (New York, 1987), 231. See W. Netherton, "Joy Gars Me Jangell", Ch. 4.

[8] G. Constable, *Letters and Letter Collections* (Belgium, 1976), 16.

[9] C. H. Haskins, *Studies in Mediaeval Culture* (Oxford, 1929), 2–3 cited in G. Constable, *Letters and Letter Collections*, 16–17.

Ego Dormio certainly contains elements of the above form but it does not adhere to key points, particularly the elaborate salutation that should open a letter. Similarly, Rolle's two other vernacular prose works, also labelled as epistles, show glimpses of the accepted formula but do not fall entirely within its constraints. *The Form of Living*, which emphasises friendship between the writer and reader, is perhaps the most epistolary in construction of the three but still does not adhere strictly to the above conventions. *The Form of Living* does indicate an identifiable initial audience by referring to Rolle's friend and disciple, the anchoress Margaret Kirkeby – "Lo, Margaret, I haue shortly seid þe fourme of lyuynge" – but her name appears only at the end of the work suggesting that it is more a dedication than a form of address (25/894). The narrative structure of *The Commandment* is more closely related to didactic and homiletic discourse than to the conventional forms common to letters of spiritual edification; it does not acknowledge a singular recipient, being instead a collection of teachings on the subject of love, initially for a monastic audience.[10] The message contained in the text of *Ego Dormio* is at most merely suggestive of a single female recipient of uncertain religious status since no formal salutation is in evidence nor is any reference to any single personage discernible.

Despite the lack of evidence to suggest a singular epistolary audience for *Ego Dormio* modern critics have relied on an imagined single female recipient as an argument to explain the intimate tone of the work. Denis Renevey suggests that Rolle's reference to the dangers of owning five or six "kirtils" when one or two would be sufficient is evidence that the recipient of the work is a personal female friend:[11]

> Þou wil nat couait þan to be riche, ne to haue many clothes and faire, [many kirtils, many] dreries, bot al þou wil set at noght, and dispise al, and take no more þan þe nedeth. The wil þynke two clothes or on ynogh, þat nowe hath fyue or six. (30/161–164)

This gendered interpretation seems unlikely. Not only does the numbering of the items of clothing appear to be random, but the Middle English word "kirtil" could denote a man's tunic as well as a woman's gown.[12] In *Meditation B*, Rolle describes Christ's own garment as a "kirtil":

---

10 See S. Ogilvie-Thomson, *Prose and Verse*, lxxix–lxxx. The subject of *The Commandment's* monastic audience will be discussed in more detail in Chapter Four.

11 D. Renevey, *The Moving of the Soul*, 218. Renevey writes: "I would like to suggest that Rolle knew personally the recipient of this epistle . . . the reference to the number of her tunics is a clear indicator of personal knowledge of the recipient on the part of the author."

12 See *Middle English Dictionary*. Ed. Hans Kurath (Ann Arbor, 1952–1998). Kirtil n. – 1.(a) a garment for men or boys, varying in length . . . a cloak or outer garment; 2. (a) a garment for women or girls, often an outer garment . . . In Ogilvie-Thomson's glossary the definition of the word "kirtil" reads "kyrtel, kyrtil n. man's tunic". The

A, der lord, swete Ihesu, what þou was woobigone when at þe begynnynge
of Herodes comaundement þy kirtil was take for þe . . . (76/279–280)

To all intents and purposes Rolle spends so little time on externals in *Ego
Dormio* that Renevey's argument seems to throw a lot more literal weight on
the reference than it can easily bear.

Modern critical identification of *Ego Dormio* as an epistle with a single
recipient has largely resulted from modern interpretation of manuscript
ascriptions. Yet, if we look closely at these ascriptions it is clear that the manuscripts containing *Ego Dormio* do not agree on the identification of the initial
recipient. University Library Cambridge MS Dd.v.64 addresses the work to a
"moniali de ȝedyngham"; another manuscript incipit concludes that the work
was one that Rolle "wrot to an ankresse"; and the Longleat manuscript
includes the work in a group of works all dedicated to Rolle's friend and
disciple Margaret Kirkeby. This is one aspect that sets Rolle's work apart from
traditional letters of spiritual edification, where explicit reference to an initial
recipient is used as a means of justifying the composition. Early in the tradition of epistolary instruction for women Jerome wrote a letter on the merits of
virginity that clearly identifies the initial recipient as the virgin Eustochium;[13]
the thirteenth-century author of *Ancrene Wisse* composed his rule at the
specific request of three "sisters of one father and mother";[14] and Aelred of
Rievaulx constructed his rule of solitary living *De institutione inclusarum* for a
woman he claims is his sister.[15] Like Rolle, these authors were also aware that
a wider audience may have been reached but their discourse of intimacy
stems from a literal or "real" relationship rather than an implied one, as in *Ego
Dormio*.

It is possible that Rolle knew, and drew on, these letters for many of his
own works, but in his vernacular writings we can begin to see a subtle shift in
emphasis from a known recipient to a generic one. In the later Middle Ages
letters were, for the most part, self-conscious, quasi-public literary documents
in which consciousness of the identifiable recipient could become of lesser

word "kirtils", meaning gowns, is accompanied by an asterisk that indicates it to be
an editorial emendation. See S. Ogilvie-Thomson, *Prose and Verse*, 244.

13 Jerome, "To Eustochium". *The Letters of Saint Jerome*. Trans. C. C. Mierow (Westminster, MD, 1963. Vol. I, Letters 1–22, 135. The letter begins "I write this to you, my lady
Eustochium . . ."

14 B. Millett and J. Wogan-Browne, *Medieval English Prose for Women*, xi–xii. Millett and
Wogan-Browne cite British Library, Cotton Nero MS A. xiv, f. 50r/23–27: "There is a
great deal of talk about you, what well-bred women you are, sought after by many
for your goodness and kindness, and sisters of one father and mother, who in the
flower of your youth renounced all the joys of the world and became recluses."

15 J. Ayto and A. Barratt, eds. *Aelred of Rievaulx's De institutione inclusarum: Two Middle
English Versions* (Oxford, 1984), xi. Ayto and Barratt describe *De institutione
inclusarum* as "a treatise on the ordering of the external and inner life of an
anchoress, written in the form of a letter to his sister".

importance to the reader.[16] Whereas earlier letters of spiritual edification had required a real or at least imagined personal association, later religious epistolary exchange explicitly transcended the initial reader in favour of a wider audience. Fourteenth-century devotional texts often address an unnamed generic sister, brother or friend, or include only minor textual reference to the initial recipient. The collection of works supposed to be written by the author of *The Cloud of Unknowing* includes two epistolary works, the *Epistle of Prayer* and the *Epistle of Discretion of Stirrings*, that both open with the generic salutation "Goostly frende in God".[17] Even conventional epistolary salutations of endearment such as these are not found in Rolle. Furthermore, none of the manuscript dedications that occur with the text of *Ego Dormio* can claim to be of an autograph copy so they might better be viewed as dedications of certain scribal editions of the work, rather than as conclusive indications that Rolle's work could only have the function of addressing a singular female monastic recipient.

This is not to say that the monastic dedication appearing in University Library Cambridge MS Dd.v.64 should be completely overlooked, but it must be recognised that the division amongst modern scholars about the religious status of the initial recipient of *Ego Dormio* stems from a determination to pinpoint a *real* singular recipient for *Ego Dormio* that reflects the afore-mentioned over-preoccupation with Rolle's life and character.[18] Furthermore, disputation based on the evidence of manuscript ascriptions overlooks a key consideration – that the varied dedications, suggesting the differing audience of nun, anchoress and disciple, might themselves indicate the known diversity of Rolle's audience in the estimation of early scribes. Assessment of Rolle's audience can not be limited to mere scribal dedications because throughout the work a discourse is developed that accommodates both the explicit and the implied audience of this text. Externalities are of little

---

16 G. Constable, *Letters and Letter Collections*, 11.

17 *Deonise Hid Diuinite*. Ed. P. Hodgson (London, 1955), 48 and 62.

18 In early Rolle scholarship Carl Horstmann supported the "nun of Yedingham" dedication but it was soon rejected by Hope Emily Allen who claimed that *Ego Dormio* contained overt references to secular customs: "Exhortations against worldliness and especially against worldly dress might suggest that the recipient was a secular lady who did not become a nun till after the epistle was written." H. E. Allen, *English Writings*, 60. Sarah Ogilvie-Thomson, in support of the Longleat manuscript dedication, has shown University Library, Cambridge MS Dd.v.64 to be a monastic text only in that it is a copy of a more "original" *Ego Dormio*, carefully adapted for a monastic audience. She also postulates that the secular woman to whom it was written could possibly be Margaret Kirkeby before she had taken her vows, using the record of their friendship as a way of explaining the intimate tone of the piece. Nicholas Watson favours a singular monastic audience by arguing that Rolle's intimate address concentrates on the second and third degrees of love. However, this notion implies that all women entering the second degree of love must be nuns, which is insupportable.

consequence to the spiritual journey in this text and instead the reader is engaged from the very beginning in a highly emotional relationship with Christ and Rolle's authorial self. The best conclusion to draw might be that the scribes recognise that the text seems to single out one reader, but that the identity of this special reader is not literally fixed. Utilising secular as well as religious traditions of love literature, Rolle woos each reader not as a real or even as a constructed specific audience, but more subtly as an individual soul whose heart is to be seduced and won for his Lord.

III

Ego Dormio derives its modern title from the quotation from the *Song of Songs* 5:2, "ego dormio et cor meum vigilat", that makes up the opening address. Manuscript ascriptions attest that the title itself is not an entirely modern construction; in the fifteenth-century manuscript British Library, Additional MS 37049, where fragments of both prose and verse from *Ego Dormio* occur, the motto "Ego Dormio" appears prominently in illustrations, which is a reliable indication that the phrase had long been associated with the work. But other incipits suggest that contemporary interest lay more with the content of *Ego Dormio* than with the biblical allusion. The twelve manuscripts containing *Ego Dormio* highlight the significance of the categorical grades of love that are the main theme of the work by describing it variously as "tractatus", "tretis", "tres gradus amoris secundum", and "thre degrees of loue as is written nowe here aftyr".[19] The Middle English word "tretis" implies a formal discourse on a circumscribed topic;[20] the Latin word "tractatus" also suggests a treatise or discourse in the fourteenth century.[21] These titles indicate that Rolle's subject matter, not his addressee, was the main consideration for the scribes. No medieval manuscript inscription suggests that *Ego Dormio* was considered an epistle.

Throughout *Ego Dormio* Rolle employs a language of love drawn from a number of different medieval traditions. Much of this language derives from the commentary tradition of the *Song of Songs*, but the work also appears to draw from the earlier vernacular tradition of devotional prose for women

---

[19] S. Ogilvie-Thomson, *Prose and Verse*, xliv. University Library Cambridge MS Dd.v.64 III, Bradfer-Lawrence MS 10, Magdalene College Cambridge, Pepys MS 2125 and British Library, Additional MS 37790 respectively.

[20] See *Middle English Dictionary*. Tretis, n. a formal discourse or written work expounding a topic, a work of instructional or informative character, a disquisition on a circumscribed topic, a treatise.

[21] R. E. Latham, *Revised Medieval Latin Word-list from British and Irish Sources* (London, 1965). Latham includes "tractatus, n. a treatise, discourse (1300–1432)".

including *Ancrene Wisse* and the "Wooing Group"; to a certain extent it also draws on elements of the medieval romance tradition. Analysis of how an implied reader emerges in this text, one that can potentially take on special relationships with Rolle's authorial self, will depend heavily on perceptions of the nature of this love-language. Nicholas Watson briefly notes the importance of this textual intimacy for Rolle's relationship with his initial female reader, and for the creation of his own self-image.[22] And while it seems clear that the intimate discourse of Rolle's inaugural vernacular work establishes his awareness of the initial reading subject as female, this does not necessarily simply provide us with proof that Rolle's sole reason for writing his vernacular works is because he claimed, in the earlier Latin work *Melos Amoris*, that he had a special ministry to women.[23] Textual evidence is lacking in the English treatises to suggest such a gendered reading.

The idea that Rolle constructs an audience that is always female is founded on his use of traditional tropes of feminine piety, such as the *sponsa Christi*, and his asking the reader to identify with Christ's Passion and his Holy Name.[24] Nuptial imagery had long been associated with devotional/spiritual works for women composed throughout the medieval period. Female readers/ writers particularly identified with this image of spirituality; traditionally nuns were married to Christ at the taking of their vows. Catherine of Alexandria, who, according to legend, was martyred in 307, and her namesake Catherine of Siena (d. 1380) were both reputed to have contracted a mystic marriage with Christ.[25] In England the fifteenth-century lay worshipper Margery Kempe wore a "bone maryd ryng to Ihesu Crist" upon which God had commanded her to inscribe "Ihesus est amor meus."[26] Christ's Passion, his human suffering, was particularly relevant to women, who were expected to join with the Virgin Mary at the foot of the cross lamenting the death of their son. Likewise, the invocation of the Holy Name, the Word made flesh, was prominent in literature for female religious. But Rolle's use of such discourse reveals his understanding of the human soul as inherently feminine, rather

---

22 N. Watson, *Invention of Authority*, 226. Watson claims that "the English work in which Rolle's sense of intimacy with a female reader and his belief in his divinely appointed mission to women both emerge most clearly is *Ego Dormio*".

23 N. Watson, *Invention of Authority*, 231.

24 See S. Beckwith "A Very Material Mysticism: The Medieval Mysticism of Margery Kempe". *Medieval Literature: Criticism, Ideology, and History*. Ed. D. Aers (New York, 1986), 36. Beckwith argues that it was women who encouraged and propagated the most distinctive aspects of late medieval piety – devotion to the human Christ as lover, husband and infant, devotion to the Eucharist in a form of piety which insists on the physical as a legitimate means of access to the spiritual.

25 M. Warner, *Alone of All Her Sex: The Myth and Cult of the Virgin Mary* (New York, 1976), 127. Warner notes that the wedding of Catherine of Alexandria and Christ is the subject of hundreds of Christian paintings from the fourteenth century onwards.

26 *The Book of Margery Kempe*, 78.

than his conception of the reading subject as explicitly female. What could be considered as gendered directives are positioned in another sphere of significance that exploits the feminine nature of these devotional tropes less literally. Hence, Rolle's English works, although apparently utilising gender-specific *exempla*, were able to appeal to a wider readership. When all souls are understood as feminine, then the apparent gender specificity of *Ego Dormio* becomes in effect a gender neutrality of utterance and implied reception.

In the opening words of *Ego Dormio* Rolle authorises his work and himself by expounding the Word. The biblical quotation that is to set the course of the piece is given in Latin, the accepted authoritative language of Scripture. The reader is simply addressed as "þe þat lust loue" and is asked to "hold þyn ere and hyre of loue", an open form of address in that no gender is specified, no socio-religious status is referred to, and no specific prior relationship to the author is implied, secular or sacred. Only after this preamble does Rolle translate the Word into the vernacular for his lover of Love, the implied reader of this work, who is presumably an *illiteratus* addressee because the Latin is translated – a technique that reflects what Vincent Gillespie describes as the emergence in the fourteenth and fifteenth centuries of texts which explicitly recognise the linguistic limitations of their audiences.[27] In distinction from traditional exegetical introductions, where authors often introduce biblical material in forms such as "as I find written" or "it is written", Rolle appropriates the Word for himself: "þat I haue set at þe begennynge of my writynge". This implies that it is not to the biblical words only, but to Rolle's special vernacular utterance of them that the reader is expected to attend. The love of which they are to hear is offered not directly by the divine word but through Rolle's authorial self as the divine messenger. It is to begin with a relationship with this messenger, made one with the message of love, that the reader is offered. Even in this early part of the work Rolle creates a threefold space for his reader to occupy: as one desiring to love, as a hearer of the Word uttered by Rolle's constructed authorial self, and as a potential *sponsa Christi*.

What does Rolle's language of "hearing" suggest in relation to his textual audience?[28] It is possible that Rolle expected that his work would be transmitted orally, perhaps by the literate reading to the illiterate as in the case of Margery Kempe. His works could also reflect the maxim, drawn from Romans 10:17, that it is by hearing that we come to faith: "Ergo fides ex auditu, auditus autem per verbum" [Faith then, is by hearing: and hearing is by the word of Christ]. Hearing was also associated with memory and the process of cognition in the medieval period because listening represented the opening of "the

---

27 V. Gillespie, " 'Lukynge in haly bukes' ", 7.
28 N. Watson, *Invention of Authority*, 228. Watson notes that Rolle is "always to be heard 'speaking' the words he has written", as a means of perpetuating the three-way relationship he constructs in the prologue to *Ego Dormio* between Christ, the reader and his authorial self.

eye of the mind". Susan Hagen suggests that, if we infer accurately from various medieval texts, the process of hearing a story and envisioning it in one's mind's eye was so much a thing of expectation, so much a mode of comprehending narrative, that the medieval writer could move with impunity from verbs of reading and hearing to verbs of seeing and imagining.[29] V. A. Kolve also notes the importance of hearing and seeing in the cognitive process because it is clear that in the Middle Ages, poetic narrative – which even a printed book assumes to be addressed to "man's hearing" – sought a response from the inner eye.[30] In *Ego Dormio*, Rolle's exhortation to hear his words suggests his acceptance of the cognitive power of the ear and prefigures the later part of the work where, once the Word has been heard, the fixing of the gaze becomes of prime importance to the opening of the heart.

Auditory reference may also be simply another exegetical aspect of Rolle's prologue, borrowed from earlier writers of literature for a female audience. Elizabeth Robertson argues that the author of the homiletic *Hali Meiðhad*, drawing on the example of Jerome's letter to the virgin Eustochium, begins his work with an allegorisation of the opening lines of Psalm 44, "Audi, filia, et vide et inclina aurem tuam" [Hear daughter, and see, and incline thine ear] as a matter of pastoral convention.[31] However, Rolle's positioning of his own changeable author-identity, as friend, teacher and the messenger of love, requires an auditory response from his audience different from the one implied by Jerome and the author of *Hali Meiðhad*. Pastoral concern does not appear to be the prime objective of Rolle's utterance; rather his words are to be heard by the reader in order that he/she may then become one with them just as the Word, proffered by the messenger of God the Archangel Gabriel, was made flesh at the Annunciation.

Here we can begin to see how Rolle develops a range of reader/writer relationships implicit within the discourse of intimacy he employs. Initially, the reader is wooed by Rolle to become the bedmate of Christ in what is perhaps the most widely quoted passage of his English works:

Forþi þat I loue þe, I wowe þe, þat I myght haue þe as I wold, nat to me, bot to my Lord. I wil becum a messager to brynge þe to hys bed þat hath mad þe

---

29 S. K. Hagen, *Allegorical Remembrance: A Study of the Pilgrimage of the Life of Man as a Medieval Treatise on Seeing and Remembering* (Athens and London, 1990), 70.

30 V. A. Kolve, "Chaucer and the Visual Arts". *Geoffrey Chaucer: Writers and their Background*. Ed. D. Brewer (London, 1974), 298.

31 See E. Robertson, *Early English Devotional Prose*, 80. Robertson notes that this type of passage is a convention in treatises on virginity. However, where it was used by patristic authors, such as Jerome, as an allegory of the soul's relationship with God, here the author uses it to express his concerns for temptations that are of special concern to women – lust and marriage.

and boght þe, Crist, þe kynges son of heuyn, for he wil wed þe if þou wil loue hym. (26/6–9)

This passage has a broad range of inter-textual suggestions. Expressing the love between the soul and God as that between lover and beloved was not uncommon in medieval mystical writings. Barry Windeatt refers to *The Doctrine of the Herte* as a text in which the impetus of love is often conveyed by associating it with the urgency of desire and courtship and also cites the concluding passage of *A Talkynge of the Loue of God* – "A swete Ihesu . . . Bi-twene þine armes ley I me, bi-twene myn armes cluppe I þe . . ." – to illustrate the commonality of metaphors of erotic and nuptial love in English devotional works of the fourteenth century.[32] The shift in emphasis from Christ's divinity to his humanity that began in twelfth-century devotional literature had introduced Christ's physical body as a subject of meditation. Spiritual union with the human Christ incorporated identification of Christ as bridegroom to the soul. Erotic language became synonymous with the identification and was widely employed by male authors writing for a female audience. It has even been suggested that in twelfth-century religious literature the *sponsa Christi* metaphor attracted to itself the suggestive dress of thinly veiled literary eroticism which was to characterise the testimony of female mystics throughout the remainder of the Middle Ages.[33] In *Ego Dormio* Rolle utilises this erotic imagery as he advises his reader to covet the role of "Goddis louer" (29/139). In the earlier vernacular tradition the author of *Ancrene Wisse* urged his audience to "streche þi luue to iesu crist. þu hauest him iwunnen. Rín him wið ase muche luue. as þu hauest sum mon chearre".[34] Similarly, the task of winning a beloved object of desire for a distant importunate lover is a familiar motif in medieval romance literature, the most celebrated example being Chaucer's *Troylus and Criseyde*. Rolle might be seen as like Chaucer's Pandarus, a procurer delivering the reader to Christ's bed, and gaining a vicarious sexual pleasure from the act.[35] The use of a trope common to both sacred and secular love literature may also suggest Rolle's anticipation of a diverse audience for this work – readers familiar with either romantic or religious writings on love and marriage who would be able to respond to the implicit sexual allusions.

Critics have focused on the overtly sexual nature of the language Rolle

---

32 *A Talkynge of the Loue of God*. Ed. S. Westra (The Hague, 1950), 68. Cited in B. Windeatt, *English Mystics*, 8.

33 J. Bugge, *Virginitas: An Essay in the History of a Medieval Ideal* (The Hague, 1975), 92. See also E. Robertson, *Early English Devotional Prose*, 189–190.

34 *Ancrene Wisse*. Ed. J. R. R. Tolkien (Oxford, 1962), 208/23–25.

35 A. Clark Bartlett, *Male Authors, Female Readers*, 67. Bartlett notes that Watson also recognises the similarity to *Troylus and Criseyde*, suggesting that Rolle "teasingly evokes a sensual relationship with his reader" in order to teach her about spiritual *amicitia*. See also N. Watson, *Invention of Authority*, 231.

employs in the prologue to *Ego Dormio* as indicative of misogynist stereo-typing and his gendering of the audience.[36] But both suggestions are misleading. Rolle's language is indeed overtly sexual in that he wishes to "haue" the reader, to bring the reader "to hys bed", and to see the reader "perfitly cowpled with God" (27/15) but only as a condition of true union within marriage.[37] The Bible explicitly teaches that while fornication is forbidden in the Christian church, "Honorabile connubium in omnibus, et thorus immaculatus" [Marriage is honorable in all, and the bed undefiled] (Heb. 13:4). Within the context of holy matrimony, the church, following Christ's own words, views sex as the act which binds the couple together and indeed marries them:

> Ab initio autem creaturae masculum et feminam fecit eos Deus. Propter hoc relinquet homo patrem suum et matrem, et adhaerebit ad uxorem suam: et erunt duo in carne una. Itaque iam non sunt duo, sed una caro. Quod ergo Deus coniunxit, homo non separet. (Mark 10:6–9)
>
> [But from the beginning of the creation, God made them male and female. For this cause, man shall leave his father and mother: and shall cleave to his wife. And they two shall be in one flesh. Therefore now they are not two, but one flesh. That therefore which God has joined together, let not man separate.]

In *Ego Dormio*, a quasi-sexual relationship within the mystical marriage is certainly alluded to in this sense. Christ's maleness suggests the need for the reader to accept a feminised role in order to become the bride, but there is no suggestion that, as the lover of Christ in the mystical sense, this reader is liter-ally female. That would be to mistake the carnal suggestions of the meta-phor's vehicle for its spiritual tenor. In transcending the literal sexual union known to the worldly, Rolle also invites transcendence of this world's gender discriminations.

In other Rolle texts the audience is urged, no matter what their gender, to consider themselves the brides of Christ; and he often uses his own mystical experience as exemplum. In *Incendium Amoris* he writes:

> . . . cum enim dulcissimi mei amplexus et oscula sencio, quasi deliciis inenarrabilibus affluo, quem sola dileccione sue immense bonitatis ueri amatores omnibus anteponunt. Ueniens ergo me ueniat, perfectum amorem infundendo, reficiat quoque cor meum perseueranciam dando, accendatque et impinguet omne impedimentum amoris auferendo.

---

36 N. Watson, *Invention of Authority*, 229. Watson describes the prologue to *Ego Dormio* as "a flamboyantly daring mystical-cum-sexual fantasy".

37 See *Middle English Dictionary*. Couple n. 1a. (a) a man and woman in marriage; also a pair of lovers; 1. (b) copulation.

[. . . when I feel the embrace and caress of my Sweetheart I swoon with unspeakable delight, for it is he – he whom true lovers put before all else, for love of him alone, and because of his unbounded goodness! And when he comes, may he come into me, suffusing me with his perfect love. May he refresh my heart by his continual gifts, and by removing every hindrance to his love make me glow and expand.][38]

In this passage Rolle's authorial self not only acts as the bride of Christ, but desires to become pregnant by him. Marriage with God was commonly seen as a metaphor for the soul's union with Him that not necessarily applied to female religious only. When Bonaventure is discussing the ineffable burning love Francis feels for Christ he expresses it as a marriage: "No human tongue could describe the passionate love with which Francis burned for Christ, his spouse."[39] Throughout the vernacular treatises Rolle's own identification with the bride is central to the acceptance of the soul as feminine and the development of intimate relationships with the reader.

Rolle thus recognises the biblical text as literally carnal. The sexual nature of the *Song of Songs* had long been debated, causing it to pose two interrelated problems for the Fathers of the early church, both of which are articulated and addressed in Origen's third-century commentary. The first arises from what the song leaves unstated and the second from what it actually says; the explication of spiritual love being the former and the literal expression of carnal love being the latter.[40] Literary employment of the *Song of Songs* in the Middle Ages was as diverse as it was profuse. That Rolle should choose to employ it in one of his few English works is most interesting in terms of his positioning of a vernacular audience that is feminised through a discourse of intimacy. Rolle's English predecessor, the author of *Ancrene Wisse*, interspersed his rule for anchoresses with direct and indirect allusions to the *Song of Songs*, leading Mary Dove to conclude that the writer sees the life of the woman anchorite, lived as it should be lived (for, like every other way of life, it is capable of gross deformation), as a literal gloss on the biblical text. Here on earth, she has responded to the bridegroom's words of invitation to the bride – *surge* (2:10) and *veni* (4:8).[41] Rolle's lover of Love, who is expected to be "neuer wery of loue" (26/4), is merely a slightly less literal reading of the *Songs of Songs'* text,

---

38 *Incendium Amoris*, 216; *The Fire of Love*, 123.
39 Bonaventure, "The Major Life of St. Francis". Trans. B. Fahy. *St. Francis of Assisi, Writing and Earlier Biographies*, IX, 2, 698.
40 See Origen, *In Canticum Canticorum*. Trans. Rufinus. *Patrologiae Cursus Completus, Series Graeca*. Ed. J. P. Migne (Paris, 1857–1866), 13, C63 cited in A. Astell, *The Song of Songs in the Middle Ages* (Ithaca, 1990), 1.
41 M. Dove, " 'Swiche Olde Lewed Wordes': Books About Medieval Love, Medieval Books About Love and the Medieval Book of Love". *Venus and Mars: Engendering Love and War in Medieval and Early Modern Europe*. Eds. A. Lynch and P. Maddern (Western Australia, 1995), 24.

"ego dormio et cor meum vigilat", that Rolle, positioning his authorial self as an extension of the Song-author, sets at the beginning of the work. Just as the author of *Ancrene Wisse* appears to draw on the *Song of Songs* to orient female (anchoritic) life to the biblical text, Rolle's incorporation of the *Song of Songs* into *Ego Dormio* appears similarly to centre around audience participation in the marriage metaphor.

This brings us to another consideration in Rolle's incorporation of the *Song of Songs* into a vernacular work, that of the vernacular religious literature tradition itself and its relationship to Latin commentary. There was a literary tradition of commentaries in the vernacular on the *Song of Songs*, written initially for female religious audiences.[42] By virtue of the accessibility of the language these had "special power" to influence medieval Christian lay piety as well as the professional religious audience for whom they were explicitly intended. Rolle is, of course, one author who actually participated in the Latin commentary genre as well as in the tradition of vernacular devotional treatises based around the *Song of Songs*.[43] However, his Latin commentary *Super Canticum Canticorum* is, in some ways, a work that does not do justice to the complexity of his thought in *Ego Dormio*, where he uses the *Song of Songs* as the central premise introducing his reader to the glories of wholly immersing oneself in the love of God. Hope Emily Allen describes *Super Canticum Canticorum* as a diffuse and rambling exposition of the first five half-verses of the *Song of Songs* and for Nicholas Watson it is like reading "a highly wrought sermon".[44] By comparison *Ego Dormio* is more an impassioned meditation, designed for use in its own right rather than to stand as an accepted biblical commentary. Rolle's description of the *Song of Songs* as the "songe of loue" (26/2) sets a theme which is essential to his purpose: the teaching of spiritual union with God. Such centrality is interesting considering that the *Song of Songs* makes only two literal entrances in *Ego Dormio*, at the very beginning and again near the end. But, as E. Ann Matter points out, the spiritual teaching of the commentaries in the tropological mode is evident throughout.[45] The words "I slepe and my hert waketh", as the beginning of the spiritual ascent of the soul to God, frame the explanation of the three levels of the spiritual journey that form the body of *Ego Dormio*. As in Bernard of Clairvaux's third

---

42 E. Ann Matter, *The Voice of My Beloved: The Song of Songs in Western Medieval Christianity* (Philadelphia, 1990), 178–200. Matter lists a number of commentaries, in various vernaculars, that were addressed initially to female religious, including the early German commentary *St. Trudperter Hohelied* which used the *Song of Songs* to spur its readers ever higher in *minnichlichen gotes erkennusse* [loving knowledge of God].

43 E. Ann Matter, *The Voice of My Beloved*, 183.

44 H. E. Allen, *Writings Ascribed*, 62; N. Watson, *Invention of Authority*, 147–148.

45 See E. Ann Matter, *The Voice of My Beloved*, 184. In quoting the first lines of *Ego Dormio* from H. E. Allen's edition (*English Writings*, 61) Matter has misquoted the description used for the *Song of Songs* as the "sang of lyf" instead of the "sang of luf".

sermon on the *Song of Songs*, the final stage of mystical rapture is not expressed through the kiss of the *Song of Songs* 1:1, but by another verse, *Song of Songs* 2:5, "for I languish with love".[46] Here, *Ego Dormio's* relationship to both Rolle's own Latin commentary work and to his other vernacular works is apparent – the same verse appears as a major turning point in *The Form of Living*.[47] For Rolle it would appear that metaphor drawn from the *Song of Songs* bridges what could be termed the exegetical gap between the Latin commentary tradition and vernacular religious discourse.

The very choice of the "ego dormio" verse of the *Song of Songs* is interesting in terms of Rolle's appropriation of a speaking voice in *Ego Dormio* as well as his construction of his authorial self as an extension of the Song-author. Literally, the Vulgate text of the *Song of Songs* 5:2 sees the woman anticipating the arrival of her lover:

> SPONSA
> Ego dormio, et cor meum vigilat.
> Vox dilecti mei pulsantis:
> SPONSUS
> Aperi mihi, soror mea, amica mea,
> Columba mea, immaculata mea,
> Quia caput meum plenum est rore,
> Et cincinni mei guttis noctium.

> [I sleep, and my heart watches: the voice of my beloved knocking: Open to me my sister, my love, my dove, mine immaculate: because my head is full of dew, and my locks of the drops of the nights.]

If Rolle's text is also taken literally, his voice appropriates the voice of the woman who is speaking, thus feminising his authorial identity. In turn, the appeal to the "sister" becomes Rolle's authorial self appropriating the voice of Christ calling to the reader. In each case he constructs utterance on behalf of the two who will form a relationship of lover/beloved, his reader and Christ. In the opening lines of *Ego Dormio* Rolle's authorial position is fluid. He at first woos the reader as a lover, "forþi þat *I* loue þe, *I* wowe þe, þat *I* myght haue þe as *I* wold" (emphasis mine) but quickly asserts that this is not to be taken literally because he loves only in the service of another and wishes to draw the reader "nat to me, bot to my Lord". The persona shifts to become the messenger who brings the beloved to his love. Ann Astell has convincingly argued that in *Ego Dormio* Rolle himself identifies with the bride of the *Song of Songs* and thus the bride to whom he brings the love of Christ in this text

---

46 E. Ann Matter, *The Voice of My Beloved*, 185.
47 The words "Amore langueo" function in the text of *The Form of Living* (15/489) in a divisionary capacity.

represents a stage of his own mystical journey towards *canor* and mystical union.[48] Caroline Walker Bynum suggests that such author/reader identities arise because the dominant religious image of the self in the late Middle Ages was female; the soul as woman or bride (or sometimes child).[49] This type of authorial self-feminisation is apparent in *The Form of Living* where Rolle identifies his own contemplative role with the bride and also refers to himself in terms of the domestic metaphor of the "sitter" (another feminised authorial role I shall discuss in detail later in relation to Rolle's *The Form of Living*). Rolle's feminising of his audience may not necessarily reflect the gender of actual readers, instead it suggests that he both accepts and promotes the soul as feminine in this text, demanding from the reader dedication of his/her own soul to the role of bride and the love of God.

The image of the bride in *Ego Dormio* is crucial to an understanding of the experiential (Rolle as "messenger"), as well as authoritative (Rolle as teacher), authorial personae within the text. The figure of the "messenger" appears both to feminise and masculinise Rolle for the reader. He is a bride of Christ himself as well as the messenger/message figure of Love. Rolle's construction of both the reader and his own authorial *anima* as the bride of Christ in *Ego Dormio* suggests that his perceptions of feminised spirituality are fairly traditional. The Canticle's commentary tradition speaks of a double marriage into which the contemplative is drawn.[50] The first marriage takes place within the reader of the *Song of Songs* in the form of a joining together of the affective and the rational faculties of the soul; the second occurs simultaneously between the soul and God.[51] The *affectus*, deemed feminine in typical medieval discussions of human nature as *imago Dei*, marriage as sacrament, and the Fall of humankind, is then joined with pure reason, the masculine. According to Ann Astell the expositions of the *Song of Songs* associate the feminine principle with the affections which are joined to the enlightened reason as their husband – even as they associate the reader with the figure of the Bride united to her bridegroom, Christ; and they use the same word to designate both: *anima*.[52] She further notes that Rolle's autobiographical writings, generally included as digressions in his Latin biblical commentaries and spiritual treatises, reveal that some of his greatest temptations are sexual. And that the spiritual friendships he later enjoyed and which led the English works to be written could not have taken place without a reconciliation within Rolle to his own *anima*, or feminine self. Rolle himself claims that the gift of *canor* had gradually led him to an affective integration which enabled him to have friendships with women without moral danger or spiritual disquiet.[53] As a result Rolle, particularly in

---

48 See A. Astell, "Feminine *Figurae*", *passim*.
49 C. Walker Bynum, *Fragmentation and Redemption*, 165.
50 A. Astell, "Feminine *Figurae*", 118.
51 A. Astell, "Feminine *Figurae*", 118.
52 A. Astell, "Feminine *Figurae*", 118.
53 H. E. Allen, *English Writings*, li–ii cited in A. Astell, "Feminine *Figurae*", 120.

his role as the "messager" in *Ego Dormio*, is himself with the reader the bride of the piece.[54] In *The Form of Living* this type of gender integration also takes place and allows Rolle to develop the nuptial theme further by suggesting that it leads to what he sees as a superior relationship with his reader, that of spiritual friend in God. In *Ego Dormio* intimacy is achieved because the reader is free to unite with both the authorial and the "messager" Rolle, who both participate in the spiritual rite of passage offered. The fluidity of the gender of Rolle's own authorial soul is, as it were, transferred to his reader through the example of its union with the messenger.

The image of the messenger as mediator borrows from biblical tradition. In his second epistle to the Corinthians (2 Cor. 11:2) Paul writes: "Aemulor enim vos Dei aemulatione. Despondi enim vos uni viro virginem castam exhibere Christo" [For I emulate you with the emulation of God. For I have espoused you to one man, to present you a chaste virgin unto Christ]. John the Baptist (John 3:28) also described himself as a mediator between the believer and Christ: "Non sum ergo Christos: sed quia missus sum ante illum" [I am not Christ: but that I am sent before him]. Rolle's offer to become the "messager" echoes both Paul and John and implies that in appropriating such a role he is as intimate with Christ as His apostles were. Furthermore, biblical sanction of the messenger role permeates the work as a whole; the "ego dormio" verse itself echoes the desire for ceaseless prayer advocated by Paul in his first epistle to the Thessalonians.[55] Drawing attention to this connection, Denis Renevey concludes that the messenger role which Rolle ascribes to himself in *Ego Dormio* results from the sophisticated combination of Old and New Testament passages while also echoing *fin amor* motives.[56] Beyond the biblical authorisation of the role, the figure of the messenger held an important place in the noble household of the fourteenth century. In secular as well as religious

---

[54] A. Astell, "Feminine *Figurae*", 121. Rolle's ability to communicate with individual women in a noble healthy way points to an affective integration within himself – the marriage of "vis inferior" with "ratio" – as a precondition for, and fruit of, his mystical marriage with Christ. Earlier in the article Astell explains her use of the terms "vis inferior" and "ratio" as derived from the teaching of Honorius of Autun whose discussion of the tropology of the *Song of Songs* discusses how the "anima", which is the lower, affective part of the soul (vis inferior), is coupled to the higher power ("interioris hominis spiritui") as her husband ("ejus vir"), from which marriage good works are engendered: "de quo conjugio spiritalis prole, id est, bonum opus gignitur". See Honorius of Autun, *Expositio in Canticum Canticorum. Patrologia Latina*, ed. J. P. Migne (Paris, 1844–1864), 172, 349–350.

[55] 2 Th. 2:12: "Nos autem debemus gratias agere Deo semper pro vobis" [Therefore we also give thanks to God without intermission].

[56] D. Renevey, *The Moving of the Soul*, 217. Renevey also notes a connection with the two verses mentioned with the "Jesus Prayer". He asserts that in the fourteenth century *perfecti* were advised to replace the "Jesus Prayer" by the simple invocation of the Name of Jesus, just as Rolle advises his reader later in *Ego Dormio*.

terms the messenger played a prominent role in the dissemination of important information. Records of the English Royal household suggest a slow but
definite improvement of the status of the messenger throughout the twelfth to
fourteenth centuries because of their increased involvement in the transmit-
ting of the private written word as opposed to the older style of verbal
message. The prestige of the role and the functional importance of the
messenger increased as epistolary production increased.[57] Accordingly, it is
likely that Rolle's medieval audience could have had an exalted idea of the
status of the messenger from a secular as well as a religious perspective.

Rolle's offering of his authorial self to the reader as the "messager" of God's
love is of course clearly representative of the most important verbal utter-
ance/message in Christian religion: the Annunciation. In effect Rolle positions his authorial self to appropriate the role of the Archangel Gabriel
bringing the message, the Word that is to become flesh, to the Virgin. Rolle's
message of love is to become flesh in his reader. The image of the angel as a
messenger of love is prominent in a wide selection of medieval literature. The
well-known lyric *Angelus ad virginem*, which circulated in both Latin and
vernacular versions throughout the fourteenth century, includes a very direct
representation of Gabriel acting as a sort of love messenger. An English translation of *Angelus ad virginem* appears with an extract from Rolle's *The Form of
Living* in a collection of vernacular pieces at the end of a manuscript
containing the works of the fourteenth-century vernacular poet John Audelay,
perhaps suggesting that medieval scribes considered there to be a connection
between Rolle and the lyric:

> The angel to þe vergyn said,
> Entreng into here boure,
> For drede of quakyng of þis mayd,
> He said, "haile!" with gret honour,
> "Haile! be þou quene of maidyns mo,
> Lord of heuen and erþ also,
> Consayue þou shalt, and bere with ale, þe Lord of my3t,
> Hele of al monkyn.
> He wil make þe þe 3ate of heuen bry3t,
> Medesyne of al our syn".[58]

Chaucer's *Miller's Tale* has the Miller describe a "poure scoler" named
Nicholas who plays a stringed instrument and sings with a fine voice:

---

[57] M. C. Hill, *The King's Messengers, 1199–1377* (London, 1961), 135.
[58] This vernacular version of *Angelus ad virginem* appears in Bodleian Library Oxford,
Douce MS 302, fols. 24–24v. The extract from *The Form of Living* occurs on fols.
32r–32v. For further information on the "Angelus ad virginem" lyric see J. Stevens,
"*Angelus ad virginem*: the History of a Medieval Song". *Medieval Studies for J. A. W.
Bennett: Aetatis Suae LXX*. Ed. P. L. Heyworth (Oxford, 1981), 297–328. I have reproduced Stevens' version of the Douce translation here.

And al above ther lay a gay sautrie,
On which he made a nyghtes melodie
So swetely that al the chambre rong;
And *Angelus ad virginem* he song;
And after that he song the Kynges Noote.
Ful often blessed was his myrie throte.[59]

Chaucer's citation of the song indicates its contemporary popularity and suggests the favourable reception of the notion of Gabriel as a love-messenger.

The idea that Christ comes to his mother Mary as her beloved was also widespread in the Middle Ages. The well-known poem in British Library, Sloane MS 2593 (c. 1400), "I sing of a mayden that is makeles", talks of Christ coming to his mother's "bowr", implying a romantic liason:

He cam also stille
To his moderes bowr
As dew in Aprille
That falleth on the flowr.

He cam also stille
Ther his moder lay,
As dew in Aprille
That falleth on the spray.[60]

In the fifteenth-century *Towneley Plays*, God's instruction to Gabriel regarding the Annunciation includes the call for him to hail Mary as his beloved:

Angell must to mary go,
ffor the fend was eue fo;
he was foule & layth syght,
And thou art angel fayr & bright;
And hayls that madyn, my lemman,
As heyndly as thou can.
On my behalf thou shall hyr grete,
I haue hyr chosen, that mayden swete,
She shall conceyf my derlyng,
Through thy word & her heryng.[61]

The cycle plays of the late Middle Ages incorporated more graphic representations of human emotion for the benefit of the devout laity.[62] The portrait of

---

[59] F. N. Robinson, ed. *The Works of Geoffrey Chaucer*, 48.
[60] R. T. Davies, *Medieval English Lyrics*, Poem 66, 155. This poem derives from the thirteenth-century poem "I sing of one that is matchless" found in Trinity College Cambridge MS 323. See C. Brown, *Religious Lyrics of the IVth Century* (Oxford, 1932), Poem 31, 55.
[61] *The Towneley Plays*. Eds. M. Stevens and A. C. Cawley (Oxford, 1994), 93–94/61–70.
[62] J. Hughes, *Pastors and Visionaries*, 236.

Mary as God's "lemman" in the *Towneley Play* is suggestive of a private, perhaps even secular, relationship based on love. Rolle's message of love in *Ego Dormio*, his suggestion of a personal relationship of love between his authorial self and the reader as a catalyst for the reader's loving relationship with God, has secular parallels. Both these annunciation narratives rely on secular notions of love as the literary bridge between religious piety and human relationships. By the late fourteenth century the clergy had assumed responsibility for communicating and adapting eremitic teaching for the laity through contemplative literature and such forms of religious expression as the Corpus Christi processions and the cycle plays.[63] The secularity of Rolle's message of love in his own annunciation narrative in *Ego Dormio*, a text popular before and at the time many of these plays were written, may well have served as a model.

Recognition of the divine message, or messages, as important and necessary steps towards spiritual perfection is not uncommon in many of Rolle's vernacular works. These "sondes" perform various functions throughout his works and each time Rolle's exhortatory voice can be heard encouraging the reader towards absorption of God's words. The last line of the short prose work *Desire and Delight* exhorts the reader to renounce all "sensualite" for the love of God and to "be payed of al Goddis sondes withouten gurchynge and heuynesse of thoght" (40/26–27). Similarly, an exhortation to put aside the world in *The Commandment* asks the reader to "thanke hym euer of al his sondes" (37/147). Created as an object not only of desire but also of gratitude, the message becomes integral to the reader's journey towards spiritual fulfilment. Similarly, one of Rolle's vernacular prose Passion meditations, *Meditation B*, depicts "sondes" as both longed for suffering during life that will better enable imitation of Christ's suffering and the ultimate reward of death:

> Now, swete Ihesu, graunt me here wilfully to suffre deseises and tribulacions for þy sake, and neuyr to gurche for sekenesse ne for wronges of man, bot euer to þank þe of al þy sondes. And graunt me, lord Ihesu, purgatory for my synnes er I deye, and hertely, lord, continuely hit to pray, and when hit cometh, lord, yif me pacience and hert hooly to þank þe of þy blesful and gracious sond. (73/179–185)

In these didactic utterances, the figure of the message performs a variety of penitential and salvific functions; these may not have the same emotive impact as Rolle's message of love in *Ego Dormio* but they nonetheless demonstrate that many aspects of Christian faith were interpreted as messages directly from God.

Once Rolle has asserted his position as the "messager" of love he invites the reader to share yet another constructed space: Rolle is to play the

---

63 J. Hughes, *Pastors and Visionaries*, 236.

messenger-angel Gabriel to his reader's annunciate Mary. In this construction, Rolle's reference to the ordering of the seraphic hierarchy becomes of more importance. The nine orders of angels he describes for the reader were first enumerated by the fourth-century Pseudo-Dionysius and it seems likely that Rolle's discussion of angels here is a brief summation of Pseudo-Dionysian theories from the *Celestial Hierarchy*.[64] Rolle may also have been influenced by certain passages from Gregory and Aelred of Rievaulx in which the soul is said to aspire to "join the choir of angels".[65] Inclusion of an explanation of the nine orders of angels in this message of love is exhortatory and demands an emotional response from the reader: "this I say to kyndel þi herte to coueit þe felewshipe of angels" (26/24–25). Again the reader must "coueit" a role suggested by the text.

The three degrees of love, which provide both the framework and the main subject of the work, are here explained in terms of orders of angels, the nine being divided into three orders. As Rolle has fashioned his authorial self as a messenger-angel, the company that the reader is exhorted to covet includes himself in an exalted position. Gabriel, the messenger of the Annunciation, as archangel, is an angel of the lowest order and situated specifically between "angels" and "virtus". Interestingly, Seraphim, the highest of all angels, have the "most brennynge hertes" (26/31) which would seem to equate to Rolle's lowest rung on the spiritual ladder, the fire of love.[66] In the prologue of *Ego Dormio* Rolle equates his authorial role in this text with the lowest of the orders of angels (archangel) and in the lowest sphere of his own mystical schema (*calor*). His use of the Annunciation tradition along with imagery from the *Song of Songs* prepares the reader for a categorical account, from the bottom up, of the mystical journey. Extensive use of this model is apparent in his later English works. The degree to which each order of angels loves God is different. In *Ego Dormio* it would appear that the messenger, the archangel of the lower order, functions as an escort to guide the reader to that higher order of Seraphim where the reader may experience spiritual *calor* and begin the glorious ascent to *canor* in the third degree of love. William Pollard argues that this is how Rolle incorporates all four of Richard of St. Victor's degrees of love even when he explicitly only draws on three because this "seraphic love is for Rolle the 'singular love' of the Victorine school with elements of the 'insatiable', and it is the *apex affectionis*".[67] Of course Rolle is quick to point out, in

---

[64] S. Ogilvie Thomson, *Prose and Verse*, 204. The names derive from Paul's description in Colossians 1:16 and Ephesians 1:21. See C. Horstmann, *Yorkshire Writers*, I, 50–51. On the occasional influence of Pseudo-Dionysian language theory on Rolle's writings see R. Boenig, *Chaucer and the Mystics*, 24–25.

[65] H. E. Allen, *Writings Ascribed*, 88. Allen notes that "angel choirs" are ecstatically dwelt on in Rolle's *Judica Me Deus* as mystically opening the door to heaven.

[66] See H. E. Allen, *Writings Ascribed*, 88.

[67] W. Pollard, "Richard Rolle and the 'Eye of the Heart' ", 91.

what proves to be a characteristically unprejudiced manner in the vernacular works, that not all will be worthy of the higher orders:

> ... for al þat ben good and holy, whan þai passe out of þis world, shal be taken in to þese ordres: sum in to þe lowest ... sum in þe myddis ... oþer to þe heghest. (26/25–28)

Rolle's explanatory categorisation of angelic membership here is the first in a number of references to his acceptance of the varying levels of reader capability which can only suggest his perception of a broad audience for this work.

The intimate language within *Ego Dormio* not only expresses to the reader the idea of how the spiritual journey should progress, but signals the deeply felt expectations Rolle, as writer/utterer of spiritual advice, has of the recipient of his message. Rolle reorients his authorial position from messenger of love to personal tutor; his intimacy expresses confidence in the reader's agency:

> To þe I writ þis speciali, for I hope in þe more goodnes þan in anoþer, þat þou wil gif þi þoght to fulfil in dede þat þou seest is profitable for þi soule, and þat lif gif þe to in þe whoch þou may holyest offre þi [hert] to Ihesu Criste, and lest be in besynesse of þis world. (26/33–36)

Anne Clark Bartlett argues that the concern of a specific male writer for an intended female reader is the basis of a "discourse of familiarity" found in many male-authored devotional texts of the later Middle Ages.[68] The formation of what Bartlett terms "a collegial relationship" between male authors and their female readers modelled on the monastic ideals of friendship and community is certainly apparent in Rolle's *Ego Dormio*.[69] But I would further suggest that although Rolle uses tropes common to male-authored texts for a female audience, his extension of these tropes to a wider audience is just as apparent. Although Rolle is almost certainly writing initially for a female audience, his purpose in writing "speciali" to a reader in *Ego Dormio* does not appear to fit comfortably into Bartlett's mould; his work is not an adaptation of a text that was explicitly written for a male audience nor is the work specifically addressed to a gendered recipient. What is "profitable for þi soule" is

---

68 A. Clark Bartlett, *Male Authors, Female Readers*, 96. Bartlett argues that Middle English devotional literature for women begins to develop a discourse of familiarity between male authors and their "religious sisters". This phenomenon occurs in two varieties. The first occurs as a broad cultural shift that prompts male authors to address female readers with greater esteem and deference than earlier writing for women exhibits. The second appears in individual texts that reveal the concern of a specific male writer for the concerns of an intended female reader. The latter type of relationship becomes particularly apparent in adaptations of texts originally designed for male audiences.

69 A. Clark Bartlett, *Male Authors, Female Readers*, 97.

Rolle's prime concern for the reader, whom he individualises only by expressing his own desire to find within that soul "more goodnes þan in anoþer". Rolle's personal address to the reader's soul, coupled with the further personal expression of confidence, has the effect of drawing the reader closer to an understanding of, and desire to fulfil, Rolle's authorial expectations.

Rolle's introduction of the soul as reader, or more specifically the soul as the recipient of what is written to the reader, indicates his acceptance of the soul as the true seat of spiritual life, following the common medieval maxim that mind and body should be submissive to the soul. God is described by Rolle as the life of soul, a life that can be snuffed out by "venymous" sin:

> For þese vices sleeth þe soule, and maketh hit depart fro God þat is lif of þe soule; and when a wreched man or womman is departed fro God, we seyn he is dede, for he is slayn fro God, withouten whom no creature may lyve. (28/77–79)

Rolle's "we seyn" implies his membership with the reader of a collective enterprise, and their sharing of one discourse; it can be read as another invitation to the reader to bond with Rolle's authorial self/selves and his message. Imitation of Rolle will lead to perfection in the imitation of Christ. *Ego Dormio*, like most devotional texts of this period, has as a focal point of spiritual reference *imago Dei*, the soul's imitation of Christ.[70] Caroline Walker Bynum has written extensively on the subject of male-authored literature for female readers which utilises the *imago Dei*; she concludes that men wrote of such things for women because, although women had been viewed by the ecclesiastical hierarchy for hundreds of years as precisely not in the image of God, women themselves did not think this the case. One example is the French beguine Douceline of Marseilles who, when she asked herself "What is the soul?", answered confidently, "It is the mirror of divine majesty; in it God has put his seal".[71] The *anima* of Rolle's work shows little of the misogynistic attitudes to female spirituality often found in the fourteenth century and has more in common with the basis on which an individual like Douceline identified herself – that every soul is made in the image of God. In *Ego Dormio* Rolle appropriates the role of mediatory mirror, inviting the reader to gaze metaphorically through his own perfection of *imago Dei* to a vision of the sinners of the world in hell. Readers are, or at least should be, secure in the solace of their own soul loving God. The often unacknowledged first lyric of *Ego Dormio*,

---

[70] See W. Riehle, *The Middle English Mystics*, esp. Chapter XI. Riehle discusses the "imago" and "similtudo" character of the soul and its "reformatio" and "deficatio" in English mysticism.

[71] *La vie de sainte Douceline, fondatrice des beguines de Marseilles.* Ed. J. H. Albanés (Marseilles, 1897) 91 cited in C. Walker Bynum, *Fragmentation and Redemption*, 155.

accompanying the first degree of love, is the affective means of drawing out and directing reader-response:

Al perisshethe and passeth þat we with eigh see; hit vansheth in wrechednesse þe wel of þis world. Robes and richesses roteth in þe diche; pride and peyntynge slak shal in sorowe. Delites and dreries stynke shal ful sone; har gold and har tresour draweth ham to deth. Al þe wiked of þis world dryueth to a dale þat þay may se har sorowynge; þer [wo] is al þe rabil. Bot he may synge of solace þat loued Ihesu Crist, when al þe wreches fro wel falleth in to helle. (28/84–91)

The reader is invited into a closer, plural, relationship with Rolle's authorial self while their collective eyes are trained on the sinners of the world. The collective verbal utterance of the soul's death quoted above is here supported by a collective sight of passing mortality. Privileging the reader further, Rolle contrasts their collective vision of common mortality with the special status of the lovers of God who "may synge of solace . . . when al þe wreches fro wel falleth in to helle".

In writing *Ego Dormio* "speciali" to the reader, Rolle is not only fostering an intimate relationship but is also appealing to the *intellectus* of the reader, as the recipient of Rolle's utterance of the Word; in the same way that the language of flattery, "I hope in þe more goodnes", engages the reader's *affectus* in a relationship of honour and shame, the reader must also intellectualise the expectations of Rolle's special words by considering his/her own sinfulness in detail. The author of *The Cloud of Unknowing* similarly addresses his audience as if they could not possibly be reading his work and be guilty of even venial sin:

I say not þis for I trowe þat þou, or any oþer soche as I speke of, ben gilty & combrid wiþ any soche sinnes.[72]

The author's implied knowledge of the reader's "goodnes" creates another subject position for the reader to occupy: personal friend. Rolle invites "þe" to read and love, and read and be loved in the fellowship of heaven:

For if þou stabilly loue God and brennyngly whils þou lyvest here, withouten dout þi sete is ordeyned for þe ful hegh and ioiful bifore þe face of God amonge [his] holy angels. (27/36–39)

Of course, Rolle has already hinted to the reader that he himself occupies an exalted place in heaven, in that he was able to appropriate the position of angel/messenger, and is therefore authorised to offer advice "withouten dout". Again, the intimate exhortation is as pedagogic as it is collegial. The

---

72 *The Cloud of Unknowing*, 37–38/21–22.

reader is expected to participate in, and respond to, Rolle's friendly discourse whilst still recognising his advice as a literary extension of the Word.

Rolle's awareness of *Ego Dormio* as literary, or bookish, is explicit in the early passages of the work. On three separate occasions, before any real discussion of the three degrees of love takes place, Rolle comments upon the medium of the written word. Firstly in acknowledgement of a literary source "I fynd hit written" (26/2), secondly referring to his own composition, "to þe I writ þis speciali" (26/33), and finally utilising the inexpressibility topos by commenting on the inability of the written word to express God's love, "How myght I than writ hit?" (27/58). Denis Renevey has argued that Rolle's English works offer insights on the interdependence between religious experience and literary competence and that the exposition of the three degrees of love depends on the capacity of the reader to decipher written signs.[73] The construction of the complex and changing relationship between the reader and the writer/messenger in *Ego Dormio* certainly seems uniquely dependent upon the reader's ability to construct meaning from the literary text. In *The Form of Living* Rolle warns the reader against over-indulgence in books. If you hold love in your heart instead of coveting books, he counsels, you will have "al done þat we may say or write" (18/624). Later, in *The Form of Living*, he makes passing reference to the meditation of "holy writynge" (24/862) as the lower "partie" of contemplative life. But in *Ego Dormio* holding love in your heart is dependant on understanding Rolle's written words. Understanding the text as written is connected to Rolle's positioning of each reader as an intimate and single reading subject. The intimate tone of *Ego Dormio* suggests that Rolle perceives his audience to be able to assimilate the language of love he uses. His inclusion of the eroticised prologue indicates that he does not expect his audience to be surprised by the use of the terms of love in such a spiritual context.[74] Rolle positions himself in this prologue as "messager", the conveyor of the Word as love, and his own words of love are elevated to become one with the Word itself. The introduction of the central theme of the work, an exposition of the three degrees of love, is prefaced by another theme – "Gif al þyn entent to vndrestond þis writynge" (27/65) – which again affirms the importance of Rolle's words. Then, for the second time, Rolle requires his reader to "hire" his words: "and if þou haue set þi desyre to loue God, hire [þese] þre degrees of loue" (27/65–66). Rolle's utterance of the three degrees of love is therefore to be a re-affirmation of the intimate three-way relationship between himself, the reader and God, and prefigures their ultimate union.

---

[73] D. Renevey, *The Moving of the Soul*, 7. Renevey further argues that "pleasure is a concomitant of the understanding of the spiritual message contained in the text".

[74] D. Renevey, *The Moving of the Soul*, 218.

IV

The three grades of love, although touched on in a number of Rolle's early Latin works, are discussed at length only in the English works and the later Latin work *Emendatio Vitae*.[75] The untitled three degrees of love in *Ego Dormio* are in fact Rolle's first explication of this common medieval ladder of perfection. Hope Emily Allen suggests that the unnamed grades of love could have been drawn from Gregory:

> Primus ergo gradus est ut se ad se colligat, secundus ut videat qualis est collects, tertius ut super semetipsum surgat, ac se contemplationi auctoris invisibilis intendendo subjicat.[76]

> [So the first step is that one should focus on oneself, secondly that one should see the nature of what one has focused upon, and thirdly that one should rise above oneself, and by straining in contemplation of an unseen authority, by struggling submit oneself.]

It has also been suggested that they simply define three types of Christian living; the lay state, the active religious and the contemplative religious.[77] Rolle's assurance that the third degree of love, representative of the contemplative life, is the most perfect state of being certainly reflects Gregory's view that "no one seeks the active life for its own sake; it is undertaken and endured as a means of attaining to contemplation".[78]

The simple categorical arrangement of the three degrees of love found in *Ego Dormio*, corresponding firstly to the nine orders of angels, secondly to the active, coenobitic and the solitary lives, and thirdly to interior states associated with those lives, parallels, but is not equivalent to, the influential distinction between the purgative, illuminative and unitive states found in Bonaventure's *De Triplici Via*.[79] Watson observes that *Ego Dormio*'s structure is also similar to a threefold division Rolle adopts from Peter Lombard in his account of the structure of the *English Psalter*:

75 H. E. Allen, *Writings Ascribed*, 201. The grades entitled "inseparable", "insuperable", and "singular" do not appear in any works except in *Emendatio Vitae*, *The Commandment* and *The Form of Living*.

76 Gregory, *Homilia in Ezechielem prophetam*, II. v. *Patrologia Latina*, 76, c. 989 cited in H. E. Allen, *Writings Ascribed*, 202. See also M. Jennings, "Richard Rolle and The Three Degrees of Love", 198.

77 M. Jennings, "Richard Rolle and the Three Degrees of Love", 199–200. See also W. Pollard, "Richard Rolle and the 'Eye of the Heart'", 91.

78 Gregory, *Faust*, xxii, 58 cited in M. Jennings, "Richard Rolle and The Three Degrees of Love", 200.

79 N. Watson, *Invention of Authority*, 226. Watson argues the divisions used here are yet another way of articulating Rolle's own spiritual career, like the twelve "gradus" which make up *Emendatio Vitae*.

Alswa þis boke is distyngid in thris fyfty psalmes, in þe whilk thre statis of cristin mannys religion is sygnifyd: þe first in penance, þe toþer in rightwisnes, þe thrid in louynge of endles lyfe.[80]

Each of the three stages described in *Ego Dormio* is accompanied by a meditative lyric designed to appeal directly to the *affectus*. This not only creates a clear framework for the exposition but alerts the reader to the central theme of the work – the instilling of love in the very seat of the affections, the heart. Rolle's preoccupation with the *affectus*, and his belief that union can only be reached through love, is encapsulated in one sentence from *The Form of Living*: "in þis þrid degre of loue, to þe which degree hit is impossibil to cum bot in a gret multitude of loue" (17/577–578). In *Ego Dormio* the third degree of love is also firmly positioned as the seat of love and the residence of the gift of *canor*. The progress of the work is thus mainly governed by an anticipatory sense of its ultimate goal in absolute love.

In describing the central tenets of his approach to God, the three degrees of love, Rolle uses his sources differently in each of his vernacular works. Unlike the description of mystical love found in *The Form of Living*, which appears to have developed from ideas of violent love explicitly found in Richard of St. Victor's *De Quattuor Gradibus Violentae Caritatis*, *Ego Dormio* does not contain a detailed discussion of mystical love.[81] However, even though Rolle does not directly draw upon Richard of St. Victor in *Ego Dormio*, it is clear that the third degree equates to Richard's *singularis* because of the mystical experience of *calor*, *dulcor* and *canor* which accompanies it:

At þe begynnynge, when þou comest thereto, þi goostly egh is taken vp in to þe light of heuyn, and þare enlumyned in grace and kyndlet of þe *fyre* of Cristes loue . . . and fillynge þe ful of ioy and *swetnesse* so myche þat no sekenesse ne shame ne angys ne penaunce may gref þe . . . þi praiers turneth in to *ioyful song* and þi thoghtes to melodi. (31/225–233)

In *Ego Dormio*, *calor* and *dulcor* also appear in the second degree of love, as does the concept of union, although the latter is probably anticipatory of that state because it is clear that the audience for this work is in the early stages of spiritual development. The descriptions of languishing for love and true spiritual rest clarify the differing intensity of feeling in each degree. Rolle writes that in the first and second degrees the soul longs to be united with God, but when it attains singular love it enters a restful state where it can say "I sleep but my heart is awake." It is interesting that this notion of "ego dormio et cor

---

[80] *English Psalter*, 4 cited in N. Watson, *Invention of Authority*, 227.
[81] Richard of St. Victor, *De Quattuor Gradibus Violentae Caritatis*, 69. In *The Form of Living* Rolle borrows the three degrees of love from Richard's "four degrees of passionate love" and the same division occurs in *Melos Amoris*, *Emendatio Vitae* and some other Latin works.

meum vigilat" is used to describe the opposite end of the affective spectrum in Bernard of Clairvaux's twenty-third sermon on the *Song of Songs*. For Bernard the waking heart represents its own intellectual endeavour which exhausts it:

> For sleep indeed she feels, the repose of sweetest wonder and tranquil admiration, but she wakes, for she suffers the weariness of ceaseless curiosity and laborious effort.[82]

For Rolle the heart's awakening represents the joy and harmony that accompanies the height of union. The heart as the locality of love may be considered as a major theme in *Ego Dormio* developed from the exegetical opening of the work. The intrinsic significance and historical importance of the symbolic representation of the heart as the locale of love in medieval literature is worth elaborating, to appreciate fully its position in Rolle's development of a discourse of intimacy in this work.

Representations of the heart in medieval writing are centred around the notion of it as the seat of human emotion. Medieval theories of the emotional make-up of human beings derived largely from Patristic interpretation of ancient (mainly Greek) works on the psychological and physiological make-up of humankind; Plato and the Stoics were major sources and, after the twelfth century, Aristotle.[83] Medieval physiology also relied heavily on ancient medical sources for its definition of certain organs or members of the body. Most physiological doctrines were derived from the Hippocratean tradition, which Galen systematised. This system included the hierarchical theory of the sexes, and grounded its medical thinking on the affirmation of a gradation of temperature between them.[84] Women were intrinsically wetter and cooler than men and, as a consequence, less perfect:

> Now just as mankind is the most perfect of all animals, so within mankind the man is the more perfect than the woman, and the reason for this perfection is his excess of heat, for heat is nature's primary instrument.[85]

In the Middle Ages Bonaventure, the Victorines and later mystical writers showed an appreciation of the psychological relations of the religious affections based on Augustinian interpretation of the Platonic division of the soul.[86] The exact function of the heart differs in many of these interpretations

---

82 Bernard of Clairvaux, *Sermo* 23, I/146, 6–9 cited in A. Louth, "Bernard and Affective Mysticism", 4.
83 H. M. Gardiner, *Feeling and Emotion: A History of Theories* (New York, 1937), 90.
84 H. M. Gardiner, *Feeling and Emotion*, 90.
85 M. Tallmadge May, trans. *Galen: On the Usefulness of the Parts of the Body* (Ithaca, 1968), II, 630–632.
86 H. M. Gardiner, *Feeling and Emotion*, 90–118. In the Middle Ages the basis of all psychological doctrine was the Platonic division of the soul into parts rational, concupiscible, and irascible. This division, according to Gardiner, is found in all the

of the affections but it is clear that it is an organ considered to be of prime importance in the disposition of human emotional states. Rolle's appeal to the *affectus* in *Ego Dormio* relies heavily on the medieval perceptions of the heart as the organ where love resides.

According to Aristotle the heart was the seat of physiological activity, the first and central organ of the body.[87] The heart became the focal point through which love reached the soul, it was the eye of the emotions. The author of *Ancrene Wisse*, drawing directly on "Salomon", understood the heart as the dwelling place of the soul which is guarded by the five wits:

> Wið alles cunnes warde dohter sei" Salomon wite wel þin heorte. for sawle lif is in hire . . . Þe heorte wardeins beoð þe fif wittes.[88]

In John of Trevisa's translation of Bartholomaeus Anglicus' *De proprietatibus rerum* the etymology of the Latin word "cor" is used to allocate "wit and konnynge" within the heart:

> The herte hatte cor latyn, and haþ þat name of cura "besines", for þerin [is] al besines and cause of wit and konnynge.[89]

In the fourteenth century, the rise of affective language in literature afforded the heart an exalted place. Romance literature in particular uses the metaphor of the heart to explain numerous tropes of self and society. In Chaucer's *Troilus and Criseyde*, the heart is described as the eye of the breast, the result of the gaze being love:

principal writers down to the middle of the twelfth century. Richard of St. Victor (c. 1173) modified the system in the twofold division of *ratio*, by which we discern or apprehend, and *affectio*, by which we love; seven principal emotions being ascribed to the latter – hope, fear, joy, grief, hate, love, and shame. In the thirteenth century Bonaventure (1221–1274) recognises this division under the names *vis cognitiva* (the power to know) and *vis affectiva* (the power to feel) with further sub-divisions. Thomas Aquinas (1225–1274) classified the passions into the faculties of concupiscible and irascible. The passions of the concupiscible faculty regard good or evil absolutely, those of the irascible regard good or evil as something arduous, something to be attained or avoided with a certain difficulty. Love is defined as aptitude or proportion of the appetite to good, a complacency in good; hate is the contrary. From the love of an object follows the movement towards it, which is desire; and from the attainment of it, the rest in it, which is pleasure, or joy (*delectatio*). Other thirteenth-century writers are discussed here in relation to Aquinas' systematisation of the affections.

87 J. Cadden, *The Meanings of Sex Difference in the Middle Ages: Medicine, Science and Culture* (Cambridge, 1993), 32.

88 *Ancrene Wisse*. Ed. J. R. R. Tolkien, 29/2–5.

89 Bartholomaeus Anglicus, *De proprietatibus rerum. On the properties of things: John Trevisa's translation of Bartholomaeus Anglicus De proprietatibus rerum: a critical text.* Ed. M. C. Seymour (Oxford, 1975), Liber Quintus, 237.

But were he fer or ner, I dar sey this:
By nyght or day, for wisdom or folye,
His herte, which that is his brestes eye,
Was ay on hire, that fairer was to sene
Than euere were Eleyne or Polixene.[90]

In *Piers Plowman* "kynde knowynge" resides in the heart:

And in the herte, there is the heed and the heighe welle.
For in kynde knowynge in herte ther comseth a might –
And that falleth to the Fader that formed us alle,
Loked on us with love and leet his sone dye
Mekely for oure mysdedes, to amenden us alle.[91]

Vincent Gillespie notes that Langland's fourteenth-century concept of "kynde knowynge" appears to derive from writings on *sapientia* by twelfth-century affective theologians who emphasised the importance of feeling and compunction in the search for wisdom.[92] Langland stresses that love, residing in the heart, is an essential and fundamental part of higher knowing.[93] In *Ego Dormio*, Rolle exhorts his reader, "as þou coutaitist be Goddis louer . . . loue his name Ihesu, and þynke hit in þi hert" (29/139–140) suggesting that he too perceived that thinking love in the heart represents a form of higher knowing which results in the redirection of the *affectus* towards God. The imagery in Rolle's text certainly appears to reflect Gillespie's suggestion that what concerned the theologians and writers of the Middle Ages was how the individual soul could be brought to this state of wisdom; how they could be moved away from sin to a firmer relationship with God.[94]

The heart was also a dominant image in medieval iconography. Gazing upon the open heart of Christ represented to the viewer an embodiment of the pain Christ suffered in his Passion. The eye of the heart is suggestive of an image of Christ opening his breast to reveal his heart for others to gaze upon. From close examination of the paintings of late-medieval nuns, Jeffrey Hamburger suggests that representations of the heart as the locus of devotional experience in medieval art can be directly linked to the epistolary genre and the message through the apostle Paul's second letter to the Corin-

90 G. Chaucer, *Troilus and Criseyde*, 114/451–455.
91 W. Langland, *The Vision of Piers Plowman*. Ed A. V. C. Schmidt (London, 1978), Passus I/164–168.
92 V. Gillespie, "Mystic's Foot", 201. Gillespie cites A. Louth, "Bernard and Affective Mysticism", 2–10, esp. 3 and A. Louth, *The Origins of the Christian Mystical Tradition from Plato to Denys* (Oxford, 1981), 132–158. See also M. Davlin, "*Kynde Knowyng* as a Middle English Equivalent for 'Wisdom' in *Piers Plowman* B". *Medium Aevum* 50 (1981), 5–17.
93 V. Gillespie, "Mystic's Foot", 202; W. Langland, *Piers Plowman*, Passus I/142–143.
94 V. Gillespie, "Mystic's Foot", 202.

thians (2 Cor. 3:3) where he enjoined his audience to show: "manifestati quoniam epistula estis Christi ministrata a nobis et scripta non atramento sed Spiritu Dei vivi non in tabulis lapideis sed in tabulis cordis carnalibus [being manifested, that you are the epistle of Christ, ministered by us, and written not with ink, but with the Spirit of the living God; not in tables of stone, but in the fleshly tables of the heart].[95] In *Ego Dormio* Rolle combines the image of the eye, the heart and the message to embody this very sentiment in the reader as the intellectual and emotional recipient of the text. Medieval depictions of reading often portray the reader in two guises, firstly in the act of reading the book and secondly as a participatory figure in what is being read. The late fifteenth-century Hours of Mary of Burgundy contains a particularly clear representation of the eye gazing on the book as the gateway to participatory consciousness. In the first miniature of the book, one of the most famous in late medieval art, the owner is shown reading next to a window in an oratory; she is richly dressed and has a small dog in her lap. The window beside her opens into a church where a woman is seen kneeling before the Virgin and Christ-child, accompanied by three women in simpler dress and a man who is also kneeling. The kneeling woman appears to represent Mary of Burgundy actively participating in a contemporary devotional ideal, personal contact with the divine.[96] Rolle's exhortation to his reader to become one with the message he delivers via his writing is suggestive of this type of window imagery. Reader agency is generated in that he/she gazes upon Rolle's own words in order to participate in a personal relationship, a marriage no less, with the divine.

In later medieval romance literature the heart and the eye often combine to wound the lover with love itself. In the thirteenth-century poem the *Romance of the Rose*, the eye is the gateway to the heart. Entering the *hortus conclusus* Amans fixes his gaze on the object of his love, the rose, and is pierced by an arrow from the bow of the God of Love:

> The God of Love, who had maintained his constant watch over me had fol-
> lowed me with drawn bow . . . when he saw that I had singled out the bud
> that pleased me more than did any of the others, he immediately took an
> arrow . . . and shot at me in such a way that with great force he sent the point
> through the eye and into my heart.[97]

The image of the lover's agony in the garden represents Christ's suffering in the Garden of Gethsemane. Just as Christ foresaw the Passion as he prayed in the garden, so the medieval viewer saw in the Agony in the Garden the sum of

---

[95] J. Hamburger, *Nuns as Artists: The Visual Culture of a Medieval Convent* (Berkeley, 1997), 126–127.

[96] *The Hours of Mary of Burgundy* (London, 1995), f. 14v. Commentary on the manu-script is provided by Eric Inglis towards the end of the book.

[97] *The Romance of the Rose*. Trans. C. Dahlberg (Princeton, 1971), 1681–1687.

Christ's sorrow. Angela of Foligno (1248–1309), or more likely the redactor of her *Liber vitae*, urged readers to use the image of Christ's prayer at Gethsemane as a mirror, because Christ "prayed for you, not for himself".[98] The function of the eye is to open the heart to love. Christ cries out to the bride in the *Song of Songs* 4:9: "Vulnerasti cor meum, soror mea, sponsa; vulnerasti cor meum in uno ocularum tuorum" [Thou hast wounded my heart, my sister spouse, thou hast wounded my heart in one of thine eyes]. In *Ego Dormio*, thinking on the Passion of Christ, in the form of the Passion meditation that accompanies the second degree of love, will cause the heart to be drawn up "so þat þe egh of þi hert may loke in to heyun" (31/215).

Early in the fifteenth century, in an omnibus of sermons collectively titled *Dives and Pauper*, a discussion takes place in which the creation of Adam and Eve is seen as a paradigm of marriage. When Dives asks "Why did God make woman out of Adam's rib rather than out of another bone?" Pauper replies ". . . Because the rib is closest to the heart, signifying that He made her to be man's companion in love, and helper."[99] This explanation was very widely disseminated and is found in Chaucer's *Parson's Tale* and in Jacques de Vitry, *Sermones vulgares*. It traces back to at least Hugh of St. Victor's *De sacramentis* and was made familiar from its use in Peter Lombard's *Sentences*.[100] Rolle's use of bridal imagery in conjunction with the image of the opening of the heart shows a certain affiliation with this tradition. The reader is to assume the role of the bride of Christ, to open his/her heart to him. A female recipient would more than likely have been aware of the imagery associated with her position as the creation of Adam's rib, a bone positioned close to the heart of God's created perfect creature, man. Rolle's feminised reader-as-soul may have found here an appropriate image of espousal to Christ.

The three degrees of love themselves, as described by Rolle in *Ego Dormio*, show little relationship to conventional male-authored misogynist thought because gender is not mentioned in relation to this spiritual hierarchy. Instead, Rolle's decision to discuss the three degrees of love here is one of form and function in that they provide a convenient framework, rather than an end in themselves. Their inclusion in the work can be described as plainer and more moralistic than the treatment they receive in *Emendatio Vitae* and *The Form of Living*, where they are given significant attention. The perfunctory nature of their appearance here caused Hope Emily Allen to suggest that *Ego Dormio* itself is elementary in manner.[101] She then used her own judgement as

---

98   See *Il Libro della Beata Angela da Foligno*. Eds. L. Thier and A. Calufetti (Rome, 1985), 466.

99   *Dives and Pauper*. Ed. Priscilla Barnum (Oxford, 1980), Commandment VI, Chapter 4 cited in A. Blamires, *Woman Defamed and Woman Defended: An Anthology of Medieval Texts* (Oxford, 1992), 261.

100 A. Blamires, *Woman Defamed and Woman Defended*, n. 142, 261.

101 H. E. Allen, *Writings Ascribed*, 251.

evidence of the work's earlier composition and simpler construction in comparison with *The Commandment* and *The Form of Living*. Yet, Watson argues that the account of the third degree of love given in *Ego Dormio* seems most characteristic of Rolle's mystical schema because it urges its reader to strive for *fervor*, *dulcor* and *canor* in a way which implies real confidence in his/her ability to achieve them. This, he suggests, is a more complex method of instruction than the one outlined in *The Commandment* which seeks only to instruct the reader in the basic tenets of loving God.[102] I would further argue that, in conjunction with Rolle's discourse of intimacy, reading the three degrees of love here engages the reader in a multi-layered web of interrelationships far beyond simple moralising. The appearance of simplicity is instrumental in opening Rolle's message of love to a wide variety of readers, because it can be read on so many different levels.

The more formal tone of the first degree of love invites an extended audience: devout Christians who wish to pursue a deeper religious life. The reader is asked to commit to the basic tenets of the Christian faith in terms that could be considered as much in accordance with secular faith within the Christian religion as with the requirements of conventual life:

> The first degre of loue is when a man holdeth þe ten commandement3, and kepeth hym from þe vij deedly synns, and is stabil in þe trouth of holy chirch. (27/68–70)

The address to "a man", the masculine everyman common to medieval representations of humankind, clearly positions the first degree of love as an early stage of spiritual development able to be accomplished by most devout Christians. The second degree of love returns us to the question of gender-specificity in *Ego Dormio* because Rolle exhorts the reader to think on the name of Jesus and become "Cristes dere mayden and spouse in heuyn" (29/143–144). He further suggests that in order to accomplish this, three enemies must be faced, "þe world, þe deuyl, and þy fleishe" (29/150–151) and "thi fleishe shal þou ouercum through holdynge of þi maydenhede" (29/155). This might be thought to imply a female addressee but it turns out to be a fleeting reference, not supported by *Ego Dormio* as a whole. The subject of virginity is not a strong theme in any of Rolle's vernacular treatises, despite his inclusion of feminised notions of spirituality. In contrast, the Latin alliterative treatise *Melos Amoris* voices an appeal to young female virgins to remain chaste and avoid sin caused by their own carnal nature:

> Virgines que vultis Vitam videre, vigiles in virtutibus, de viciis vindicate, animum erigite ut habitet in alto, sola celestia sapida sentite, semper

---

suspirantes Dilectio deduci, pulcras vos proferentes ornatasque amore ut cito vos suscipiat qui castas concupiscit.[103]

[You virgins who want to see [true] Life, vigilant in your virtues, make judgement of your faults, shake up your minds to live on a higher plane think only of heavenly pleasures, always sighing for Love to go away, presenting yourselves, beautiful and ornamented by love so that he who longs for the chaste may swiftly find you.]

Even Rolle's *Contra Amatores Mundi*, a work which makes no reference to an intended audience but implicitly addresses the work to humankind in general, includes a similar exhortation addressed to chaste female virgins. The implication of the passage is that females are naturally susceptible to the lure of wanton idle chatter:

Vos igitur, o pudice virgines, que Christo sponso vestro amorem vovistis, lasciviorum iuvenum consorcia fugite; nec illorum stultiloquiis aures inclinate, ut dum [in vanis] colloquiis confabulari non intenditis, interius in cordibus vestris Christi inspiracionem senciatis.

[I say then, O chaste virgins who consecrated your love to Christ your Spouse, flee the company of wanton young men, and do not incline your ears to their foolish babblings; so that since you do not endeavour to converse in idle talk, you may feel the inspiration of Christ in your innermost hearts.][104]

The single reference to the maidenhead of the reader in *Ego Dormio* seems merely a rote inclusion of a common religious ideal designed to exhort the reader to maintain a chaste lifestyle. Whereas the sentiment expressed in *Melos Amoris* implies that the virginity of a female religious is always at risk from her own carnal nature, any such accusation is immediately tempered by Rolle in *Ego Dormio* in his anticipation of "anoþer þat redeth þis" (31/218) – the implied reader from a broader audience who may or may not be a virgin:

Thi fleishe shal þou ouercum throgh holdynge of þi maydenhede for Goddis loue only, or, if þou be noght mayden, þrogh chaste lyuynge in þoght and in dede, and þrogh discrete abstinence and resonable seruice. (29–30/154–157)

In the earlier tradition of English works written for women the paradigm of virginity in the reader's relationship with God is more rigid. The author of *Hali Meiðhad* considers virginity as an unbreakable physical bond between the female virgin and Christ:

---

103 *Melos Amoris*, 79/17–21.
104 *Contra Amatores Mundi*, 102/1–5; Translation of *Contra Amatores Mundi*, 188/1–6.

Ant tu | þenne, eadi meiden, þet art iloten to him wið meiðhades merke, ne brec þu nawt þet seil þet seileð inc togederes. Halt þi nome þurh hwam þu art to him iweddet; ne leos þu neauer for a lust, ant for an eðelich delit of an hondhwile, þet ilke þing þe ne mei neauer beon acoueret.[105]

In *Ancrene Wisse*, written slightly later than *Hali Meiðhad*, the virginity of the soul is said to be redeemable through good works and true faith:

> For as Seint Austin seið, swa muchel is bitweonen – bituhhen Godes neoleachunge ant monnes to wummon – þet monnes neoleachunge makeð of meiden wif, ant Godd makeð of wif meiden. *Restituit, | inquit Iob, in integrum*. Godes werkes ant treowe bileaue – þeose twa þinges beoð meiðhad i sawle.[106]

The passage in *Ego Dormio* can be seen as a further development of these virginity paradigms for a fourteenth-century vernacular audience. Rolle acknowledges *Hali Meiðhad*'s view that virginity has long been considered desirable, if not mandatory, for female religious but accepts that his reader, the lover of love, may or may not be a virgin. He then expands on the passage in *Ancrene Wisse* that suggests that the virginity of the soul is redeemable by offering a bridge to those who are not physical virgins. Margery Kempe, a devout but married woman who knew Rolle's works, could well have heeded such a passage as advice as to how one could live an exemplary life even without her virginity intact. Thirteenth-century mystic Mechtild of Hackeborn was once reassured by a vision that the married are not further from Christ than virgins because the "Word is made flesh".[107] In this spirit, Rolle's vernacular utterance on virginity, and his expansion of a vernacular tradition that was itself beginning to accord lesser importance to literal virginity in defining spiritual worth, has displaced his own Latin teaching. The virgin of the Latin *Melos Amoris*, ever in danger of her own carnal desires, has become in the vernacular a woman/feminised soul who may or may not be in a state of virginity. A wider female audience for Rolle's vernacular works is certainly suggested here. An even wider ungendered and non-religious audience is not discounted either. The narrow view of virginity explicated in *Melos Amoris* seems intended for a clerical audience with a narrow view of female sexuality, and provides no model for understanding the more liberal vernacular text. In contrast, *Ego Dormio* appears to be a relatively open invitation to all those who would seek purity in their souls, love God and forsake worldly living.

---

[105] *Hali Meiðhad. Medieval English Prose for Women*. Eds. B. Millet and J. Wogan-Browne (Oxford, 1990), 8/29–34.
[106] *Ancrene Wisse*. Ed. J. R. R. Tolkien, 118/4–8.
[107] C. Walker Bynum, *Fragmentation and Redemption*, 155. For a more detailed account of the life and works associated with Mechtild of Hackeborn see C. Walker Bynum, *Jesus as Mother*, 210, 215.

The final consideration in regard to Rolle's construction of the audience in *Ego Dormio* is his inclusion of affective lyrics that accompany each degree of love. These lyrics are designed as modes of address to appeal directly to the *affectus* of the reader, to touch the heart. Structurally they represent the idea that the function of *Ego Dormio* is that of devotional manual: a prose exhortation to engage the *intellectus* of the reader followed by a lyrical exercise to waken and inflame the *affectus*. This simple function is most apparent in the first lyric, the interpolated "Alle perisshethe" (quoted in full earlier in this chapter), an illustration of the first degree of love in *Ego Dormio* that has been described as a well-wrought but not elaborate moralising lyric.[108] This is not surprising considering that the first degree of love described here is in itself a conventional appeal to readers to love their neighbour, purge sin and reject the world. The alliterative verse's rhetorical function thus reaffirms the purgative state of the first degree of love.

Rita Copeland notes that the severe stylistic restraint and literalism of this part of the work, in which Rolle treats the theme of worldly passion (purgation), gives way, with the transition to the second stage of love (illumination), to an eloquent metaphoric style, in which certain key affective terms make their first appearance in the work: "lyghtly", "gastly", "swetnes", "joy", "byrnand", and "lufe" (28/95–129).[109] The culmination of this is the longer lyric, "My kynge þe watyre grete", a Passion meditation which accompanies the second degree of love, somewhat of a patchwork of borrowings from popular Latin texts including Rolle's own *Incendium Amoris*. The first lines (30/175–181) derive from the Latin meditation *Respice faciem Christi*, ascribed in the Middle Ages firstly to Augustine and then later to Anselm, which Rolle used also, only slightly altered, in *Incendium Amoris*.[110] The description of the crucifixion (30/182–184) derives from an older Passion poem, *Candet nudatum pectus*, which follows the same text, and of which many vernacular translations are in existence.[111] The translation of popular Latin lyrics for this purpose suggests a reader who is perhaps familiar with the Latin texts but unable to engage fully with them because of language difficulties. The occurrence of translation and assimilation of Latin lyrics within the vernacular

---

108 R. Copeland, "Richard Rolle and the Rhetorical Theory of Levels of Style", 68. Copeland suggests that by contemporary standards the poem is distinctive, but by the standards of Rolle's poetic canon it is an uncomplicated production, using as its only ornamental device the alliteration which is the hallmark of Rolle's lyric writing.

109 R. Copeland, "Richard Rolle and the Rhetorical Theory of Levels of Style", 68.

110 S. Ogilvie-Thomson, *Prose and Verse*. 205. See also C. Brown, *Religious Lyrics of the XIVth Century*, 241–242 and H. E. Allen, *Writings Ascribed*, 148–149.

111 S. Ogilvie-Thomson, *Prose and Verse*, 205. See also R. Woolf, *The English Religious Lyric*, 162. Woolf notes that although this Passion poem does not confine itself to the crucifixion, Rolle borrows the description of the event from *Candet nudatum pectus*.

works signals Rolle's commitment to a continuity of traditional affective themes and strategies, while opening such writings to a wider audience of *illiterati*.

Throughout Rolle's corpus, meditation on the Passion is recommended as an early exercise, and he does not return to it to signify the highest reaches of love, either in his Latin or in his English writings. The exhortation in *Ego Dormio* "thynk oft þis of his passione" (30/174) pertains to a preliminary or intermediate stage.[112] This seems most appropriate for the second degree of love, where the reader's *affectus* is just beginning to be awakened. And it is here, within the Passion meditation, that Rolle intimates that it is in the second degree of love that Jesus will receive the heart of, and become the lover of, the reader:

> Ihesu, receyue my hert, and to þi loue me brynge;
> Al my desire þou art, I couait þi comynge . . .
> In loue þou wound my thoght, and lift my hert to þe;
> þe soul þat þou hast boght, þi louer make to be.
>
> (31/196–197 and 31/203–204)

Focusing on Christ's human suffering, thinking often of it, is in effect focusing the heart of the reader so that they may be ready to receive *canor* in the next degree. The role of meditation on the Passion in *Ego Dormio* should therefore be viewed as preparatory. As Denis Renevey points out, the lyric itself manages to lift the audience from the lowest range of the second degree to the fringe of the third degree because it is composed in two parts, the first precise and factual, and the second affective and elusive.[113] The emotional response demanded of the reader intensifies throughout the first part of the lyric as the description of Christ's suffering intensifies. Initially, Christ exudes "watyre" and "swete", then he is beaten "at þe piller", his face is "fouled with spetynge", he is crowned with thorns, nailed to the cross, his side is pierced and finally, red blood drips down his side and out of "his woundes depe and wide" (30/175–185). The full textual effect is achieved in the second part of the lyric where the reader, having experienced and been touched by Christ's departure from the world, is drawn towards his/her own renunciation of the world for Christ's sake, "þis world I for þe fle" (31/205), and then made ready to begin his/her own preparation for the third and final degree of love.

The final lyric, "My songe is in seghynge, my lif is in langynge", which accompanies the third degree of love, concludes *Ego Dormio*. Its purpose is to drive the *affectus* forward to experience *canor*. Bathed in the language of intimacy, Rolle's third degree of love exhorts the reader "gif þi hert to Ihesu", to throw off the worldly cloak of "lustes", "delites", and "richesse". According to

---

112 R. Copeland, "Richard Rolle and the Rhetorical Theory of Style", n. 56, 79.
113 D. Renevey, *The Moving of the Soul*, 248.

Rolle the reader "wil couait þe deth, and be ioyful when þou hirest men name deth" (32/247) in this degree. The intimate address is once again collegial as Rolle envelopes his reader in the final degree of love in which he, and by implication the reader, will dwell in worldly death and eternal bliss:

> And I wene, fro þou or I or anoþer be broght in to þis ioy of loue, we mow nat lyue longe after as oþer men doth, bot as we lyue in loue, also we shal dey in ioy, and passe to hym þat we haue loued. In þis degre of loue al drede, al sorow, al wo, al ydel ioy and al wicked delites is put fro vs, and we lyve in swetnesse of heuyn. (32/249–254)

Here Rolle offers another gesture to a broader, yet still special audience. He widens the circle of intimates without losing the sense of their particular and distinctive bond. In turn, life and death are transposed in the entering of the third and final degree – temporal death for spiritual life eternal. Now that this point is reached Rolle is able to introduce the final lyric: "Now I writ a songe of loue þat þou shalt haue delit jn when þou art louynge Ihesu Criste" (32/265–266). The lyric itself echoes many of the affective traditions I identified earlier. The reader is the "I" figure in the text, the singer, who calls on Christ to fulfil their love with words drawn from the *Jesu Dulcis Memoria*:

> When wil þou cum, Ihesu my ioy, and keuer me of kare,
> And gyf me þe, þat I may se, hauynge for euer more? (32/272–273)

The reader desires a personal relationship with Christ:

> Ihesu my sauyour, Ihesu my confortour, of fairnesse þe floure,
> My helpe and my sokour, when may I se þi toure?
> When wil þou me kalle? Me langeth in to þi halle . . . (33/276–278)

Devotion to the Holy Name is encouraged through the repetition of the word "Ihesu" in the text:

> Ihesu, Ihesu, Ihesu, whyne ware I til þe ledde?
> .   .   .   .
> Ihesu, my dere and my drery, delites art þou to synge;
> Ihesu, my myrth, my melody, when wil þou cum my kynge?
> Ihesu, my hele and my hony, my quert, my confortynge,
> Ihesu, I couait for to dey when hit is þi paynge. (33/285 and 292–295)

The lyric certainly succeeds in drawing on the traditions of affective piety, such as the intense devotion to the person and the name of Christ, but its rhythmical language also succeeds in engaging the reader in a passionate outpouring of love. Rolle does not ask the reader meekly to recite a simple lyric of love; the power of the song demands that he/she will experience real "delite" in singing out his/her love for Christ.

In offering his own "songe of loue" to close *Ego Dormio* Rolle again appropriates the role of the Song-author, since the *Song of Songs* was commonly considered as *the* song of love in the Middle Ages. Accordingly the reader is invited to participate in both the Song tradition itself, with its own intimation of a loving and personal relationship with Christ, and in Rolle's own song which exhorts the reader to strive to attain the highest reaches of the spiritual journey where he/she will "sit and synge of loue langynge" (33/284). The further implication here is that the reader will be united with Rolle himself, and eventually with God, in spiritual song, *canor*, because *canor* is both the ultimate gift in the Rollean schema, and a gift he tells us in *Incendium Amoris* that he has already received. The lyric mode itself can therefore be seen as integral to spiritual fulfilment in Rollean terms. Thinking on the Passion every day exhorts the reader to a "gret swetnesse, þat shal draw þi hert vp", presumably to the next level, the third degree of love. The task of drawing the reader towards spiritual fulfilment has required subtle textual shifts culminating in this final lyric which Copeland describes as one of Rolle's most rhetorically intense products, and also one of his finest for its control.[114] The union of the reader and writer is complete; the song of love that the reader will experience ("haue delit jn") will fill the heart with love and the reader will join with Rolle in the joys of eternal song.

That *Ego Dormio* should conclude with a lyric, the experiential culmination of the gift of *canor*, suggests the depth to which Rolle understood affective literature in terms of his own mystical schema. His desire to form a close bond of love, an intimate union, with the reader in *Ego Dormio* is also illustrative of the pedagogical qualities of the ladder of ascent he provides based on his own experience. Through the explication of the three degrees of love, which provide the frame for this work, the adoption of the role of mediator between the lover and the beloved, and through his sharing of his own experience of nuptial union and ecstatic song, Rolle develops a discourse of intimacy with his reader that stops just short of a union in itself. In the final lines of the lyric "My songe is in seghynge", where the reader is exhorted to sing when he/she is actively "louynge Ihesu Criste", Rolle hints at an eventual tri-part union that will take place in heaven where his authorial self, the reader, and Christ will never be parted:

> My sete ordayn for me,
> And set þou me þerin, for þan may we neuer twyn,
> And I þi loue shal synge þrogh syght in þy shynynge
> In heuyn withouten endynge. (33/310–313)

The image evoked is one of Rolle and the reader seated in an exalted place in heaven, an image Rolle uses to full effect later in *The Form of Living*, having finally achieved the gift of *canor* and the resulting ability to see the shining

---

114 R. Copeland, "Richard Rolle and the Rhetorical Theory of Style", 69.

light of God. Rolle's authorial self, the "messager", has consummated the affective message itself because, in terms of textual closure at least, the reader is in the process of achieving the unitive state. A process, not a finished product, because the ultimate reward can only be achieved in death – but the very continuity of the loving song, with its present continuous tense formations, may simulate the eternal joy of heaven.

V

Ego Dormio is a short, pointed, didactic work composed to guide a beginner in the spiritual life, but it is also clearly an affective work of some skill and complexity. It may have been the first of Rolle's vernacular treatises but as demonstrated it can be read as a more intricate and mature rendering of Rolle's mystical advice than has been previously thought. The implied audience for the advice offered in *Ego Dormio* is of prime importance in understanding not only Rolle as author in penning a single exhortatory text but also Rolle as textual construct. His didacticism is of a kind that exhorts the reader to unite with his words as well as with the subject of his words. He in effect gives an explicit agency to the reader that had remained rather more implicit in the earlier mystical writers who influenced his English works such as Bernard of Clairvaux and Richard of St. Victor.

In offering such a reading, it has not been my intention to argue against the view that *Ego Dormio* was probably composed for a female reader in the early stages of her spiritual career. Certain aspects of the discourse of intimacy Rolle employs, the utilisation of medieval tropes of feminine piety, and the vernacular address, would all be congruent with such an assessment. But this initial function should not be confused with the whole function of the work or be allowed to narrow the sense of its potential audience. Internal textual evidence suggests that for the author of this work the initial reader was a starting point not a limitation. Rolle's construction of the reader in the variety of roles I have suggested supports the notion of wide parameters for the work and a wide potential audience. The discourse of intimacy employed by Rolle in order to engage the *affectus* of the reader with both his authorial self and Christ invites an implied gender-neutral audience to participate not only in Rolle's own mystical schema as set out in the body of the text, but also in a variety of intimate relationships that directly promote a deep emotive response throughout the reading process.

As a message of love directed to a reader who is to be the individual recipient of that love, *Ego Dormio* embodies tropes of romantic literature of the thirteenth and fourteenth centuries, and of the spiritual love expressed in the patristic epistles of spiritual friendship and of Cistercian notions of *caritas*. What appears to be a very straightforward reading of the three degrees of love in terms of Rolle's own mystical schema is in fact a complex invitation for the reader to become not only intimate with Christ but also with the author of the work in a number of guises. Drawing on traditional imagery, Rolle becomes the messenger, the message itself and the author of the message. All this is formulated in metaphorical and rhetorical devices designed to embrace the reader within the bosom of the text. The implied reader who actively inhabits the series of subject positions offered will, at the end of the work, be able to join with Rolle's authorial self in a heartfelt song of love (32/265). Rolle, the messenger, guides each and every reader in his or her quest to be "perftily cowpled with God".

4

"A noble tretis of loue":[1] *The Commandment*

I knew Thi comaundement, that is full brade, for it is luf of God and oure neghbure. I knew that it is end of all perfeccioun, for in charite is all goed will and goed werk rotid and festid.[2]

I

THE SECOND of Rolle's vernacular treatises was a shorter work of plain instruction which is known today by the title *The Commandment*.[3] Unlike its predecessor *Ego Dormio*, which had sought to woo the reader to become the lover of Christ through the use of affective language, *The Commandment* engages the lover of God in a more sober and formal discourse. The text itself follows a fairly simple narrative structure. Rolle opens the work with an exposition of Christ's utterance of the great commandment from Matthew 22:37 which both sets the tone of the work as didactic and informs the reader of its dominant theme – the "wylful styrrynge of oure thoght in to God" (34/1–8). Initially, moderate penitential practice is recommended and the reader is exhorted to avoid sin, embrace silence and be "ful of charite" (34/8–23). The three degrees of love are named briefly in the early part of the work but do not appear to have the same significance as they do in Rolle's other vernacular treatises (34–35/24–41). In the body of the work, the joys of the mutual love between Christ and the soul are praised but Rolle's explicit concern is with the efficacy of prayer and meditation, especially on the Passion, and the stripping away of all worldly ties (35–39/42–213). In this latter connection, where Rolle warns against having too many fine clothes, he draws extensively on biblical *exempla* to explicate the dangers of how outward appearance can mask inner truth. The final exhortation encourages the reader to participate in one of the most constant elements of Rolle's devotion, meditation on the Holy Name (39/214–224).

---

1   The incipit preceding *The Commandment* in Bradfer-Lawrence MS 10, fol. 28r cited in S. Ogilvie-Thomson, *Prose and Verse*, xlvi.
2   *English Psalter*, Psalm 118:96. See also H. E. Allen, *English Writings*, lxii.
3   The title *The Commandment* was first used with this work by Carl Horstmann, *Yorkshire Writers*, I, 61–71.

In modern scholarship, *The Commandment* has been seen as a dry, didactic and highly conformist work that apparently lacks the intimate address and emotional tone usually associated with Rolle's vernacular prose.[4] Internal evidence and manuscript ascription suggest that the work was written for the initial edification of a nun and this has been used to explain the emphasis on practical instruction.[5] Indeed, Rolle's approach to his audience seems to be one of basic spiritual edification and the work contains none of the explicit references to his own mystical experience that we have come to expect.[6] This lack of reference to personal experience has even caused *The Commandment* to be considered less Rollean.[7] Lack of mystical content has caused it to be considered of less general interest and its didactic tone has caused it to be deemed perfunctory.[8] For what purpose then would Rolle choose to include such a text in his vernacular canon? In general terms I suggest that the effect he achieves in writing *The Commandment* needs to be viewed in terms of two potential audiences which its discursive strategies engage. The first audience is a young female religious whom Rolle addresses on the subject of love. Secondly, he appeals to an implied reader who is any individual soul in need of guidance, allowing the work to open itself to a potentially wide readership. Throughout the work Rolle appears to have been influenced by both the gender and spiritual maturity of his initial audience, but on the whole the implied audience is not explicitly gendered. Instead Rolle's teaching is focused firmly on the objects of God's love in the great commandment itself; the heart, the mind and the soul. As always, his textual objective is firmly set on turning the reader to the love of God, over and above any other concerns he raises.

---

[4]   See H. E. Allen, *Writings Ascribed*, 253–254; N. Watson, *Invention of Authority*, esp. 236.

[5]   There seems little reason to doubt the ascription at the end of the text of *The Commandment* in the University Library Cambridge MS Dd.v.64, "Explicit tractatus Richardi Hampole scriptus cuidam sorori de Hampole", as internal evidence suggests an initially monastic audience. The influence of Rolle's initial audience will be discussed in further detail later in the chapter. See also H. E. Allen, *Writings Ascribed*, 254–255.

[6]   H. E. Allen, *Writings Ascribed*, 253–254. Allen comments that *The Commandment* "shows unmistakable evidence of Rolle's authorship, but it discusses holiness with fewer references to .the more esoteric details of mysticism that are usual in his works".

[7]   Watson's perception of the narratorial voice adopted by Rolle in *The Commandment* as assuming the "institutional authority of a preacher issuing general instructions – albeit urgent and affective ones – not inducements to spiritual growth based on Rolle's personal experience" also suggests the opinion that the content of the work falls outside of the "usual" Rollean criterion. See N. Watson, *Invention of Authority*, 236.

[8]   See S. Ogilvie-Thomson, *Prose and Verse*, lxxvii.

To discern how Rolle achieves his textual effect requires a close examination of the instructional language he uses; in particular how the image of worldly dress, elaborated for the reader through biblical *exempla*, is used to illuminate the theme of *contemptus mundi* and to speak for his own abhorrence of hypocrisy. The dominant concerns of the work are not limited to practical teaching on external virtues but are concentrated more on the interior life of the reader. Rolle's preoccupation with the corrupt will is most notable in this connection. In turn, his condemnation of clothing, beauty and vanity, which could be construed as addressing a specifically female audience, reveals that the gender of the reader is of little concern. Instead, feminised metaphors in the text follow the direction begun in *Ego Dormio*, and suggest an idea of the soul as feminine rather than a consideration of the audience as entirely female. The inclusion of seemingly gendered literary tropes and the influence of the initial female audience certainly impacts on the work as a whole but beyond this Rolle succeeds in creating *The Commandment* as a work of broader appeal. While the practical instruction offered throughout the text seems uncharacteristically impersonal and distant, he carefully constructs a specific writer/reader relationship, which instructs and appeals to the reader's *affectus* within the constraints of homiletic discourse, and permits the subtle emergence of the more personal qualities found in his other vernacular treatises. It is this latent affectivity that marks *The Commandment* as an assuredly Rollean devotional text.

The dominant theme in each of Rolle's vernacular treatises is the love of God; the broad affective message contained within *The Commandment* is therefore the same as that found in *Ego Dormio* and *The Form of Living* but constructed through a different discourse. The major distinguishing factor between the three vernacular treatises is the construction of their writer/reader relationships. In *Ego Dormio* he employs a discourse of intimacy to draw the reader into a union with both the divine and with the diverse authorial personas presented throughout the text. In *The Form of Living* a collegial discourse of friendship encourages the initial recipient, his disciple Margaret Kirkeby, and by implication all those who will become his disciple by reading this work, towards the attainment of the contemplative life. Such close bonding may well be absent in *The Commandment* but Rolle offers instead a variety of subtle textual relationships designed to fulfil the affective objective of turning the reader/soul to the wilful love of God. The reader is constructed as pupil to Rolle's self-construction as pedagogue, a practical solution to his task of composing a formal exposition of a biblical text popular in the medieval period, the great commandment. But despite this seemingly formal relationship, affective exhortation is never far from the surface; the choice of plain instruction for *The Commandment* merely acts as a framework in which Rolle presents the reader with a textual disquisition on the subject of the interiority of love, genuinely characteristic of Rollean doctrine and thought.

II

The Commandment has long been considered a mere patchwork because it relies heavily upon a number of borrowings from other writers as well as passages from Rolle's own works.[9] The most common connection to his other vernacular works is the explication of the three degrees of love for the reader. Despite being its most prominent link to both *Ego Dormio* and *The Form of Living*, their brief delineation in *The Commandment* suggests that they do not hold the same significance within the present work as in the other English prose works. Yet, curiously, it is here in *The Commandment* that for the first time Rolle uses the terms "insuperabile", "inseparabile" and "syngular" to name the three degrees of love:

> And þat þou may wyn to þe swetnesse of Goddis loue, I set here þre degrees of loue, in þe which þou be euer wyxynge. The first degre is cald insuperabile, the toþer insperabile, þe þrid synguler. Thi loue is insuperabile when no þyng may ouercum hyt; þat is neþer wel ne wo, ese ne anguys, loue of fleishe ne lykynge of þis world . . . Thi loue is inseperabile when al þi þoghtes and willes be gedered togeddre and festned holey in Ihesu Criste, so þat þou may no tyme foryet hym . . . Thi loue is synguler when al þi delite is in Ihesu Crist, and in non oþer thynge fyndeth ioy and comfort.
>
> (34/24–26, 30–32, 34–36)

This nominal recognition of the three degrees of love might simply expose the humble didactic function of *The Commandment*, which would make extraneous detail irrelevant. But the brief reference also establishes Rolle's persona as speaker in the work, and allows the three degrees of love to act as a type of endorsement of his own mystical schema of *calor, dulcor* and *canor*. Rolle uses similar language to *Ego Dormio* in setting the material before the reader, which affirms his own authorial presence in the text and marks the three degrees as his own. He perhaps expected a reader who was familiar with the earlier work, supporting the idea that the three works may have been initially composed as a vernacular series, as the Longleat rubrics suggest. In the introduction to the three degrees of love the reader's goal is the attainment of "þe swetnesse of Goddis loue", suggesting that *The Commandment* is centred around the second of Rolle's own mystical experiences, *dulcor*. This possibly reflects the implicit monastic themes in the work because the emphasis on *dulcor* implies that the work is mainly restricted to the second of *Ego Dormio*'s

---

[9] Watson describes *The Commandment* as "more a patchwork of borrowed passages and ideas, in which some of the seams are still exposed, than an original composition". He recognises borrowings from *Compendium Theologicae Veritatis, Emendatio Vitae, Super Canticum Canticorum* and the pseudo-Bernadine *Meditationes Piissimae*. N. Watson, *Invention of Authority*, 237–238.

degrees of love which appears to represent the coenobitic state.[10] References to the lesser of Rolle's mystical experiences of *calor* and *dulcor* occur far more than references to *canor*, which also suggests that the work is aimed at an audience in the early stages of the mystical journey. Margaret Jennings argues that the three degrees of love used by Rolle in the English works do not correspond directly to his own definition of *calor*, *dulcor* and *canor* and bear only marginal relationships to them.[11] Indeed it would seem that the definitions do not correspond directly but it does seem that in *The Commandment* some interplay between Rolle's *dulcor* and accepted notions of the second degree of love as the middle or coenobitic stage is definitely present.

The three degrees of love also act as a form of signature or authorial reference for Rolle in that they occur in a number of his works. In fact, this whole passage is borrowed from the descriptive listing of the three degrees of love given in *Emendatio Vitae*:

> Sunt siquidem tres gradus amoris Christi . . . Primus vocatur *insuperabilis*, secundus *inseparabilis*, tercius *singularis*. Tunc quippe amor insuperabilis est quando nulla affeccione alia potest superari . . . Amor vero inseparabilis est quando iam uehementi dileccione succensa mens atque Christo inseparabili cogitacione adherens . . . Ad singularem ergo gradum amor ascendit quando omnem consolacionem, preter vnam que est in Ihesu, excludit, quando nichil preter Ihesum sibi sufficere poterit.

> [There are soothly three degrees of Christ's love . . . The first is called, unable to be overcome; the second, unable to be parted; the third is called singular. Then truly is unovercomable when it can not be overcome by any other desire . . . Love truly is undeparted when the mind is kindled with great love, and cleaves to Christ with undeparted thought . . . Love ascends to the singular degree when it excludes all comfort but the one that is in Jesu; when nothing but Jesu may suffice it.][12]

The passage is again drawn upon in *The Form of Living* (16/525–551) where the three degrees of love are also named. Despite a few stylistic variations, the first two degrees of love in *Emendatio Vitae*, *The Commandment* and *The Form of Living* are generally similar. Only the description of the third degree differs greatly between the texts. In *The Commandment* the portrait of "syngular love" is drawn from imagery found in the *Song of Songs* that describes love as being as strong as death, where one desires to suffer for God's love; in *The Form of Living*, the fire of love is said to burn in the soul, while thought turns into a melody of love; in *Emendatio Vitae*, the complete self becomes suddenly despicable, and the soul, in suppressing all that is contrary to God's will, finds true

---

10 N. Watson, *Invention of Authority*, 236.
11 M. Jennings, "Richard Rolle and the Three Degrees of Love", esp. 195.
12 *Emendatio Vitae*, 57/36, 58/40, 58/46–48, 59/69–71; *The Mending of Life*, 230–231.

joy.[13] From this we can see that Rolle's use of the degrees of love varies throughout his canon but is an integral part of his thought, particularly in the vernacular. In *The Commandment* the inclusion of the three degrees of love should not be viewed as a mere borrowing but as a marking of the work as Rollean. In turn, his decision to highlight only the second degree of love in *The Commandment* suggests his commitment to writing a separate work for a separate purpose.

From her analysis of the manuscript tradition of *The Commandment* Sarah Ogilvie-Thomson concludes that the work shows a relatively simple textual history, perhaps drawing from a single early copy. This leads her to believe that the simplicity and didacticism of the work may have made it less appealing than Rolle's mystical treatises in general terms, but of more practical interest to its initial audience the nun, or nuns, of Hampole.[14] Her argument favours the notion that *The Commandment* was aimed at a monastic audience, but its manuscript dissemination also suggests wider interest. While it may not have been as popular as *Ego Dormio* in the Middle Ages (fifteen manuscript copies of *Ego Dormio* survive to thirteen of *The Commandment*), it does appear as the only Rolle work in three manuscripts (University Library Cambridge MS Dd.v.55, University Library Cambridge MS Ii.vi.40 and Trinity College Cambridge MS B 15 42), whereas *Ego Dormio* only ever occurs in manuscripts with *The Form of Living*.[15] Each of the manuscripts in which *The Commandment* alone represents Rolle contains other well-known and widely read instructional works which are not specifically monastic. University Library Cambridge MS Dd.v.55 contains Hilton's *Scale of Perfection*; University Library Cambridge MS Ii.vi.40 has a version of the *Speculum* of St. Edmund which is wrongly ascribed to Rolle; and in Trinity College Cambridge MS B 15 42 *The Commandment* is one of the few works composed in the vernacular (the others are either Latin or Latin with English excerpts). The singular recognition of *The Commandment* in these manuscripts would seem to suggest a reputation based on its general didactic qualities rather than on local monastic interest.

The vast number of manuscripts of instructional religious literature in the vernacular that survives from the medieval period supports the notion that although modern scholars have often found such literature to be aggressively didactic, digressive and repetitious and of limited general interest, it is certain

---

[13] M. Jennings, "Richard Rolle and the Three Degrees of Love", 194–195. See also H. E. Allen, *English Writings*, esp. 63–107.

[14] S. Ogilvie-Thomson, *Prose and Verse*, lxxvii. Ogilvie-Thomson writes: "It is easy to imagine such a text being in heavy demand as word spread round the nunneries of Yorkshire, and copies would proliferate, not only in a short period of time, but within a confined geographical area."

[15] N. Watson, *Invention of Authority*, 236.

that medieval readers did not.[16] W. A. Pantin points to the popularity of didacticism in devotional practice when he describes the fourteenth century as the classic age of preaching in medieval England, when sermons were abundant, vigorous and influential.[17] Similarly, literature such as manuals of sin, books of vices and virtues, treatises on the ten commandments and other didactic literature focusing on salvation proliferated during the later English Middle Ages and was increasingly addressed to secular as well as monastic audiences.[18] That such works enjoyed a fairly high socio-religious status in the fourteenth century can be seen in Chaucer's famous retraction at the end of *The Canterbury Tales*. Here Chaucer informs his audience of his decision to disown the works he has written of "worldly vanitees" in favour of those such as "the translacion of Boece de Consolacione, and othere bokes of legendes of seintes, and omelies, and moralitee, and devocioun".[19] Through this retraction, by which he makes it clear that didactic and devotional prose is the genre of literature by which he wishes to be remembered, Chaucer elevates the context of repentance and salvation.[20] I am not directly concerned here with Nicholas Watson's thesis that Rolle consciously constructed himself as a medieval *auctor*, but if the status of vernacular works of devotion could reach the heights Chaucer seems to imply, this may well have been a consideration of Rolle's in choosing to add such a work to his own already prodigious output. In fact, it is more likely that the apparently broad appeal of a work such as *The Commandment* is linked more closely to its didacticism than to any other aspect of its composition.

Like *Ego Dormio*, *The Commandment* does not appear to have been recognised as an epistle in the manuscript tradition. Ascriptions found in the surviving manuscripts generally refer to the work as a "tretis" or "tractatus", with one fifteenth-century exception where it is given the status of a rule: "A good rule for men þat desireþ to lyue perfit lif".[21] The task of locating *The*

16 A. Clark Bartlett, *Male Authors, Female Readers*, 1. The first chapter of this book deals with the scholarly neglect of Middle English devotional literature in general. Here Bartlett names works such as *Speculum devotorum, A Devout Treatyse Called the Tree and the xii Frutes of the Holy Goost, The Chastising of God's Children, The Fervour of Love, The Seven Poyntes of Trewe Wisdom, The Abbey of the Holy Ghost, The Doctrine of the Hert, The Commandment, The Form of Living* and *Contemplations of the Dread and Love of God* as among the many works that have long been considered as barely worthy of literary analysis except for studies of sources and stylistics.

17 W. A. Pantin, *The English Church*, 236.

18 As I noted in my introduction, Vincent Gillespie has linked the rise of vernacular works of religious instruction in the fourteenth and fifteenth centuries (miscellanies in particular) to the growing awareness among authors and compilers of a wider audience for such texts. V. Gillespie, " 'Lukynge in haly bukes' ", 17.

19 G. Chaucer, *The Canterbury Tales. The Complete Works of Geoffrey Chaucer.* Ed. F. N. Robinson, 265.

20 R. Boenig, *Chaucer and the Mystics*, 13.

21 Magdelene College Cambridge, Pepys MS 2125.

Commandment within the tradition of didactic literature itself is, however, a difficult one, just as making the distinction between works of religious instruction and works ostensibly linked to devotional aspects of the Christian faith is difficult. Many have argued that any such distinction is artificial: but it is essentially one between works defining the content of faith, and those ordaining mental or spiritual reactions to this content.[22] Of course, all works related to religion throughout the medieval period contained elements of Christianity which might stimulate and confirm belief, but how these works achieved their ends was often diverse and incomparable.

Generic or sub-generic definitions such as "didactic", "homiletic" and "devotional" are idealistic constructions which can offer a misleadingly compartmentalised view of religious works from the later medieval period. Let us say that the term didactic implies an authoritative voice of instruction; that the term homiletic refers to familiar discourse and the art of preaching; and that the term devotional has to do with engaging the will to serve and worship God. A text such as *The Commandment* does not seem to conform to any one of these closed definitions but instead discloses analogous elements of each. The practical instruction offered in the text is in places reminiscent of a sermon, and Rolle's textual objective, the drawing of the individual soul towards union with God, is achieved through the use of didactic language. The extensive use of biblical *exempla* similarly places it in the tradition of homiletic discourse. When contemporary and near-contemporary manuscript ascriptions for the work vary, it seems unnecessary for modern readers to limit *The Commandment* to a single definitive genre. We can best locate *The Commandment* not under a single defined heading but as one individual text amongst many vernacular works of didactic/devotional character.

The earlier tradition of works of religious instruction in the vernacular, the thirteenth-century texts of the "Wooing Group",[23] and its close linguistic associates the "Katherine Group"[24] and *Ancrene Wisse*, can be closely linked to Rolle's vernacular works in terms of the initial female audience for these texts and the affective focus on the humanity of Christ in the Bernadine fashion.[25] Firmly based in the anchoritic context, most of these works instruct the reader through a discourse of enclosure, relying on the psychological effects born out

[22] R. N. Swanson, *Religion and Devotion in Europe, c.1215–c.1515.* (Cambridge, 1995), 72.

[23] The four lyrical prose pieces that make up the "Wooing Group", Þe Wohunge of Ure Lauerd, On wel Swuðe God Ureisun of God Almihti, On Lofsong of Ure Louerde and On Lofsong of Ure Lefdi, dwell particularly on the theme of Christ's love for the soul and are the first extant Middle English works to demonstrate the practicability of contemplation outside the monastery.

[24] The "Katherine Group" comprises the lives of the virgin martyrs Katherine, Margaret, and Juliana, the letter on virginity called by its editors Hali Meiðhad, and an allegory on the custody of the soul, Sawles Warde. See B. Millett and J. Wogan-Browne, eds. *Medieval English Prose for Women*, xii.

[25] D. Renevey, *The Moving of the Soul*, 82–83.

of strict confinement in the reclusorium.[26] For example, *Ancrene Wisse* is essentially an anchoritic rule composed for three reclusive sisters. Didactic elements within *Ancrene Wisse* bear some resemblance to monastic rules and include (or assume) a regular daily horarium of prayers and devotions, reading, and meditations. The reader is instructed in both the regulation of the spiritual and the corporeal self. *Ancrene Wisse* is fundamentally an instructional work and this can be seen clearly in its very structure which presents a holistic frame wherein an outer rule, which governs the body (exterior), envelopes an inner rule which governs the heart (interior). An essentially persuasive work, *Ancrene Wisse* has been described as more obviously expository and didactic than other, more emotive works associated with the "Katherine Group" and the "Wooing Group" in that we have at least the semblance of rational arguments.[27] On the other hand a text such as *Hali Meiðhad*, composed to extol the virtue of virginity, is generally considered to be essentially a form of preaching by written instruction in which the audience is addressed in terms of occupational or "estates", categories which for women were usually wife, widow, or virgin.[28] It is the didactic elements of these works to which *The Commandment* has closest resemblance.

There is wide diversity in the instructional discourses found in the "Wooing Group" and the "Katherine Group", and a vast array of literary approaches evident in these texts. The most prominent text of the "Wooing Group", *The Wohunge of Ure Lauerd*, and its fourteenth-century offshoot, *A Talkynge of the Loue of God*, offer didactic instruction which relies heavily on the imagery of the *Song of Songs* blended with secular love practices. In this work the implied female reader is invited to engage affectively with the text and simulate the role of the Virgin Mary in her relationship with her son, Christ. In contrast, the noisy allegorical household of *Sawles Warde*, derived from a Latin treatise in dialogue, *De custodia interioris hominis*, is an allegorical reworking of the original into a homily.[29] The work is designed to evoke sense-images of heaven and hell in the mind of the reader. Following traditional allegorical models of the medieval household, Wit, the master of the house, is married to the unruly Will whose servants, the five senses (representing the outer) and the other senses (representing the inner) are apt to take advantage of her

---

26 N. Watson, "The Methods and Objectives of Thirteenth-Century Anchoritic Devotion". *The Medieval Mystical Tradition in England: Papers Read at Dartington Hall, July, 1987*. Ed. M. Glasscoe (Cambridge, 1987), 132–154. In this article Watson examines the anchoritic characteristics of *Hali Meiðhad, Ancrene Wisse, Sawles Warde*, the Saint's Lives and the "Wooing Group".

27 See G. Shepherd, ed. *Ancrene Wisse Parts 6 and 7* (London, 1959; repr. Exeter, 1985), lx; B. Millett and J. Wogan-Browne, eds. *Medieval English Prose for Women*, xxxii.

28 B. Millett and J. Wogan-Browne, eds. *Medieval English Prose for Women*, xv.

29 B. Millett and J. Wogan-Browne, eds. *Medieval English Prose for Women*, xxv. It is noted that the homily was an "important vehicle of instruction and persuasion in the vernacular".

misrule. Unlike more formally instructional works such as *Ancrene Wisse*, both *Þe Wohunge of Oure Lauerd* and *Sawles Warde* are didactic but are not rules of living. Instead, the type of instruction offered in these works emphasises sensory manifestations typical of those later found in Rolle's works.

Allegorical representation remained a popular form for didactic works in the fourteenth century, especially in the type of literature that was increasingly addressed to lay worshippers. This is clearly demonstrated by *The Abbey of the Holy Ghost*, a work composed to teach a devout lay person who is not free to embrace the coenobitic or contemplative life how to create an abbey in his or her own conscience. It is a text built on the tension between the inner and outer life of the lay reader which the author acknowledges in his opening sentence by addressing the work to "all tho þat ne may noght be bodyly in religyone, þat þay may be gostley".[30] Yet, plain instruction was also a favoured medium – one of the most popular didactic works of the later Middle Ages *John Gaytryge's Sermon*, known also as *The Lay Folks' Catechism*, is a translation made by John Gaytryge, a Benedictine monk, of the Latin catechism of Archbishop Thoresby of York. Widely disseminated in fourteenth-century England, this work, which is described by the author as a sermon, provides the reader with a systematic arrangement of the elements of the Christian faith which every Christian, priest and parishioner, must know.[31] It lacks any literary adornment and is firmly based on factual material, neatly categorised, that will be of use in teaching the reader "how scrifte es to be made and wharof and how many thyngez solde be consederide".[32] The author is neither interested in constructing any sort of relationship with the reader nor provoking any emotive response to elements of the Christian religion. This English translation, made at Thoresby's request, functioned primarily as a means of making the catechism known as widely as possible; its singular purpose is to instruct. Some of the most popular didactic works in the vernacular were the numerous translations of, and works derivative of, the French *Somme le roi* (made by Friar Laurent in 1280 for the use of Philip III)

---

[30] C. Horstmann, ed. *Yorkshire Writers*, I, 321. See also F. Riddy, *Sir Thomas Malory* (Leiden, 1987), 26.

[31] See N. F. Blake, *Middle English Religious Prose*, 9. *The Lay Folk's Catechism* (or *John Gaytryge's Sermon*) is a rythmical prose translation and expansion of Archbishop John Thoresby's instructions to the clergy of the province of York concerning the education of the laity. The instructions were modelled on Archbishop Pecham's Lambeth Constitutions of 1281 and provided brief expositions of the articles of the Creed, the Ten Commandments, the Seven Sacraments, the Seven Works of Mercy, the Seven Virtues, and the Seven Deadly Sins, concluding with the promise of an indulgence of forty days to all who learned them. They were issued in 1357 together with the vernacular version made at Archbishop Thoresby's request by John Gaytryge a monk of St. Mary's Abbey, York. See *A Manual of the Writings in Middle English*, Vol. 7, 2270.

[32] "John Gaytryge's Sermon". *Middle English Religious Prose*. Ed. N. F. Blake, 72/2-3.

such as the *Book of Vices and Virtues* (c. 1375), *A Myrour to Lewd Men and Wymmen* (late fourteenth-, early fifteenth-century) and the compendium known as *Speculum Vitae* (which itself includes an extract from Rolle's *The Form of Living*).[33] These works are similar to *John Gaytryge's Sermon* in that they primarily offer instruction on practical aspects of Christianity in the form of expositions on such subjects as the Ten Commandments, the Seven Deadly Sins, and the Articles of the Creed.

The Commandment certainly contains elements of the approaches taken in the works discussed above. It has even been suggested that a lesser colleague of the author of *Ancrene Wisse* might also have written *The Commandment* because Rolle appears to have borrowed from the work and because both are instructional works in the vernacular associated with an initial female audience.[34] But *The Commandment* displays a notable difference, when compared to the majority of these works, in that the didacticism of Rolle's prose is largely oblique. His type of instruction is marked by subtlety, particularly when compared to more aggressively didactic texts such as *John Gaytryge's Sermon* or the near-contemporary *Book of Vices and Virtues*. He is rarely concerned with externalities or petty detail and is more focused on discussion of the interior life of the reader. In fact, when we look closely at *The Commandment* it is explicitly a didactic work but also has much in common with the more affective works of the earlier tradition such as *Þe Wohunge of Ure Lauerd* which opens with a lyrical appeal to "swete Jesu" that is reminiscent of Rolle's second degree of love, *dulcor*:

> Jesu, swete Jesu, mi druð, mi derling, mi drihtin, mi healend, mi huniter, mi haliwei. Swetter is munegunge of þe þen mildeu o muþe.[35]

The Commandment itself has numerous references to the sweetness of God's love; for example, Rolle calls on the reader to experience "þe lestynge in swetnesse of deuocioun" (34/8) and "þe delitable swetnesse of his loue" (37/120). As I have noted, this attests that the work could be considered as grounded in Rolle's second degree of love, *dulcor*, which, in his mystical schema, is the degree generally associated with the purgative process and the coenobitic state. The inclusion of the sensuous concept of *dulcor* in *The Commandment* demonstrates that although the tone of the work is at times distant, affective exhortation is never far from the surface, making the work more one of firm but affective encouragement rather than one of simple instruction only.

From the small sample discussed it can be seen that the diverse range of

---

33 For brief descriptions of the contents and manuscripts of these works see *A Manual of the Writings in Middle English*, Vol. 7, 2258–2262.

34 N. Watson, *Invention of Authority*, 236.

35 *Þe Wohunge of Ure Lauerd*. Ed. W. M. Thomson (London, 1958), 20/1–5.

didactic works available in the vernacular in late medieval England performed a variety of functions for a variety of audiences. Rolle's vernacular prose canon functions in much the same way; each text performs a different function by developing a separate discourse. Like Rolle's three vernacular treatises, many of the works in the earlier tradition can be linked by the commonality of their initial audience: female religious. But later works in the vernacular reflected trends towards a wider community of readers of didactic literature, as can be seen in *The Abbey of the Holy Ghost* which explicitly addresses both men and women. Vernacular works of instruction can be seen to have shifted in emphasis from a specifically female religious audience in the thirteenth century to a more generic, often mixed audience in the later Middle Ages. *The Commandment* appears to reside comfortably in company with the various types of didactic literature on offer in fourteenth- and fifteenth-century England whilst maintaining a sense of individuality through the affective strategies that can be seen operating within the text. Rolle's distinctive speaking persona in *The Commandment*, his skill in offering practical yet affective instruction, and his subtle acknowledgement of a mixed or seemingly gender-neutral audience also make *The Commandment* a genuinely Rollean work.

As with all of Rolle's works, critical assessment of *The Commandment* has been plagued by the desire to ascertain information about Rolle himself. In modern scholarship *The Commandment* has been closely linked to Rolle's initial audience, the nun of Hampole, from University Library, Cambridge MS Dd.v.64, or Margaret Kirkeby according to the Longleat rubrics.[36] Rolle's choice of language for a short vernacular work ostensibly dealing with penitential practice suggests that he has been influenced by the gender, education and spiritual erudition of a female religious audience. Like many of the didactic texts mentioned above this work can be located, partly at least, in the tradition of male-authored religious works in the vernacular for a female religious audience. Internal evidence clearly suggests that the initial recipient was a woman in a religious order rather than an anchoress or lay-woman with religious aspirations:

---

[36] As with *Ego Dormio*, University Library Cambridge MS Dd.v.64 ascribes the work to a nun of a named convent whereas the Longleat manuscript states that the recipient is Margaret Kirkeby. Supporting both ascriptions, Ogilvie-Thomson points out that the ascriptions of these two manuscripts are not mutually exclusive; Margaret Kirkeby was a nun at Hampole during Rolle's association with the convent and therefore it would seem more likely that the work would have been written for this acknowledged favourite than for any other. If so, it supports the theory that the Longleat manuscript is possibly descended from an autograph collection that was compiled for Margaret. Ogilvie-Thomson suggests that *The Commandment*, with its emphasis on practical instruction, could have been composed for Margaret shortly after her entry into the convent c. 1343. S. Ogilvie-Thomson, *Prose and Verse*, lxxix.

> If þou haue delite in þe name of religioun, loke þat þou haue more delite in
> þe dede þat falleth to religioun. Þi habit seith þat þou hast forsaken þe
> world, þat þou art gyffen to Goddis seruyce . . . (37/152–155)

Later in the text, when discussing outward appearance and hypocrisy, Rolle
again alludes to coenobitic practices when he charges the reader "if þi body be
cled withouten as þyn ordre wille, loke þat þi soule be nat naked within, þat
þyn ordre forbedeth" (38/158–160). The solitary life, which he generally
considers as the most perfect, is not mentioned in any great detail in *The
Commandment*. There is even a suggestion that the reader may find it difficult
to be alone:

> If þou may nat dure to sit bi þin on, vse þe stalwarthly in his loue, and he
> shal so stabily set þe þat al þe solace of þis world shal nat mowe remeve þe,
> for þe wil nat list þerof. (35/58–60)

The implication that this anxiety focuses on a coenobitic audience is clearly
discernible in the advice that follows:

> When þou art by þyn on, be euer, til slepe cum, oþer in praier oþer in gode
> meditaciouns. (35/61–62)

In essence, the focus on practical instruction such as prayer and meditation
succeeds in limiting the reader of this text not only to practices common to
coenobitic discipline but also to the very basics of mystical experience. This is
clear when we consider that while recommending *imaginatio*, *The Commandment* does not suggest the possibility of mystical union this side of death,
another reason why it has been regarded as more devotional than mystical. It
does mention the possibility of "syngular" love, again drawing upon Richard
of St. Victor, but only states that through meditation on the Passion the reader
will "rer þi thoght abouen erthly lykynge, and make þi hert brennynge in
Cristis loue, and purchace in þi soule delitabilte and sauour of heuyn"
(38/191–193). It does not discuss union in terms of *canor*, or a sight into heaven
comparable to that found in either *Ego Dormio* or *The Form of Living*, although
the idea of corporeal sight as leading to sight of God is prominent. Towards
the end of the work Rolle states that through devotion to the Holy Name of
Jesus the reader will experience both comfort in this life and join with angels
after death in seeing God endlessly:

> O þynge I rede the, þat þou foryet nat his name Iesus . . . Who-so loueth hit
> verrayly is ful of Goddis grace and vertuȝ, in gostly comfort in þis lif, and,
> when þei dey, þei ben taken vp in to þe ordres of angels, to see hym in endles
> ioy þat thay haue loued. (39/216–215, 221–224)

In this passage the exhortation to worship the Holy Name is direct and
uncomplicated, suggesting an audience of limited mystical advancement.

111

However, he is still recommending that the reader follow the same type of affective meditation as the recipient of *Ego Dormio*. Rolle, it would seem, is able to suggest meditation on the Passion and on the Holy Name, meditations that require an affective response from the reader, at different levels of the mystical journey. From this we can conclude that his understanding of *imaginatio* does in fact lie in his regard for the *affectus*, making his debt to Bernadine affectivity of as much importance in this work as in his other prose treatises. In short, Rolle's commitment to the *affectus* in *The Commandment* may not have the same emotive force as in his other vernacular works but it is not absent. The use of plain language, the concentration on basic instruction and the allusion to coenobitic practice still support the affective objective that drives all of his vernacular prose treatises: the implied reader, the reader beyond the initial reading subject, the individual soul, is guided towards the love of God.

III

The opening passage of *The Commandment* is a literal exposition of Matthew 22:37: Ait illi Iesus diliges Dominum Deum tuum ex toto corde tuo, et in tota anima tua, et in tota mente [Jesus said to him: Thou shalt love the Lord thy God with thy whole heart, and with thy whole soul, and with thy whole mind], some of it drawn from the *Compendium Theologicae Veritatis*.[37] It offers basic instruction in a form reminiscent of a sermon and provides a useful example of Rolle's gender-neutral discourse. In choosing the first commandment of God, Rolle has not opted for a gender-specific example as one might have expected from a male author to a female audience. Instead, he appeals to aspects of a mixed readership's spirituality: the heart, the soul and the mind. The body is not mentioned. The clothing metaphor itself, which is discussed in detail later, appears to refer to the nakedness of the soul in the sight of God rather than the nakedness of the corporeal body. That the focus of the work is immediately directed away from externalities such as the body emphasises Rolle's commitment to the interior life of the reader. He is not concerned with the "outer rule" as other didactic works such as *Ancrene Wisse* are.[38] In fact, the clothing of the corporeal body itself is only a vehicle in *The Commandment*, through which he maintains that it is from within that the love of God is apparent, not from without on the body. Here the link to Rolle's fear of hypocrisy is most clearly recognisable.

It is not just the great commandment itself that provides the context for

---

[37] See Hugh of Strasbourg, *Compendium Theologicae Veritatis. Opera Omnia Sancti Bonaventurae.* Ed. A. C. Peltier (Paris, 1864–1871), Vol. 8, 60–246.
[38] See above.

Rolle's message in *The Commandment*. The whole text of Matthew 22 revolves around how falsity of appearance is reflected in and reflects the interior life of the lover of God. The parable of the wedding garment, in which a wedding guest is inappropriately clothed for the occasion, occurs early in the verse and pre-empts Christ's utterance of the great commandment to love God with all one's heart, soul and mind:

> Intravit autem rex ut videret discumbentes, et vidit ibi hominem non vestitum veste nuptiali. Et ait illi: Amice, quomodo huc intrasti non habens vestem nuptialem? At ille obmutuit. Tunc dixit rex ministris: Ligatis manibus et pedibus eius, mittite eum in tenebras exteriores: ibi erit fletus et stridor dentium. Multi enim sunt vocati, pauci vero electi. (Matt. 22:11–14)

> [And the king went in to the guests: and he saw there a man not attired in a wedding garment. And he saith to him, Friend, how camest thou in hither not having a wedding garment? But he was dumb. Then said the king to the waiters, Bind his hands and feet, and cast him into the utter darkness; there shall be weeping and gnashing of teeth. For many be called, but few elect.]

Here clothing directly represents the idea that many who have been called to religious life will be found spiritually unprepared and unworthy. Rolle's own association of clothing with hypocrisy in *The Commandment* appears to be influenced by this part of the text of Matthew which functions as a preamble to Christ's denunciation of the Pharisees as hypocrites because they hope to trap him into an indiscretion. The utterance of the great commandment itself is a direct result of a Pharisaic plot to tempt Christ into placing himself in a human context by choosing one of the ten commandments as the greatest. This Christ avoids by creating a holistic commandment:

> Pharisaei autem audientes quod silentium imposuisset sadducaeis, convenerunt in unum: et interrogavit eum unus ex eis legis doctor, tentans eum: Magister, quod est mandatum magnum in lege? Ait illi Iesus: Diliges Dominum Deum tuum ex toto corde tuo, et in tota anima tua, et in tota mente tua. Hoc est maximum, et primum mandatum. Secundum autem simile est huic: Diliges proximum tuum, sicut teipsum. In his duobus mandatis universa lex pendet, et prophetae. (Matt. 22:34–40)

> [But the Pharisees hearing that he had put the Sadducees to silence, came together: and one of them a doctor of law asked of him, tempting him, Master, which is the great commandment in the law? Jesus said to him, Thou shalt love the lord thy God from thy whole heart, and with thy whole soul, and with thy whole mind. This is the greatest and the first commandment. And the second is like to this, Thou shalt love thy neighbour as thyself. On these two commandments dependeth the whole Law and the Prophets.]

Christ's utterance of the great commandment not only locates charity in the interior self but implies that the external (words) must become an internal part (in the heart, the soul and the mind) of the hearer. Rolle's text can be seen to be operating in a similar way in that his own words, the text of his own commandment, in mediating Christ's, are also to become an internal part of the reader. Rolle's interpretation of Christ's words demands that "we" love "oure" Lord; he provides the reader with the means to engage with the great commandment through his utterance of it:

> The comandement of God is þat we loue oure Lord in al our hert, in al oure soule, in al oure thoght. (34/1–2)

As in *Ego Dormio*, the collegial tone constructs an individual relationship with both Rolle's authorial self and the divine, again directly engaging the individual reader's interior self. The omission of the second part of Christ's commandment here, to love thy neighbour, is also significant in Rolle's focus on the interior aspects of reader's spirituality in that he chooses to leave out the aspect that seeks to focus the reader on others, and on society. It is only included later in the passage as part of a general exhortation:

> . . . and he þat speketh euer þe good, and holdeth euery man better þan hym self, he sheweth wel þat he is stabile in goodnesse in his hert, and ful of charite to God and his neghbore. (34/21–23)

Rolle's experience as an exegete can also be seen as of prime importance to the broad appeal of *The Commandment*. No Latin is used for any of the biblical quotations and his translations are literal and his expositions elementary; he may have anticipated that many of his readers would have no Latin and be of relatively limited scriptural education.

From the very beginning it seems unlikely that any reader would doubt that this text was intended to be instructional rather than mystical; a commandment of any kind implies didacticism. Yet, the specific function of this opening passage is not so much to command as to introduce the loving will of God as the central theme. In this common theme the work displays its most explicit relationship to Rolle's other vernacular works. The tone itself is set early in the piece with Rolle drawing on accepted notions of human emotional, spiritual and intellectual faculties, the "hert", the "soule" and "thoght", to explain to the reader how each of these faculties is to be understood in relation to loving God:

> In al oure hert: þat is in al our vndrestondynge, withouten errynge. In al our soule: þat is in al our wille, withouten syggynge ayeyne. In al oure thoght: þat is þat we thynke on hym withouten foryetynge. (34/1–5)

Appealing directly to the reader's *intellectus*, which in turn touches the *affectus*, the gloss culminates in a description of love as "a wylful styrrynge of oure thoght in to God" (34/6) which "is perfeccioun of þis lif" (34/9). Accordingly, both truthful love and perfection itself are depicted as the very "werk of mannys will". The will itself is of crucial importance to Rollean schematics[39] and is in many regards the crux of the message contained within the text of *The Commandment*. Rolle's preoccupation with the corrupt will shows his comprehensive understanding of the ways in which an affective response could be generated.[40] Of course, this type of devotion contains both subjective and objective elements. Subjectively, the responsive acts of the mind and the will constitute the reader's "wylful styrrynge"; objectively God's love, here expressed as inner truth, forms the point on which this devotion centres. Self-knowledge becomes an individual responsibility in that truthful love can only be achieved if the will is incorrupt. In *The Cloud of Unknowing* the repeated phrase "a nakid entent to God" matches Rolle's idea of the "wylful styrrynge" in that it signifies an elevation of the will towards the being of God.[41] In Book Two of the *Scale of Perfection*, Walter Hilton talks about a similar inner process in terms of remaking – reforming those elements of the self which he calls the "miȝtes" (powers) of the soul – mind, reason and will – in such a way that they reflect the likeness of God in whose image they were created.[42] It is in Rolle's concern with the corrupt will that the fear of the hypocrite originates. Hypocrisy is especially abhorrent in the context of self-knowledge here because medieval views on this matter were principally drawn from the Book of Genesis and from the Epistles of St. Paul which state that God has given people free will.[43] He strives to emphasise how wilful lust and sin can even deny the true will:

> Restreyne þi wille a while fro al lust and lykynge of syn, and þou shal haue aftreward al þi wille, for hit shal be clensed and mad so fre þat þe shal lust do no thynge bot þat is paynge to God. (35/53–55)

Throughout much of the work Rolle exhorts the wilful reader to embrace God in the form of loving truthfully and without any shadow of deception, echoing Paul's warning of "false brethren".[44]

---

39 See H. E. Allen, *Writings Ascribed*, 326. Allen suggests that Rolle's preoccupation with the concept of "good will" was probably influenced by Anselm.

40 V. Gillespie, "Mystic's Foot", 207. Gillespie argues that "again and again throughout the Latin and vernacular works, the same basic premises are annunciated: man's will is corrupt, it must be reformed through a rejection of carnal affections and an acceptance of the love of Christ, a yearning love of Christ will lead to further kindling of love as a gift from God, this new kindled love will fix our intellects and the eye of our soul on the contemplation of God and will help us achieve wisdom".

41 *The Cloud of Unknowing*, 17/2. For an explanation of the *Cloud*-author's use of this phrase see the note to 17/2 on page 185 of this edition.

42 M. Glasscoe, *English Medieval Mystics*, 120.

43 Gen. 3:1–8; 2 Cor. 3:17; Rom. 20–23.

44 2 Cor. 11:26: "In itineribus saepe periculis fluminum periculis latronum periculis ex genere periculis ex gentibus periculis in civitate periculis in solitudine periculis in mari periculis in falsis fratribus" [In journeying often, in perils of waters, in perils of

Appealing to the more general aspects of the subject of love, and perhaps a more general audience, Rolle uses the third person in the passage directly following the opening exposition to appeal to "al þat wil loue God perfitly" (34/11–12). Here he subtly shifts the emphasis of the opening exposition of the first commandment which reiterates the message of the love of "oure Lord" in "oure hert . . . soule . . . thoght" to the third person impersonal "ham behoueth" and "al þat loueth har owne state". The reader-writer relationship thus moves between a collegial one and an instructional one. This shift in address then allows him to construct the penitential platform upon which *The Commandment*'s theosophy is built: intention or the action of the will. Rolle's concern with intention may have been influenced by Augustine who emphasised will as the principle by which we act.[45] This influence can also be seen in Peter Abelard's twelfth-century work *Ethica*, also known as *Scito te ipsum*, where the overriding ethical concern is with intention behind an act. Works are themselves morally neutral; what matters is the intention with which they are performed. Abelard maintains that the term "sin" is used improperly when discussing those who sin in ignorance or through negligence because properly speaking, a sin involves a deliberate evil intention.[46] In *The Commandment*, sin, as the enemy of the wilful stirring of thought, is neatly categorised:

> And þis is perfeccioun of þis lif, to þe whiche al dedly synnes ben contrarie and enemy, bot nat venyal synnes, for venyal syn doth nat away charite, bot only letteth þe vse and þe brennynge þerof. Forþi al þat wil loue God perfitly, ham behoueth nat alonly flee al dedly synnes, bot I also, as myche as þay may, al venyal synnes, in þoght, in word and in dede . . . (34/8–14)

Here heart, soul and thought are neatly juxtaposed with thought, word and deed. Interestingly, in terms of intention, mortal sins and venial sins are categorised differently, with Rolle recommending that the reader flee all deadly sins but all venial sin "as myche as þay may". Clearly, moderation is developing as a characteristic trait of Rolle's vernacular utterance. Just as the reader of *Ego Dormio* is not necessarily expected to be a virgin, here the reader is expected to sin only as little as possible. In contrast, Rolle's attitude to wilful sin in *Incendium Amoris* is more firm:

robbers, in perils from my own nation, in perils from the Gentiles, in perils in the city, in perils in the wilderness, in perils in the sea, in perils from false brethren.]

45 Augustine, *De duabus animus*, xi. 15 (PL 42. 105). See P. Abelard, *Ethica. Peter Abelard's Ethics*. Ed. D. E. Luscombe (Oxford, 1971), xxxiv. In his introduction Luscombe writes that for Augustine sin consists in the will to retain or to pursue that which justice forbids and from which one is free to abstain.

46 See P. Abelard, *Ethica. Peter Abelard's Ethics*, esp. xxxii and 8/5–20 where Abelard uses the example of the servant who kills his lord unwittingly to emphasise this point.

Si enim recte amaremus Deum, deberemus magis uelle magnum premium in celo amittere quam saltem uenaliter peccare . . .

[And if we are really to love God, we ought to be willing to lose the great reward of heaven than to commit a single sin however venial . . .][47]

In *Contra Amatores Mundi* the true lover of God casts out every sin:

Omne penitus peccatum vere amans respuit; secularis solacii nescit vanitatem.

[The man filled with true love casts out every sin from within his heart; he knows not the vanity of worldly pleasures.][48]

This could suggest that Rolle's Latin works envisaged a more specific audience of professional religious readers who would be expected to accept such harsh judgements on sin. In contrast, he plays down the role of penitential practice in *The Commandment*, favouring love over repentance in an active sense:

Bot þynke euer þat of al þynge most coueiteth God loue of mannys harte, and forþi seke more to loue hym þan to do any penaunce, for vnskylful penaunce is litel worth or noght, bot loue is euer þe best, wheþer þou do penaunce litel or mych. (35/64–67)

Rolle's reference here to the generic "mannys harte" and his later reference to a "Christen mannys soule" (35/73) suggests a more general audience than the one traditionally accepted. Gender, socio-religious status and spiritual experience are variously alluded to within the text but do not appear to control its function, to draw the individual soul to the love of God. The subject position of the individual reader is constructed from within the discourse, rather than merely surviving as a vestige of the initial addressee. In this sense the reader's identity is a direct function of discourse and Rolle's explicit silence about its gender serves to lay his text open to a wider readership.

As in *Ego Dormio*, Rolle employs throughout *The Commandment* tropes that are often found in feminised religious discourse. These tropes have encouraged the idea that *The Commandment* was composed for a female audience only. For example, the soul is washed clean with "loue tears", and the heart, the seat of emotion, is "where teres spryngeth" (38/184). Tears and weeping, although associated with both male and female religious in earlier periods, had become increasingly connected with the active devotion of religious women in the later Middle Ages. Margery Kempe regarded her tears as a gift from God, although many sought to condemn her for her excessive weeping:

---

47 *Incendium Amoris*, 165; *The Fire of Love*, 66.
48 *Contra Amatores Mundi*, 70/17–18; Translation of *Contra Amatores Mundi*, 151/22–23.

And in schort tyme ower mercyful Lord vysytyd þis creatur wyth plentyous teerys of contricyon day be day, in so mech þat sum men seyden sche mygth wepen whan sche wold & slawndered þe werk of God.[49]

As Kempe is known to have had Rolle's works read to her, she, and readers like her, may well have considered his exhortation to weep tears of love literally. But is it an entirely gendered exhortation? Kempe also tells us that "a preyste" (the eventual scribe of her book), who initially doubts the validity of the sanctity of her tears, is then himself "visityd" by the Lord with tears of devotion:

> He wept wondirly so þat he wett hys vestiment & ornamentys . . . þan he leuyd wel þat þe good woman, whech he had be-forn lityl affeccyon to, myth not restreyn hir wepyng . . . þan knew he wel þat God ʒaf hys grace to whom he wolde.[50]

Accepting tears as a gift of God, the priest then reads of other men who endorse weeping such as Bonaventure, the author of *The Prick of Conscience* and Richard Rolle: "he red also of Richard Hampol, hermyte, in Incendio Amoris leche mater þat meuyd hym to ʒeuyn credens to þe seyd creatur".[51] Through his own experience of weeping, as well as his reading of others who endorse weeping, Kempe's priest comes to an understanding of God's grace. As Sarah Beckwith has noted, claims to sanctity or to a singular grace from God were accompanied by an intense scrutiny in the late Middle Ages, yet tears of compassion had long been considered a special sign of grace, for they were a sign of the strength of a soul's love for God, and of the effectiveness of prayer.[52] Andrew Lynch argues that because the highest endorsement of tears came from God, and Christ himself had wept (John 11:35), weeping in medieval religious texts was the gesture above all which devalued differences of class, wealth, and sex. It was available to all people, to rich and poor, young and old, men and women. It betokened humility, but also conferred a kind of status of sensibility.[53] Kempe's example effectively highlights how the exhortation to weep in *The Commandment* need not always be read as offering a gendered position for the reader. The issue is not about whether crying is more suited to men or women; it is about the spiritual worthiness of individuals to receive gifts (such as weeping) from God.

In this same passage another seemingly gendered exhortation occurs in that the reader's gaze is firmly set on the beauty of Christ. But firstly, the

---

[49] *The Book of Margery Kempe*, 2/21–24.
[50] *The Book of Margery Kempe*, 153/18–27.
[51] See especially *The Book of Margery Kempe*, 152/8–154/29.
[52] S. Beckwith, *Christ's Body*, 88–89.
[53] A. Lynch, " 'Now, fye on youre wepynge!': Tears in Medieval English Romance". *Parergon: Bulletin of the Australia and New Zealand Association for Medieval and Renaissance Studies*. New Series 9/1 (1991), 51.

reader is exhorted to array his or her own soul to appear beautiful in the sight of Christ:

> Dight þi soule faire; make þerin a toure of loue to Goddis sun . . . thynke euer to cum to syght of his fairhede. (38/164–172)

Again it seems possible that the gender of Rolle's initial audience has informed the discourse to a certain degree, but as we have come to expect in his vernacular works it is the "soule" which is implicitly addressed. Renevey claims that Rolle's use of the "toure of loue" image, generally associated with medieval romance heroines, appeals directly to a female recipient familiar with the romance genre who is able to identify with the image.[54] But I would argue that this is a narrow assessment of the context because in *The Command-ment* Rolle is only speaking against feminine vanity if the work is read as *always* addressing women. He is so generally concerned with hypocrisy and falsity of habits in this work he could well be speaking against a beauty culture apparent in his own time that makes both men and women vain and superficial. In *Incendium Amoris* Rolle tells us that as a young man a female patron once commented that his own beauty covered a lack of potency, spiritual or otherwise: "Nihil habes nisi pulchrum uisum et pulchrum uerbum: opus nullum habes" [You are no more than a beautiful face and a lovely voice; you don't have what it takes].[55]

Rolle may well employ seemingly gendered tropes but his explicit construction of the reader as the beautiful soul – "fairhede of the soule, þat he couaiteth" – suggests, as it did in *Ego Dormio*, that he thinks of the soul as feminine rather than of his audience as entirely female. Rolle's reference to the beauty of the soul is also reminiscent of his construction of authorial self in *Ego Dormio* as that of an extension of the Song-author. The beloved, the soul, is recognised as beautiful since in the *Song of Songs* (1:4) the *amica* had said of herself "Nigra sum, sed formosa" [I am black but beautiful]. The soul only regains its original beauty when it frees itself from sin and is prepared to live according to God's will.[56] Rolle explains in *The Commandment* that this beauty is

---

54 D. Renevey, *The Moving of the Soul*, 211.
55 *Incendium Amoris*, 179; *The Fire of Love*, 82. I have slightly altered the Wolters translation.
56 For a discussion of the *Song of Songs* and metaphors for love see W. Riehle, *The Middle English Mystics*, 34–55. To highlight differing interpretations of the Song-author in the fourteenth-century Riehle contrasts Rolle's exposition of beauty in *The Commandment* to Hilton's more traditional approach in taking the contrast "nigra" – "formosa" of the *Song of Songs* and interpreting the blackness as representing the inner disposition towards perfection.

fairhede of þe soule, þat he couaiteth, that is to be chaste and meke and myld and suffrynge, neuer gurche to do his wille, euer hatynge al wikednesse. (38/169–171)

The blackness of sin may cloud this view in the same way that corporeal clothing may disguise the truth within. Here the concern is the beauty of the reader's soul, its purity, the emphasis being firmly fixed upon the appearance of the soul in the eyes of God. The beauty of the soul itself reflects the eternal beauty of Christ. In the affective passage that follows the brief exposition of the three degrees of love, Rolle employs the *contemptus mundi* theme to exhort the reader to choose Jesus, who offers all which can be desired, and whose beauty is everlasting:

Therfor, if þe list loue any þynge, loue Ihesu Criste, þat is þe fairest, rychest and wisest, whose loue lesteth in ioy endles. (35/42–43)

This is similar to the series of offers Christ makes in Part VII of *Ancrene Wisse*, which forms the basis for the first half of *Þe Wohunge of Ure Lauerd*, where the mediator chooses Christ since "inwið þe ane arn alle þe þinges igedered þat euer muhen maken ani mon luuewurði to oðer", working his/her way through Christ's beauty, wealth, largesse and other desirable male qualities.[57] There are no exact parallels between the two texts, but Rolle lists several of the same characteristics in the same order, and may have taken the topos either from *Þe Wohunge of Ure Lauerd* or from its fourteenth-century offshoot *A Talkynge of the Loue of God*. This adds weight to the suggestion that in writing a text like *The Commandment* Rolle has in some ways positioned himself as a progressive extension of the earlier tradition of vernacular male-authored works of instruction for an initial female audience.

In the opening passage of *The Commandment* Rolle warns against the dangers of vain or idle speech, in what looks like a gendered trope. Speech had long been associated with female temptation and was a prevailing theme in works of instruction for women. Aelred of Rievaulx was extremely firm on the importance of silence, particularly for a female recluse. Implying that female speech may be associated with sexual activity, he urges speech only with carefully chosen words.[58] A similar warning exists in *Ancrene Wisse*:

---

[57] N. Watson, *Invention of Authority*, 237. See *Þe Wohunge of Ure Lauerd*, 20/10–13.

[58] Aelred of Rievaulx, *De institutione inclusarum*. Bodley MS 423, cap. 4. For a discussion of sin and female speech in male-authored texts for a female audience see A. Clark Bartlett, *Male Authors, Female Readers*, 44–46. Bartlett compares the repressive perspective on female silence in male-authored works for a female audience with the celebration of silence in literature for men and refers readers to Paul Gehl, "*Competens silentium*: Varieties of Monastic Silence in the Medieval West". *Viator* 18 (1987), 125–160.

Ofte we þencheð hwen we foð on to eornen speoken forte speoke lutel & wel isette wordes. ah þe tunge is slubbri for ha wadeð i wete. & slit lihtliche forð from lut word in to monie.[59]

Both authors encourage what Carla Casagrande refers to as medieval *taciturnitas*, a moderate and humble speech that befits women.[60] But in *The Commandment* Rolle's concern with idle chatter is not explicitly gendered. He singles out idle speech as a venial sin in very general language, encouraging the reader "[to] be of litel speche. And þat silence be in occupacioun of good thoghtes" because "hit helpeth gretly to Goddis loue" (34/14–15). Another fourteenth-century writer, the author of *The Tree* and *The XII Frutes of the Holy Goost*, argues that the virtue of silence applies equally to men and women:

> . . . speak sparingly . . . So it is that our lord gave to a man and a woman two ears and one tongue, so that they should be quick to hear and slow to speak.[61]

Anne Clark Bartlett uses this example to suggest that this type of advice derives from a monastic tradition of silence applicable to both sexes, rather than from negative stereotypes so prevalent in earlier English devotional writing for women.[62] For Rolle the exhortation to practice active silence is effectively a vehicle in *The Commandment* to turn external vice (idle speech) into internal virtue (the occupation of good thoughts). The subsequent warning that "vayn speche and il wordes ben signe of a veyn herte and il" (34/19–20) also suggests that Rolle's interest in idle chatter is less concerned with gender and more focused on fostering in the reader an awareness of the whole self – that outer actions should reflect inner worth.

Characterisation of the sinners of the mouth, referred to as "ianglers and bacbiters" in this opening passage, opens the theme of hypocrisy in *The Commandment*. The sin of calumny is also mentioned by Rolle in both *Ego Dormio* and *The Form of Living* in vitriolic terms.[63] Each of these echoes the

---

59 *Ancrene Wisse*. Ed. J. J. R. Tolkien, 40.
60 C. Casagrande, "The Protected Woman". Trans. C. Botsford. *A History of Women in the West: Vol. II, Silences of the Middle Ages*. Ed. Christine Klapische-Zuber (Massachusetts, 1992), 100.
61 *The Tree & the XII Frutes of the Holy Goost*. Ed. J. J. Vassier (Groningen, 1960), 10. *The Tree* is the first part of a two-part spiritual guide known as *A Devout Treatyse Called The Tree and XII Frutes of The Holy Ghost*. The anonymous author addressed this double treatise to a nun, his former spiritual daughter. See *A Manual of Writings in Middle English*, IX, 3087.
62 A. Clark Bartlett, " 'A Reasonable Affection': Gender and Spiritual Friendship in Middle English Devotional Literature". *Vox Mystica: Essays for Valerie M. Lagorio*. Eds. Anne Clark Bartlett, Thomas H. Bestul, Janet Goebel and William F. Pollard (Cambridge, 1995), 141.
63 In *The Form of Living* (12/353–356) backbiting is listed alongside "flattrynge, lesynge, myssiggynge, wreyynge, disfamynge, cursynge, manacynge, sowynge of discord,

tenth chapter of the Latin *Incendium Amoris* in which Rolle rails against the hypocrisy and the covetousness of those who falsely portray themselves as holy:

> De Deo loquentes uideri uolunt et interius in tantum amore pecunie capiuntur quod eciam quandoque pro dispendio litigant; qui os suum aperientes Deo hiant, et penitus deuocione carentes, cum nullum feruorem fidei et caritatis habeant, sanctissimos tamen incessu et habitu et sermone se ostentant.

> [The wish to appear to speak of God, though their hearts are so possessed with the love of money that sometimes they will fall out over a farthing! They serve god with their lips, but are wholly devoid of devotion. And though they have no real faith or love they seem by the way they behave and dress and speak to be the most holy of men.][64]

Interestingly, dress and speech are also coupled here in condemning those who are not what they seem. In terms of gender Rolle appears to be referring to male religious, which is not surprising for a Latin text; he would certainly have been conscious that the audience for *Incendium Amoris* would have much more likely been male religious than women or even lay men.

In *The Commandment* Rolle is more concerned that "wicked wordes" will directly affect the reader's "sight of the loue of God in har soule" (34/19). As discussed in relation to *Ego Dormio*, seeing into heaven was a spiritual preoccupation in fourteenth-century religious writing. The eye of the heart was opened by love, usually through the medium of the eye itself and its corporeal function – sight. Here in *The Commandment*, the didactic function of the text is recognisable in the construction of an implied reader who is one that will both see God with a true heart and be seen by others as truly a lover of God. Rolle's point is to set the enlightenment of the individual soul against the hypocrisy of vanity, idle chatter and worldly possessions. This fear of hypocrisy leads him to encourage readers to be especially mindful of not only how they are perceived by others but how they themselves perceive others. In this we can see him building slowly and carefully on the theme of interiority suggested by the commandment itself; he proceeds by attacking external manifestations of deceit that may poison the heart, the soul or the thoughts of the reader against choosing the love of God over the love of the world.

In keeping with his focus on being spiritually sighted Rolle chooses the image of the blind, night-loving bat to describe the "ianglers and bacbiters" that he so detests:

tresone, fals witnes, il consail, scornynge, [and] vnbuxomnes with word". In *Ego Dormio* (27/74–75) it appears alongside "oþer venymous synnes".
[64] *Incendium Amoris*, 172; *The Fire of Love*, 75.

... and al þat loueth har owne state bifor al oþer, þai haue no more sight of þe loue of God in har soule þan þe eigh of a bak hath of þe son. (34/16–19)

On the surface this bestial image is little more than a sardonic metaphor. But there is a subtle thread running through the work, begun here but later elaborated by the clothing imagery. Rolle suggests that those whose outward visage blinds others to what they really are become little more than beasts. Clothed, blinded, the soul which should stand naked and pure in the sight of God becomes somehow unnatural. Despite the popularity of imagery drawn from bestiaries in the Middle Ages, Rolle is not often inclined to use bestial imagery. His most notable contribution to the genre is a short prose piece on the industry of the bee to illustrate the pre-eminence of the contemplative life.[65] In *The Commandment* the zeal with which he displays his utter disgust at those that "appeireth other mennes lif" marks this bestial image of the bat as distinctly pejorative. Homiletic use of this type of analogy was well known in the medieval period. A late fourteenth-century sermon from the collection found in British Library, Royal MS 18 B. xxiii includes a similar "ensampull in nature" of the sightless bat to illustrate how pride makes men spiritually blind. Physiologically, the sermoniser explains, bats have weak eyes because what should give them sight passes into their wings. This is likened to the loss of the grace of God's light in those who are overly proud:

> Thes backes hath febull yӡen, as philisofres seyn, and þe cause is for þe humour is like cristill, humor cristallinus, and þat shuld be cause of þere siӡthe passeþ in-to here wynges, as it semeþ well, for þer wynges be as þei were made of leddir. And so for þer flying þei haue lost here siӡth. Trewly on, like wize þise prowde men, euer thei besy hem to flye vppward to astates oþur dignities. Euon somuche þe grace of Goddes liӡthe is taken a-way from hem . . . And þe cause why þat riche men laboreþ not abowte hevenly þinges is for þe see it not with þe eyen of here mynde.[66]

Those whose sight is spiritually impaired by their own pride, primarily represented in *The Commandment* by dress and false image, are naturally less spiritually sighted. The author of the *Book of Vices and Virtues* uses the image of the blind bat to explicate the "secounde heued of þe wikked best . . . envy":

---

65 H. E. Allen, *English Writings*, 54–56. *The Bee* (or *The Bee and the Stork*) is found only in the Thornton (Lincoln Cathedral 91) and Cosin Library Durham manuscripts. Allen describes it as illustrative of Rolle's use of the popular medieval imagery found in bestiaries. No exact source for Rolle's interpretation of the bee is offered but Allen suggests that Pliny and Aristotle are echoed and that the account of the stork is derived from the *Morals* of Gregory. In the *English Psalter* Rolle interprets the nature of the basilisk and the weasel also in the style of the Bestiaries.

66 *Middle English Sermons*. Ed. W. O. Ross (London, 1960), Sermon 40, 231/31–232/4.

Þe enuyous may not see good bi oþere, ne see who-so helpeþ hym, no more þan a bake may suffre to see þe schynyng of þe sonne.[67]

Blinded by pride and envy, the hypocrite fails to see the light which will illuminate the mind. Not being able to see with the mind again implies Rolle's concern for the *intellectus* of the reader. But the bat is by nature a beast; its natural blindness is a sharp contrast to what Rolle appears to perceive as the unnaturalness of those who are not what they seem. The implication is that the spiritually blind become unnaturally bestial. Pursuing this analogy the reader is promptly reminded that "vayn speche and il wordes ben signe of a veyn herte and il, þat is withouten the grace of God" (34/19-20). Theologically, grace is defined as the gift of God to intellectual creatures (men/women, angels) for their eternal salvation. The loss of grace, as emphasised by the metaphor employed here, amounts to a type of bestial regression.

To be spiritually sighted is linked to Holy Writ. In Psalm 18:9 the commandment of the Lord is represented as "illuminans oculos" [illuminating the eies] and the example of Christ is given as a model for imitation in I Peter 2:21:

In hoc enim vocati estis: quia et Christus passus est pro nobis, vobis relinquens exemplum ut sequamini vestigia eius.

[For unto this are you called: because Christ also suffered for us, leaving you an example, that you may follow his steps.]

Rolle recommends this imitation, somewhat briefly, later in the work:

Also festyn in þi hert þe mynd of his passioun and of his woundes; gret delite and swetnesse shal þou fele if þou hold þi þoght in mynd of þe pyne þat Crist suffred for þe. (38/175-177)

Just as the Psalms formed the backbone of the Divine Office, so the Psalms traditionally formed the basis for popular paraliturgical devotion.[68] Here, Rolle, who had already a close association with the Psalter, having written both a Latin and a vernacular commentary on it, directs his reader through this common emphasis on it. In this passage it is the reader's intellective faculty, "þoght in mynd", that is directly appealed to in recommending *imaginatio*. At this juncture *The Commandment*'s adherence to balancing the negative and positive aspects of despising the world is most notable. Earlier Rolle called upon the reader to pursue negative *imaginatio*, focusing the gaze upon hypocrites "þe which ben like to sepulcre þat is peynted richly withouten, and within reten stynkynge bones" (37/151-152). Now, Christ is offered as a possible example and clothing is again alluded to in that the richly

---

[67] *Book of Vices and Virtues*. Ed. W. Nelson Francis (London, 1942), 22/19-21.
[68] V. Gillespie, " 'Lukynge in haly bukes' ", 8.

painted tomb is likened to the reader's "habit" which functions as a signifier "þat þou art gyffen to Goddis seruyce" (37/155). Rolle's use of the term "habit" is worth exploring in relation to the theme of interiority. According to the Middle English Dictionary the word habit has three separate definitions; in the first instance "habit" denotes religious attire, in the second it refers to outward form, appearance, or likeness, and the third definition variously alludes to "habit" as the bodily constitution, mental or moral disposition, customary practice, behaviour and innate property of a person. Rolle's use of the word in *The Commandment* seems reliant on an interplay of each of these definitions. Because hypocrisy is a major theme in the work it seems clear that the "habit" he refers to here means more than just the likeness of religious garb. Outward appearance, the literal "habit", reflects the inner worthiness of the reader to be in "Goddis seruyce" and this is achieved only by effort in the forming of good habit(s).

Habit, in the sense of formed behaviour, recalls Aristotle's *Nichomachaean Ethics* in which he discuses virtue and habituation:

> Virtue has two kinds, intellectual and moral. Intellectual virtue in the main owes both its birth and its growth to teaching (for which reason it requires experience and time), while moral virtue comes about as a result of habit, whence also its name (ethike) is one that is formed by slight variation from the word ethos (habit).[69]

Aristotelean ethics were a principal source for the Middle Ages. The mainstay of fourteenth-century theology itself had grown out of the thirteenth-century scholastic synthesis of Aristotle's works, and the Arabic commentaries on Aristotle's works, provided by Thomas Aquinas.[70] During his time as a student at Oxford in the early fourteenth century, when the university had already become a centre for the development of the Aristotelean-based concept of theology as a science, Rolle had certainly read some Aristotle.[71] With Rolle's exhortation to "loue hym trewly . . . in thynkynge, in spekynge and in worchynge" (37/137–138) comes the appeal to "chaunge þi thoght . . . chaunge þi mouth . . . [and] chaunge þi hand . . . " (37/139–143) which openly encourages the reader to redirect the *affectus*, to change existing habits by their own will and subsequently "bitake al in to Goddis wille" (37/156). In the passage relating to the hypocritical holy men quoted from *Incendium Amoris* above, Rolle also uses the word "habitu" to denote dress, in a context which could also suggest the Aristotelean notion of the word. Using strikingly

---

69 Aristotle, *Nichomachaean Ethics. Aristotle's Ethics*. Trans. J. L. Ackrill (London, 1973), Book II, 61/14–19.
70 J. Coleman, *Medieval Readers and Writers 1350–1400*, 236.
71 Rolle cites Aristotle in *Incendium Amoris*. See *Incendium Amoris*, 185; *The Fire of Love*, 89.

similar language in *The Form of Living* Rolle discusses how clothing, the "habite of holynesse", should be a signifier of inner holiness:

> . . . and whate wrechednesse hit is for to haue þe name and þe habite of holynesse and be nat so, bot couer pride, wreth or envy vndre þe cloþes of Cristes childehode. (5/89–91)

Throughout *The Form of Living* Rolle is concerned with how outward appearance can bear false witness to inner virtue implying that "habit of holynesse" refers to more than dress.[72] His pragmatic hortatory appeal to be true to "þi habit" in *The Commandment* runs deeper than a literal exhortation and reflects the Aristotelean ethical model. It is an instance of Rolle's preoccupation with the corrupt will and his abhorrence of hypocrisy, and acts as a semi-dramatic extension of the theme of Pharisaism.

Rolle's anxiety regarding clothing is pivotal to the construction of readerly and writerly identity in *The Commandment*. Being able to know or recognise the truth that lies in the heart of one dedicated to God has express importance in his personal religious milieu. It is possible that as a self-professed hermit, Rolle's own lack of formal ecclesiastical status is of some consequence in his choice of a clothing metaphor. One of the best-known passages of literature relating to Rolle is the conversion narrative contained in the late fourteenth-century *Officium* where Rolle, the young would-be recluse, fashions two of his sister's dresses to make the required habit of a hermit. The tantalising part of this tale lies in what is left unsaid, that it is unclear that Rolle ever gained formal approbation for this new status, even if it was tacitly accepted. Hermits were required under ecclesiastical law to receive authorisation for their way of life.[73] As in Rolle's case, however, it seems clear that individuals did become hermits by their own choice, for their own purposes. Rolle was himself subject to criticism about the authenticity of his eremitism. In the Latin *Judica Me Deus*, written as a postil upon Psalm 42:1, he writes to a friend that others have labelled him unworthy of the title of hermit because of his frequent changes of abode.[74]

Hypocrisy in the form of false hermits calls to mind another famous fourteenth-century passage, William Langland's vituperative attack on those

---

72 Rolle's concern with hypocrisy in *The Form of Living* is discussed in detail in the next chapter. It is argued that Rolle's highlighting of the theme in *The Commandment*, which deals with the second degree of love, can be seen as a preamble or forewarning for those entering the last degree, the contemplative life, which is the focus of *The Form of Living*.

73 R. M. Clay, *The Hermits and Anchorites of Medieval England*, 85–90.

74 *Judica Me Deus*. Ed. and trans, J. P. Daly (Salzburg, 1984), 2 and 81. Rolle defends his frequent changes of abode in the first section of *Judica Me Deus* known as *Judica A*. See also M. G. Sargent, "Contemporary Criticism of Richard Rolle". *Analecta Cartusiana* 55 (1981), 166–168.

of holy dress but unholy habits, in the *Prologue* to *Piers Plowman*. At the beginning of the *Prologue* Will is introduced before his dream vision as a man dressed "in habite as an heremite unholy of werkes" in order to roam about the country-side unmolested.[75] Once he falls asleep Will has a vision of a "fair feeld ful of folk" which includes both genuine hermits and anchorites "that holden hem in hire selles, | Coveiten noght in contree to cairen aboute | For no likerous liflode hire likame to plese" and those of false habit:

> Heremytes on an heep with hoked staves
> Wenten to Walsyngham – and hire wenches after:
> Grete lobies and longe that lothe were to swynke
> Clothed hem in copes to ben knowen fron othere,
> And shopen hem heremytes hire ese to have.[76]

Such an allusion implies that the general attitude toward those who fashioned themselves as hermits was that they were often motivated by a desire for a life of ease rather than one of ascetic endurance. In Langland's visionary milieu the genuine hermit was only discernible through his/her maintenance of the enclosed state. Lack of a secure spiritual space was linked to false spiritual life and in turn to false representation of this life through dress. It is probably this type of wandering that Rolle himself was criticised for, dressed, as he would have been, in the garb of a hermit. His concern for false dress in *The Commandment* may well be a reflection of his own problems in this area. And though it is not my intention to press the point, this could well be the sought after personal reference common to the majority of Rolle texts, thought to be lacking in this one.

On another autobiographical note, if it is accepted that Rolle was closely associated with the nuns of Hampole, as the *Officium* and manuscript ascriptions attest, Rolle's concern with clothing in *The Commandment* could also suggest that he was aware of charges levelled against the nuns of Hampole regarding their dress codes, especially because the initial recipient appears to have been an inmate of the convent.[77] It is well documented that the nuns of Hampole were known to be lax in possessing goods deemed unnecessary by the ecclesiastical authorities. Eileen Power notes that Yorkshire nunneries in particular were apt to be undisciplined and worldly and that the many great ladies who resided within them considered themselves above ecclesiastical protocol.[78] In 1320, Archbishop Melton warned the prioress of Hampole to correct those nuns who wore "new-fangled clothes", contrary to the accustomed use of the order, "whatever might be their condition or state of dignity". Codes of conduct regarding dress amongst cloistered communities

---

75 W. Langland, *Piers Plowman*, 1/3.
76 W. Langland, *Piers Plowman*, 2–3/28–30 and 53–57.
77 See H. E. Allen, *Writings Ascribed*, 255 and 513.
78 E. Power, *Medieval English Nunneries c. 1275–1535* (Cambridge, 1922), 329.

in general had been of concern since at least the thirteenth century. The standard decree on the subject was issued by the council of Oxford in 1222:

> Since it is necessary that the female sex, so weak against the wiles of the ancient enemy, should be fortified by many remedies, we decree that nuns and other women dedicated to divine worship shall not wear a silken wimple, nor dare to carry silver or golden tiring-pins in their veil. Neither shall they, nor monks nor regular canons, wear belts of silk, or adorned with gold or silver, nor henceforth use burnet or any other unlawful cloth. Also let them measure their gown according to the dimension of their body, but let it suffice them to be clad, as beseems then, in a robe reaching the ankles; and let none but a consecrated nun wear a ring and let her be content with one alone.[79]

Rolle's admonition to those who "trail as myche behynd" them as Jesus wore could even be considered as a direct reference to the above decree that pinpoints the length of a garment as a particular offence. In support of this idea a fifteenth-century German woodcut illustrating a moral tract depicts a woman leaving the altar with a demon riding the tail of her long cloak that is trailing behind her.[80] Women, it seems, were considered prone to the lure of frivolous dress. In this sense, Rolle's focus on clothing in *The Commandment* could also be viewed as a gendered trope, perhaps originating from his association with the convent at Hampole. But it must be stressed again that the clothing metaphor itself does not appear to be explicitly gendered in the text and is instead a function of Rolle's general directive against hypocrisy. In contrast, Rolle's Latin *Contra Amatores Mundi* does treat clothing in an explicitly gendered manner in that it openly condemns the frivolous dress of women: "Ut quid ergo, muliercule, ut amenum vos ornatis?" [And how is it, little ladies, that you adorn yourselves so delightfully?][81] And in *Super Canticum Canticorum* he berates "those solemn women in curled hair, walking with lifted horns [who] desire to be adorned only for carnal love".[82] In Rolle's canon, use of gendered language would therefore appear to be a result of the type of audience that language itself dictates. When Rolle writes in Latin it appears that he expects a male audience that accepts traditional anti-feminist

---

[79] E. Power, *Medieval English Nunneries*, 585–587. The revised decree of 1237 reads, "Item, we forbid to monks, regular canons and nuns coloured garments or bed clothes, save those dyed black. And when they ride, let them use decent saddles and bridles and saddle-cloths. And nuns are not to use trained and pleated dresses, or any exceeding the length of the body, nor delicate or coloured furs; nor shall they presume to wear silver tiring-pins in their veil."

[80] "Devil and Woman", Seelen-Wurzgarten (Ulm, Conrad Dinckmut, 1483) cited in *Witchcraft in Europe 1000–1700: A Documentary History*. Eds. A. C. Kors and E. Peters (Philadelphia, 1992), fig. 12, 91.

[81] *Contra Amatores Mundi*, 102/14–15; Translation of *Contra Amatores Mundi*, 188/16–17.

[82] *Super Canticum Canticorum*, 57.

ideas. In the vernacular, lack of gendered language suggests his awareness of a mixed audience for his works.

Anxiety regarding dress and dress codes was, of course, not peculiar to religious women or indeed, religious orders in the fourteenth century. Male and female readers of Rolle's works would have been aware of the literal as well as the metaphorical weight of his attack on clothing. Alan Hunt's recent work on the history of sumptuary law, both sacred and secular, suggests that because clothing is so strongly visible it offers the prospect of both reflective and unreflective readings of the communication that is embedded in it.[83] Sumptuary law in Europe first appeared as a part of Charlemagne's extension of the range of governmental action to secure the general conditions of feudal relations, particularly in the regulation of labourers. From early in the ninth century there appears evidence of periodic attempts to link dress to rank, and in the eleventh century to impose restrictions on the colours peasants were permitted to wear. In the thirteenth century sumptuary enactments come from both the church and the state; in 1274 Pope Gregory X issued an edict banning "immoderate ornamentation" throughout Christendom. Thereafter sumptuary law became increasingly secular. In its simplest form a sumptuary dress code provided a codification of the dress restrictions for males and females in each designated social category. Many ordinances were gender neutral, others gender specific, with those statutes that target women frequently employing strongly misogynistic attitudes and language.[84] England's first significant sumptuary enactment against excessive apparel, a gender neutral decree, appeared in 1363:

> Also, for the outrageous and excessive apparel of divers people against their estate and degree, to the great destruction and impoverishment of all the land . . .[85]

This law states what the ecclesiastical decree of 1222 does not, that dress codes were primarily concerned with class and its representation through clothing. Archbishop Melton's concern regarding the "condition or state of dignity" of the Hampole women in question also implies class-related concern. Rolle even pre-empts the secular decree of 1363 by using the term outrageous to describe those who possess too many clothes, "for to trauaille þerabout is outrageous bisynesse þat he forbedeth" (36/108–109). His concern in *The Commandment* is representative of both the ecclesiastical concerns and of class-consciousness. This is paralleled by other secular concerns voiced in the

---

83 A. Hunt, *Governance of the Consuming Passions: A History of Sumptuary Law* (New York, 1996), 42–43.
84 A. Hunt, *Governance of the Consuming Passions*, 25–27. This section is indebted to Hunt's condensed history of pre-Early Modern sumptuary law.
85 *English Historical Documents IV, 1327–1485*, Ed. A. R. Myers (London, 1969), 1153–1154.

work such as anxiety regarding the reader's willingness to leave worldly attachments:

> Bot perauentur þou wil say "I may nat despise þe world. I may nat fynd in myn hert to pyne my body; and me behoueth loue my fleishly frendes, and take ease when hit cometh". (39/194–196)

But in doing so he assumes an almost satirical tone, expropriating the voice of the reader who is heard lamenting the loss of earthly loved ones. In a literal sense, the giving up of garments, central to the spiritual journey set out in *The Commandment*, could be viewed as no more than the suggestion of an elementary step for the hand-wringing reader to take in loving God. But the fact that a satirical tone is used implies that Rolle expects more of his reader. Is this a return to the collegial relationship hinted at in the first lines of the work? The "ubi sunt?" passage he employs to counter the plaintive cries of the reader certainly suggests that this is the case:

> . . . I pray þe þat þou bethynke þe, fro þe begynnynge of þis world, whare þe worldes louers ben now, and whar þe louers ben of God. Certes, þei wer men and wommen as we ben . . . and in a poynt þai fel into helle.
>
> (39/197–202)

The didactic language Rolle uses here does not entirely mask his confidence in the reader's independent ability to construct meaning from his text. Assured in this conviction he comments, almost blithely, to the reader, "now þou may se" and "thou sest", that loving the world is meaningless. Friendly discourse of this kind modifies the strictly didactic effect of the work just as the affective, quasi-intimate tone of the passage marks it as assuredly Rollean. Clearly, Rolle's preoccupation with the *affectus* is never too far from the surface of his vernacular works.

The "ubi sunt?" passage is perhaps the most notable representation of the popular medieval theme of *contemptus mundi* in *The Commandment*. Rolle draws frequently throughout his works on the Book of Job, and here his translation of verse 21:13 (Ducunt in bonis dies suos et in puncto ad inferna descendunt) towards the end of *The Commandment* as "and they lad har days in lust and delites; and in a poynt þay fel in to helle" (39/201–202) adds biblical weight to the passage on the evils of loving the world. Of course Rolle had written his own liturgical commentary on the nine readings from Job which form the *lectiones* of the Office for the Dead, *Expositio super Novem Lectiones Mortuorum*. This work is itself an apt Latin comparison to the vernacular *The Commandment* because the conventionality of *Expositio*'s universal call to repentance is echoed in *The Commandment*'s *contemptus mundi* theme.[86]

---

[86] See M. Moyes, *Richard Rolle's Expositio*, I, 91–104. Moyes notes that, consistent with both the *De Contemptu Mundi* theme and with Rolle's expressed attitude throughout

Themes contained within *The Commandment* can be located within Rolle's broader canon, but this is not the only way in which these Latin and vernacular texts connect. *Expositio super Novem Lectiones Mortuorum* was written for an initial audience of secular canons and at times reveals what has been discussed as Rolle's anti-feminist sentiment. By necessity of their vocation, secular canons regularly came into contact with the opposite sex. To accommodate this concern he incorporates strident passages of an anti-feminist nature in the *Expositio* intending to exemplify both the illusory nature of worldly beauty and the dangers posed to the well-being of the soul. He uses temptation by women as the perfect occasion for the *contemptus mundi* themes of mutability and the vanity of worldly desires.[87] *The Commandment* is written initially to a young female religious yet the theme is the same: the dangerous seduction of beauty. The difference here is that the gender of this beauty is not discussed. Again the gender-neutrality of Rolle's vernacular prose is as clear as the gendered specificity of the language of his Latin works. The soul itself is viewed as inherently feminine throughout Rolle's entire corpus but the language in which he discusses subjects such as beauty, temptation and sin in the Latin works differs markedly in terms of gender. Male and female are clearly defined as separate in the Latin works. In them, women function primarily as vehicles of male sin. In contrast, phrases such as "euery synful man and womman" (3/1), taken from the opening lines of *The Form of Living*, are more common in the vernacular works and appear to describe and define

his English and Latin works, the misery of the damned is contrasted with the blessedness of those who are saved. He suggests that Rolle was acquainted with the most widely read and copied expressions of the theme: the *De Miseria Humane Conditionis* of Innocent III, the Pseudo-Bernadine *Meditationes Piissimae* and the *Speculum Peccatoris*, variously ascribed to Augustine, Bernard and in some manuscripts, to Rolle. See also H. E. Allen, *Writings Ascribed*, 353–354; N. Watson, *Invention of Authority*, 55, 198 and 208.

87 *Richard Rolle's Expositio*, I, 100. Moyes gives the following example: Non respicias uinum, id est, non admittas peccandi delectacionem, cum flauerit in uitro, id est, fallibili & fragili corpore, quamuis sit pulcrum & ornatum. Et hoc est contra multos qui cum ornatam mulierculam uiderint, statim in eius concupiscenciam exardescunt. Et quia pulcritudinis temptacioni fallacis non resistunt, se ipsos a diuina gracia abiciunt et in fetentem turpitudinem ruunt. Mundana namque uanitas prestigium est & similis parieti dealbate, quia & si exterius apparet amabilis, intus tamen plena est amaritudine & horrore squaloris. [You should not consider the wine, that is to say, you should not permit the pleasure of sinning, even if it glows golden in the glass, that is to say in an unreliable and fragile body, no matter how beautifully presented. And this is a warning for the many who, as soon as they see a beautifully dressed specimen of womanhood, instantly flare up with lust for her. And because they do not resist the temptation of false beauty, they cast themselves away from divine grace and wallow in fetid disgustingness. For in fact worldly vanity is an illusion rather like a whitewashed wall because, even if on the outside it seems desirable, on the inside it is filled with the bitterness and horror of filth.] See M. Moyes, *Richard Rolle's Expositio*, II, 276/9–11.

the envisaged readership. The absence of explicit references to male or female attributes in the vernacular treatises suggests Rolle's acceptance of a non gender-specific audience.

Gender aside, Rolle's attack on elaborate clothing in *The Commandment*, by implication clothing that is beautiful, speaks as much for his general fear of worldly beauty as for his preoccupation with dress per se. His concern with love of the world and its spiritual dangers is illustrated by the stark contrast of the transient rewards of worldly attire with the beauty of Christ. The *contemptus mundi* theme and the "ubi sunt?" are part of a traditional poetic strategy. From the eleventh century the theme of contempt of the world became common in exhortatory religious poetry. It is clearly represented in the thirteenth-century poem that also draws on Job, known as "Where beth they, beforen us weren":

> Where beth they, beforen us weren,
> Houndes ladden and havekes beren,
> And hadden feld and wode?
> The riche levedies in hoere bour,
> That wereden gold in hoere tressour,
> With hoere brighte rode?[88]

Here, as in *The Commandment*, worldly riches prevent heavenly reward. The poet draws on contemporary ideas of worldly wealth such as the keeping of hounds and hawks, and of women wearing golden head-bands, to describe those who "heore paradis . . . nomen here" and have long since fallen into hell. Those who choose to despise the world are given a glimpse of their reward:

> Thereinne is day withouten night,
> Withouten ende strengthe and might,
> Ande wreche of everich fo,
> Mid God himselven eche lif,
> And pes and rest withoute strif,
> Wele withouten wo.

Themes within *The Commandment* bear striking similarity to this devotional poem which has been described as designed to move the penitent heart.[89] Rolle is known to have drawn on other thirteenth-century works in the vernacular, and perhaps considered that a work such as *The Commandment* might serve as a prose extension of this common poetic form.

In summary, Rolle's condemnation of fine clothing in *The Commandment* has both a long tradition and a multitude of meanings. The didactic function of the clothing metaphor lies in both its literal and its metaphorical sense.

---

88 R. T. Davies, *Medieval English Lyrics*, Poem 8, 56.
89 R. T. Davies, *Medieval English Lyrics*, 311–312.

Rolle's references to dress, the reader's literal "habit", is in turn comple-
mented by the metaphorical sense which drives forward the affective message
to the will (which controls habits) that the soul should be clothed in the love of
God. To foster this directive the nakedness of Christ is contrasted with the
vision of the richly clothed body. Exegetical aspects of the clothing metaphor
in *The Commandment* are mainly represented by Rolle's use of biblical *exempla*,
closely linked to homiletic discourse. Rolle may well have had the parable of
the wedding garment (Matthew 22:2–14) in mind when using dress to eluci-
date images of hypocrisy and the masking of inner truth. In the Bible this
parable of the elect directly precedes the speaking of the "commandment" of
the title of Rolle's *The Commandment*, linking the issue of dress with its main
theme of the love of God.

Less explicit allusions to biblical texts, subsumed within the body of Rolle's
text, are also apparent in *The Commandment*; they add weight to his emphasis
on inner truth and his abhorrence of hypocrisy. Alford describes the commen-
tary-like structure used by Rolle as a network of submerged biblical texts,
joined by association and transformed by substitution and amplification.[90] In
The Commandment the use of proverbial *exempla* provides the explicit biblical
archetypes for the reader. The seeking and finding of Christ in the appropriate
manner – "certes, if þou seke hym right, þou shalt fynd hym" (36/86) – is
largely an expansion of Proverbs 8:17 which is achieved partly by means of
biblical stories and partly by transforming a passage of penitential emphasis
in *Super Canticum Canticorum* about the soul's search for Jesus.[91] For Rolle, it
seems that the Bible had a narrative existence and vast imaginative potential.
With the express purpose of drawing the soul towards Jesus, Proverbs 8:17[92] –
"Ego diligentes me diligo, et qui mane vigilant ad me, invenient me" – is
translated for the reader as:

> He saith þat he loueth ham þat loueth hym, and þay þat erly waketh to hym
> shal fynd hym. (36/84–85)

Of course, in its biblical context, this verse does not refer to Christ; it is
wisdom itself who loves those that seek wisdom. Rolle's substitution of Christ

---

90 J. A. Alford, "Biblical *Imitatio*", 12.
91 See N. Watson, *Invention of Authority*, 149 and 237. Watson quotes the passage from
Super Canticum Canticorum in full on page 149. He also notes (319, n. 11) that in *The
Commandment* Rolle may be indebted to Aelred's *De Ihesu Puero Duodenni* "O dulcis
puer, ubi eras? ubi lateras? quo uterabaris hospito? quorum fruebaris consortio? . . ."
De Ihesu Puero Duodenni. Aelredi Rievallensis Opera Omnia, I, 1/28–30.
92 Alford cites the possibility of Cant. 3:1–2 ("By night on my bed I sought him whom
my soul loveth: I sought him, but I found him not. I will rise now, and go about the
city in the streets, and in the broad ways I will seek him whom my soul loveth: I
sought him, but I found him not") as one of the texts that is likely to have influenced
Rolle in the following passage due to Rolle's "special fondness for the Canticles".
See J. A. Alford, "Biblical *Imitatio*", 18.

for wisdom, which Alford claims is well supported by exegetical tradition, makes the idea of wisdom Christocentric. For Rolle the search for wisdom is the search for Christ, a blending of *intellectus* and *affectus*. The proverbial gloss itself is supported by a number of implied associations with biblical texts that sustain his focus on the great commandment, the seeking of love/Christ with the heart and the soul. The Old Testament text (Deut. 4:29) "Cumque quaesieris ibi Dominum Deum tuum, invenies eum: si tamen toto corde quaesieris, ei tota tribulatione animae tuae" [And when thou shalt seek there the Lord thy God, thou shalt find him: yet so, if thou seek him with all thy heart, and all tribulation of thy soul] prefigures the great commandment itself. Christ's own words in Luke 11:9, "quaerite, et invenietis" [Seek, and you shall find], are echoed by Rolle's commandment to "sek inwardly" (34/94).

The link to Rolle's concern with hypocrisy can also be seen in the range of biblical texts he draws on to further this theme of seeking and finding Christ in the appropriate manner. Luke 2:44–46 is interpreted by Rolle as a parable of the soul's search for Christ: Mary could not find Christ for all her searching "til at þe last she come in to þe temple" (36/91–92).[93] The shepherds found him "liggynge in a crib bitwix two bestes" (36/97) and the three kings found Christ "swedled in cloutes sympilly as a pouer barne" (36/100). Each of these texts fixes the reader's gaze on seeing Christ as he should be seen. Rolle uses the image of Christ "sittynge . . . hyrynge and answerynge" (36/92–93) in the temple to exhort the reader to "sek inwardly in trouthe and hope and charite of holy chirche" (36/94). Lying between the two beasts, Christ is the very example of how truth can only be found in "pouerte and nat . . . riches" (36/98–99). In the manger he is found "swedled in cloutes sympilly" (36/100) an image Rolle uses to emphasise how "pride and vanyte" will prevent the reader from finding Christ, and of course it acts as a convenient precursor to Rolle's attack on abundance of clothing drawn from Luke 3:11: "Qui habet duas tunicas, det non habenti" [He that hath two coats, let him give to him that hath not]. Rolle draws on the text from Luke with a view to playing on both the literal and metaphorical sense of clothing imagery:[94]

> He seid to his disciplesse þat þai shold nat haue two kyrtels: þat is þat oon shold nat haue as many cloþes as two myght be sustened with. (36/106–108)

---

[93] Luke 2:44–46: Existimantes autem illum esse in comitatu, venerunt iter diei, et requirebant eum inter cognatus et notos. Et non invenientes, regressi sunt in Ierusalem, requirentes eum. Et factum est, post triduum invenerunt illum in templo sedentem in medio doctorum, audientem illos, et interogantem eos. [And thinking that he was in company, they came a days journey, and sought him among their kinsfolk and acquaintance. And not finding him, they returned into Jerusalem, seeking him. And it came to pass, after three days they found him in the temple sitting in the midst of the Doctors, hearing them, and asking them].

[94] D. Renevey, *The Moving of the Soul*, 212.

Christ's advice to his own disciples is glossed by Rolle who appropriates it as his own advice to his own disciple/pupil, the reader. It could also be tentatively argued that the image of a Christ-like Rolle dressed in the simple costume of his sister's cast-offs is evoked here, exhorting the reader to follow Rollean example. This would of course rely on the reader's knowledge of Rolle's conversion narrative, which we cannot assume from the context. The focus of this passage is placed firmly on the conversion of the reader who is urged to turn away from the worldliness of fine clothing and embrace the simple garments worn by Christ:

> How may þou for shame, þat art bot seruaunt, with many cloþes and riche folow þi spouse and þi lord, þat yed in a kyrtel, and þou trail as myche behynd þe as al þat he had on? Forþi I rede þat þou part with hym ar þou and he mete, þat he reproue þe nat of outrage, for he wil þat þou haue þat þou hast mestier of, and no more. (36/101–106)

The literal and the metaphorical are then placed side by side to enhance the metaphorical aspect of the image:

> If þi body be cled withouten as þyn ordre wille, loke þat þi soule be nat naked within, þat þyn ordre forbedeth. Bot naked be þi soule fro al vices, and warm lapped in loue and mekenesse. (38/158–160)

Denis Renevey has argued that the achievement of the espousal with Christ, which stands as the main goal described by the narrative voice for the reader, is reached by a refined understanding of the didactic message contained in the clothing imagery.[95] However, his conclusion, which refers to externalities such as clothing to stress Rolle's personal relationship with the initial recipient based on his knowledge of her individual background, then unnecessarily limits the audience able to respond to the clothing imagery to women only.[96] Yet, the clothing metaphor contained in *The Commandment* performs a more complex function if read in terms of fourteenth-century anxiety concerning the wearing of garments not suitable to one's socio-religious status, Rolle's own deep-seated concern with hypocrisy and his focus on the seeking of love inwardly. In turn, the explicit and implicit biblical exposition Rolle relies on to expound the notion of seeking and finding Christ not only embodies the visual aspect of the theme of interiority but also illuminates the explicit function of his instructional discourse: to provide a reader with the means to find Christ specifically through the "rede" offered by Rolle's text. No explicitly

---

95 D. Renevey, *The Moving of the Soul*, 213.
96 D. Renevey, *The Moving of the Soul*, 215. Renevey writes that "from the few details provided within *The Commandment* we can be certain that Rolle had at least a knowledge of the personal background of the recipient, and possibly personal contacts with her as a spiritual guide".

gendered directive is dicernible in this. Instead Rolle achieves a kind of universality for his text in that he assures each and every reader's spiritual fulfilment whilst at the same time affirming the intercessory necessity of his authorial guidance.

The exegetical and didactic manner of *The Commandment* is therefore shadowed by Rolle's unmistakable authorial presence as a companion to his reader rather than a distant instructor. Before giving the examples above, he adopts a quasi-intimate tone when he asks the rhetorical question "thou art erly wakynge oft sithes: whi þan fyndes þou nat hym?" (36/85–86), assuming the voice of a personal acquaintance questioning the reader. Such an utterance gives agency to the reader to question him/herself, and suggests that the boundary between the authorial Rolle and the reader is permeable here. It emphasises the importance of experiential spirituality, common to the Rolle canon, in *The Commandment*. Moving on from the early part of the work, in which sin was the focus, the reader is now urged to seek Christ only with a pure heart that has cast out all sin:

> Sek inwardly in trouth and hope and charite of holy chirche, castynge out al syn and hatynge hit in al þi hert, for þat holdeth hym fro þe, and letteth þe þat þou may nat fynd hym. (36/94–96)

Truth, hope and charity, like heart, thought and soul, form another affective triptych designed to direct the reader's gaze inwardly. In terms of Rolle's construction of reader agency, seeking Jesus also serves to focus the reader inwardly, recasting his/her gaze upon the self first, before they are worthy of gazing upon the crucified Christ, which is recommended only later in the work. The primary point of Rolle's composition of *The Commandment* is the transformation of a commandment heard and understood from an external source (the didactic) into a spontaneous interior will of the heart (*ex toto corde*). Therefore the text is explicitly didactic, but transforms itself into an affective work. Rolle's commitment to the reader's *affectus*, and to his own role as an affective author, is sustained, but in a deliberately understated way.

Rolle's theme of interiority is sustained by an adherence to homiletic/didactic discourse and by a modified form of the affective language common to his vernacular canon. From this blended discourse emerges the characteristic Rollean design to teach the love of God in terms of his own Christocentric doctrine:

> I wot no thynge þat so jnwardly shal take þi hert to couait Goddis loue, and to desyre þe ioy [of heuyn], and to despise þe vanytees of þis world, as stidfast þynkyng of þe mescheuous and greuous woundes and of þe deth of Ihesu Crist. (38/187–191)

Here we find Rolle desiring the reader's desire – he is always the mediator between the reader and the divine. The exhortation to "stidfast þynkyng" on the Passion elaborates Rolle's own pedagogic knowing or understanding of love. This draws readers to that understanding themselves but because of the pervasive nature of the narratorial utterance the reader's achievement of this knowledge occurs only through Rolle's wisdom. The propriety of his utterance is therefore responsible for the knowledge his reader will receive. In this he may have been following Augustine who in insisting that "the multitude of the wise is the welfare of the whole world" noted that speech/utterance was instituted so that "each might bring his own thoughts to the knowledge of another".[97] Again the knowledge possessed by Rolle's authorial self is the deciding factor in constructing the reader's agency.

The final passage of *The Commandment* is less of a conclusion than a parting instruction: "I rede the, þat þou foryet nat his name Iesus" (39/214). Rolle's "rede" functions here as a formal return to the didactic language that permeates the work as a whole, after the more collegial discourse briefly indulged in the previous passage. The final exhortation to love the Holy Name in terms of a substantive entity, "þi special and þi dere tresour", neatly complements the advice to avoid loving worldly vanities, such as fine clothing, which is the basis of Rolle's teaching. Yet, although the language of this final exhortation is didactic, a submerged affectivity is present in the allusion to union after death, the heavenly reward not yet explicitly referred to in this work:

> Who-so loueth hit verrayly is ful of Goddis grace and vertuȝ, in gostly comfort in þis lif, and, when þei dey, þei ben taken vp in to þe ordres of angels, to see hym in endles ioy þat thay haue loued. (39/221–223)

The passage reads as an affirmation that grace and virtue both return to the reader who loves the Holy Name. It also signifies how worship of the Holy Name in *The Commandment* positions Christ himself as both the means and the goal of the work. Allusion to the power of the Holy Name, "hit chaseth deuylles, hit desrueth temptatiouns", is also reminiscent of Rolle's personal experience in that he too called upon the Holy Name in order to ward off an evil apparition. The *Officium* recounts this story of how Rolle was personally tempted by a demon in the form of a beautiful woman, quoting from his own *Super Canticum Canticorum*:

> ... feeling that she might entice me to evil, I told myself to wish to rise and bless us with the sign of the cross, invoking the holy Trinity. But she so strongly bound me that I felt neither my mouth nor my hands for moving. Seeing this, I thought that not a woman but a devil in the form of a woman was there tempting me. Therefore I turned to God and with him in my mind, I said, "O Jesus, how precious is your blood," pressing the cross onto my

---

97 Augustine, *Faith, Hope and Charity*. Trans. Bernard M. Peebles. *The Fathers of the Church: A New Translation*. Vol. 2, ch. 7, 22/389; *De Doctrina Christiana*. Trans. John J. Gavigan, *The Fathers of the Church*, Vol. 2, book 4, ch. 8/174.

breast with my finger, which now I could move a little, and behold, suddenly all disappeared and I gave thanks to God, who freed me.[98]

This is a significant pre-empting of Rolle's commitment to the cult of the Holy Name which culminates in his last vernacular work, *The Form of Living*. It is interesting that devotion to the Holy Name should occur at the end of *The Commandment*, albeit as an after-word, considering Watson's theory that Rolle's invocations of Jesus, which seem to suggest more advanced spiritual states but are generally devoid of any theological content, are connected most closely with his own experience of *dulcor*.[99] In Rolle's own mystical schema *dulcor* is the middle ground of spiritual experience and the one most closely linked to *The Commandment*. Its introduction here not only brings the work to a neat didactic end in itself, but also marks a middle point in Rolle's vernacular canon. As subdued as *Ego Dormio* is flamboyant, *The Commandment* paves the way for the integration of spiritual friendship to be found in Rolle's continuing relationship with his vernacular audience in *The Form of Living*.

IV

The function of *The Commandment* in Rolle's vernacular canon appears to be grounded in a decision to offer a work that continues the theme of love found in *Ego Dormio* through plain instruction. Of course, Rolle's intention in writing this work will never really be known; it may have been simply to broaden his own vernacular canon or, more likely, it represents his willingness to adapt his message to a variety of occasions. Ostensibly, the purgative process is illuminated for a reader on the verge of spiritual commitment by developing a *contemptus mundi* theme and by offering instruction in practices often associated with the coenobitic life. Below the surface of the outwardly monastic emphasis lies a more subtle suggestiveness; by using monastic language Rolle is able to incorporate an awareness of his own second degree of love, *dulcor*, and of the theme of interiority, by addressing the reader's "habit" in almost every sense of the word. By directing attention to both the literal and metaphorical meaning of clothing, the gaze of the reader is trained inwardly and Rolle's abhorrence of hypocrisy is clearly illuminated. Urged to examine their own "habits", readers are given the agency to seek within themselves for the truth of their own convictions whilst still being instructed by Rolle on sin and vice. It is this subsumed affectivity that permits the subtle emergence of a formal yet personal reader/writer relationship where the reader is encouraged to engage affectively with the spiritual guidance offered.

[98] *Super Canticum Canticorum*, 106–107.
[99] N. Watson, *Invention of Authority*, 55.

It is primarily Rolle's skill as an affective author that succeeds in encouraging the reader towards affective response despite the apparently more distant address of this didactic work. It could be suggested that Rolle sought to embody in *The Commandment* Bernard of Clairvaux's thoughts on the importance of feeling and compunction in the search for wisdom when he said that "instruction makes us learned but feeling makes us wise".[100] In appealing directly to the *affectus*, the passionate *Ego Dormio* sought to inflame the heart; in contrast *The Commandment*'s message seeks to arouse the mind, then to install truth within the heart, the seat of love. Rolle's concern with the gaze of the reader, and its effect on the heart, in this work reveals the emergence of a continuing thread in his vernacular thought. In *Ego Dormio*, the eye of the heart is opened through powerful erotic images that urge the reader to turn to the love of God and accept the role of the bride. In *The Commandment*, didactic instruction then directs the gaze inwardly, promoting greater self-awareness, so that the open heart will be able to maintain the integrity needed to ascend the spiritual ladder.

The Commandment's reader may not to be invited to join Rolle in an intimate and personalised journey but he/she is certainly constructed as a personal focus of Rolle's homiletic concern. The readerly eye is focused on the clothing of the corporeal body and its spiritual ramifications to illuminate the point that the truth of "Cristen mannys soule" is what allows the heart to be truly turned to God. Whereas the reader/lover of *Ego Dormio* is addressed in an affirming tone as "þe þat lust loue", the reader/pupil of *The Commandment* is addressed in more distant terms, "if þe list loue". The reader is engaged in, if not an intimate, at least an individual lesson on the appropriate methods in seeking out and eventually finding love. Didactic language, which at times is certainly influenced by the gender and socio-religious status of the initial audience, constructs the reader as an individual soul in need of guidance. Rolle's pervasive utterance is found constantly constructing and affirming reader agency within the text and his own narratorial presence. Any sense of individuality or self-hood in the text is reliant on the reader's willing search inwardly to find the love offered by both the great commandment itself and Rolle's guide to it. Just as the affective focus on individual response does not necessarily exclude a wider audience for *Ego Dormio*, but invites any individual reader to participate in a relationship with God and Rolle's authorial self, the seemingly conventional didacticism of *The Commandment* also widens the audience to encompass all Christians who seek guidance in the journey to the love of God.

---

100 Bernard cited in V. Gillespie, "Mystic's Foot", 201. Gillespie does not supply an exact reference for this quote. See also A. Louth, "Bernard and Affective Mysticism". *The Influence of St. Bernard*. Ed. B. Ward (Oxford, 1976), 2–10, esp. 3.

5

"A man or a womman þat is ordeynet to contemplatif lif":[1] *The Form of Living*

Uera enim amicicia non potest esse sine mutua delectacione amicorum, et eorum collocucione desiderabili, atque consolatoris affatu, et hec amicicia si gracia Dei informata et tota in Deo fiat, et ad Deum referatur et tendat, dicitur tunc sancta amicicia, et est multum meritoria.

[For true friendship cannot exist without mutual enjoyment and pleasant fellowship and helpful conversation. And if this friendship is founded in God's grace, and is wholly his, related and directed to him, it can then be called a holy friendship, and it is very rewarding.][2]

I

LIKE *EGO DORMIO* and *The Commandment*, *The Form of Living* is a composite work that deploys material from Rolle's own Latin canon as well as from other sources. But, also like its predecessors, *The Form of Living* is a unique text which develops a singular discourse, in this case a discourse of friendship, to fulfil its affective purpose of turning the reader to the love of God. *The Form of Living* is the longest, and in many ways the most complex, of Rolle's vernacular treatises and holds the unique position in his canon of being the only work whose date and occasion of composition are known to us; it was written in late 1348 or early 1349, in the last months of his life, on the occasion of his friend and disciple Margaret Kirkeby's enclosure at an anchorhold in Richmond.[3] It was widely read and disseminated in the later medieval period as is attested by the number of surviving manuscripts;

---

[1] *The Form of Living*, 25/875.
[2] *Incendium Amoris*, 262; *The Fire of Love*, 175.
[3] N. Watson, *Invention of Authority*, 248. The probable identity of Margaret Kirkeby is outlined in detail by Hope Emily Allen in the preface to *The Form of Living* in her edition of Rolle's English writings. She writes that from archiepiscopal registers at York Rotha Mary Clay discovered the actual orders by the archbishop for the enclosure on December 12, 1348 of "Margaret le Boteler nun of Hampole . . . in a certain house [or room] adjacent to the chapel of East Layton in the archdeaconry of Richmond". See H. E. Allen, *English Writings*, 82–83.

Ogilvie-Thomson lists forty-four manuscripts in which the work occurs.[4] In twenty-one of these manuscripts *The Form of Living* is the only Rolle material to appear. It is also found in a number of pious manuscript compilations and early printed works of a devotional nature which circulated amongst the laity, such as the fourteenth-century English manual of popular religious instruction known as *The Pore Caitif*,[5] the popular Latin mystical compilation *Speculum Spiritualium*,[6] and the theological compendium *Speculum Christiani*.[7] The latter, thought to have been composed to fulfil Archbishop Pecham's directions on teaching the common people, has English passages that are derived from *The Form of Living*, although that could well suggest only a common source rather than a direct borrowing.[8] No other English treatise by Rolle enjoyed such a singular reputation; it was even translated into Latin on two known occasions during the medieval period.[9] Such diverse recognition of *The Form of Living* clearly indicates its popularity which in turn supports the idea that Rolle envisages a wider audience in this work, one that transcends

4   S. Ogilvie-Thomson, *Prose and Verse*, xxxvi–xliv.
5   The compiler of *The Pore Caitif* uses passages from *The Form of Living* but does not mention Rolle by name as the author. For further discussion of how the anonymous author of *The Pore Caitif* made extensive use of Rolle's *Emendatio Vitae*, *The Form of Living* and *The Commandment* see M. T. Brady, "Rolle and the Pattern of Tracts in *The Pore Caitif*". *Traditio* 39 (1983), 456–465 and, by the same author, "Rolle's *Form of Living* and *The Pore Caitif*". *Traditio* 36 (1980), 426–435.
6   *Speculum Spiritualium*. Syon Monastery MS M. 118, fol. xxxvii[v] cited in H. E. Allen, *Writings Ascribed*, 263 and 405–406. Allen describes the compendium *Speculum Spiritualium* as "mystical" rather than "popular". The author states in his preface that he withholds his name, and that he wishes to provide a compendium for those who cannot afford many books: it is composed with the contemplative specially in view, but the active will also find it useful. Other material by Rolle appears throughout the compendium, including an almost complete version of *Emendatio Vitae*.
7   *Speculum Christiani* is a translation of a widely circulated Latin-English pastoral manual compiled in the late fourteenth century for the use of the clergy. The compiler made extensive use of an earlier fourteenth-century Latin manual entitled *Cibus animae* and drew other material from Archbishop Pecham's *Constitutions*, Peter Lombard's *Sentences*, Robert Grosseteste's *Templum Domini*, the *Speculum Sacerdotis*, an anonymous *Treatise on the Priesthood*, and William Flete's *De Remediis contra temptacionis*. See *A Manual of the Writings in Middle English*, Vol. 7, 2265. See also V. Gillespie, "The Evolution of the *Speculum Christiani*". *Latin and Vernacular: Studies in Late-Medieval Texts and Manuscripts*. Ed. A. J. Minnis (Cambridge, 1989), 39–62.
8   H. E. Allen, *Writings Ascribed*, 404. A quotation from Rolle's *Incendium Amoris* appears in the 1485 printed edition as "Ricardus de hampole. Ille deuote orat qui non habet cor vacabundum".
9   H. E. Allen, *Writing Ascribed*, 262. The two manuscripts containing the Latin version of *The Form of Living* are Caius College Cambridge MS 140, ff.108–15b (15th century): "Explicit Ricardus heremita de modo viuendi ad margaretam inclusam"; British Museum, Harley MS 106, f.1 (15th century) which is a fragment only of another translation.

his own friendship with Margaret Kirkeby, and opens the work to every reader who "wilt do as I teche the in þis short fourme of lyvynge" (9/264–265).

The content of *The Form of Living* falls into two parts, divided by the Latin phrase "Amore langueo" which Rolle uses to move the discussion from more practical aspects of devotion to an explication of the contemplative life. In the first, more didactic part of the work Rolle assumes the role of the practical guide and is primarily concerned with the dangers of falling into temptation and sin, and the wiles of the devil.[10] Beginning the work with a grandly open gesture Rolle outlines sin in the form of the "þre wrechednesse" that can bring "euery synful man and woman . . . vnto þe deth of helle" (3/1–17). He then warns the reader of confusing holiness with penance and abstinence, by expanding on chapter four of *Emendatio Vitae* where the practice of discretion is advised (4/48–5/86). This is followed by a detailed discussion of the devil's clever deception of "vnwise men and wommen" (3/29–5/104). The solitary life is praised (6/122–150) but the emphasis on sin and temptation is maintained by Rolle's specially considering the devil's wiles against those who are solitary (7/161–181, 8/203–232). *Emendatio Vitae* is again the source of a long section that offers practical and positive advice to the beginner solitary (9/267–15/484) in which Rolle also draws upon the *Compendium Theologicae Veritatis* for lists of sins and vices to amplify the didactic message.[11]

The extensive listing and categorising of the evils of the world and the devil has caused this first section to be labelled as "laborious",[12] but although the medieval preoccupation with listing sins, vices and temptations can appear tedious and repetitive to a modern reader, the specific importance of this section should not be overlooked. Within it Rolle clearly reveals his own preoccupation with the *affectus* at an elementary level as well as his concern for the spiritual direction of human will. In fact, all Rolle's admonitions in this early part of the work stem from the same basic concern, that the human will should be aligned with the will of the divine. The key to such alignment is Christ, and it is devotion to Christ which Rolle charges the reader to make the foundation of his/her spirituality in this section: "Atte þe begynnynge turne þe entierly to þi lord Ihesu Criste" (9/267). Without this Christocentric focus Rolle holds out little hope of salvation for the reader:

---

[10] Watson gives an excellent summary of the content of *The Form of Living* in his short explication of this text. I am indebted to him in my own attempt to condense this work into a brief outline here. See N. Watson, *Invention of Authority*, 250–255.

[11] Hugh of Strasbourg, *Compendium Theologicae Veritatis. Opera Omnia Sancti Bonaventurae.* Ed. A. C. Peltier (Paris, 1864–1871), Vol. 8. III, ch. 30–33.

[12] Watson writes that "much of the first half of *The Form of Living* is frankly laborious, as Rolle deals with basic materials in which he has only temporary interest". However, whatever the interest-threshold of Rolle's prose for a modern reader, Watson's assumptions about their "temporary interest" for Rolle himself appear to be largely speculative. See N. Watson, *Invention of Authority*, 252.

For he þat loueth nat Ihesu Crist he leseth al þat he hath and al þat he is and
al þat he myght get; he nys nat worth þe lif, ne to be fed with swynes mete.

(3/14–16)

Only after this moral groundwork has been laid does Rolle consider the
contemplative life. Explicit instruction appears to end before the "Amore
langueo" section: Rolle stresses that the reader has now "herd how þou may
dispose þi lyf" (15/485) and is now ready to embrace the inner world of
languishing in the love of God.

In the second part of the work Rolle shifts the emphasis from sin and vice to
contemplation and love. His introduction of this section with words from the
Song of Songs, the medieval book of love, also signals a shift in the emotional
tone of the work. Here the composite nature of *The Form of Living* is most
discernible in that this second part of the work is extremely close to the prominent topics of the last chapters of *Emendatio Vitae*.[13] However, the coverage of
the contemplative life is more extensive. Rolle begins with a brief extension of
the theme found in *Ego Dormio* of how those who burn with love for God will
become part of the angelic hierarchy in heaven:

Forþi the dyuersite of loue maketh þe dyuersite of holynesse and of mede. In
heuyn þe angels þat ben most brennynge in loue ben next God.

(15/499–501)

Following Richard of St. Victor, the three degrees of love are described as insuperable, inseparable, and singular (16/525–597). An exhortatory lyric, "When
wil þou cum to comfort me?" (18/598–609), accompanies the third degree and
the soul's experience of love is explained in terms of Rolle's own mystical
schema of burning, sweetness, and melody. Rolle does not suggest overtly
that the reader should engage in *imaginatio* here to progress to the third and
highest degree of love, "syngular loue", but recommends devotion to the Holy
Name, "þis name Iesus, fest it so feste in þi herte þat hit cum neuer out of þi
þoght" (18/611–612). Much of the remainder of this part of the work is structured as a dialogue, a common medieval form for didactic literature, often
with a constructed friend and disciple, in which Rolle answers a series of
imagined questions. All five questions are on love, "what is loue?" (19/633–677),
"whare is loue?" (20/678–704), "how shal I verraily loue God?" (20/705–
22/772), "how þou myght knowe þat þou ware in loue and charite?"
(22/773–818) and "in whate state men may moste loue God in?" (23/819–
24/835). Rolle concedes that these "bene hard questions to louse to a feble man

13 See N. Watson, *Invention of Authority*, esp. 252–253. Watson discusses Rolle's borrowing from *Emendatio Vitae* for *The Form of Living* in some detail. He argues that like *The
Commandment* Rolle's treatment of the three degrees of love in *The Form of Living* is
expanded and adapted from the eleventh chapter of *Emendatio Vitae*, which in turn
becomes a rhapsodic account of *canor*.

and a fleisshely as I am" (18/629–630). To conclude the work Rolle discusses the differences between the active and contemplative lives, and the benefits of meditation. The goal is the ultimate reward for the true lover of God, the beatific vision for all eternity (24/836–25/893).

It is not until here, at the very end of the work, that Margaret Kirkeby is mentioned: "Lo, Margaret, I haue shortly seid þe fourme of lyuynge and how þou may cum to perfeccioun" (25/894–895). She is neither addressed nor referred to throughout the rest of the work but this one mention of her name has both influenced and limited modern perception of *The Form of Living* in many ways. In modern scholarship the work is most often described as "written for Margaret Kirkeby" through which it has become confined as a work for a single, gendered recipient. Of course, there is no reason to doubt Rolle's desire to dedicate this work to her, or that Margaret, as his friend and disciple, was the intended initial recipient of the work. The name Margaret appears in a number of contemporary manuscripts containing *The Form of Living*, either in part or in full.[14] This dedication to Margaret, as well as Rolle's presumed friendship with her and the many feminised images he employs throughout the text, has caused the work to be considered as written for a gendered audience. Mary Knowlton argues that Rolle's gendered consciousness is extended to his treatment of the reader as a personal friend because female religious were more likely to be receptive to the "intimate nature of his prose".[15] Yet the content of *The Form of Living* itself suggests that far from expecting a specifically female, contemplative audience for this work, Rolle sought to open his text, and his friendship, to all those who wish to love God as he does.

Rolle's development of a singular discourse within the text enables it to move beyond the initial recipient because the work is opened by way of subtle paths and directions, that any reader can follow, designed to invite the reader to take Margaret's place and become the individual addressee. Clearly, our knowledge of Margaret's "real" relationship with Rolle, which is constructed entirely from Rolle's canonisation document, the *Officium*, has been too heavily projected into modern perceptions of *The Form of Living* as a work of singular friendship. The tradition of spiritual *amicitia* itself, as well as the ideal of mixed-sex friendship and the discovery of self-love within friendship, will be considered here in order to locate a context for Rolle's own discourse of friendship that shapes the reader/writer relationship found in *The Form of Living*. Rolle does not allude specifically to mixed-sex friendships in this work because his concern is not with earthly relationships, which are transient and inconsequential, but with an eternal friendship between his authorial self, his reader (the human soul) and their mutual spouse, Christ. In this Rolle would

---

[14] S. Ogilvie-Thomson, *Prose and Verse*, xxiv.
[15] M. A. Knowlton, *The Influence of Richard Rolle*, 60.

appear to draw on traditions stemming from the twelfth century where, as Caroline Walker Bynum points out, the heights of spiritual fulfilment were defined in terms of the individual's friendship with God. She argues that the writings of Bernard of Clairvaux and other "new monks" of this period stress discovery of self – and of self-love – as the first step in a long process of returning to love of and likeness to God, a love and likeness in which the individual is not dissolved into God but rather becomes God's partner and friend.[16] In *The Form of Living* Rolle not only relies on the subtle appropriation of concepts that reflect accepted notions of medieval *amicitia* and *amicitia Dei* to draw the reader towards spiritual enlightenment but he also seeks to escort the reader to an acceptance of, and fulfilment in, the vocation in which this friendship is most likely to take place – Rolle's own vocation, the contemplative life.

Feminised images in this work, particularly nuptial imagery, reflect Rolle's desire for a shared experience of the mystical marriage in the contemplative life, rather than a desire to gender his audience. As in *Ego Dormio* and *The Commandment*, Rolle accepts the soul as inherently feminine in *The Form of Living*. In particular, his depiction of his authorial self as "the sitter" in this work is a metaphor that alerts us to Rolle's own authorial identification with the bride of Christ, sitting enthroned in heaven, and his acceptance of his own contemplative role as feminine. From this it follows that the union of Rolle, and by association his reader, with the divine is the focus of any feminised images in the work. Gender is not an issue in Rolle's identification with the reader as sharing in his own experience, because he accepts the reader as an equal in the contemplative life. This allows him to develop a collegial tone, one that implies that the status of the reader is elevated even more than in the passionate discourse of *Ego Dormio*. Such a reader is then able to participate in the detailed discussion of *canor*, the pinnacle of his mystical experience, in the second part of the work.

The Form of Living is not so much a response to a single (gendered) friendship, but a work that seeks to create friendship itself on the page. Even in the early, more didactic part of the work a friendly atmosphere pervades the instruction offered, so that later, when the text is structured as a dialogue, the effect of his careful drawing of readers to a close engagement with the text itself allows them to occupy a space in Rolle's own authorial company, to become, like Margaret, his friends and disciples in the contemplative life. As we shall see, manuscripts of *The Form of Living* show evidence of this when the names of other readers are inserted in place of Margaret's. Both the construc-

16 C. Walker Bynum, *Jesus as Mother*, 86. For further discussion of "the individual" in medieval thought Bynum refers readers to Colin Morris, *The Discovery of the Individual: 1050–1200* (New York, 1973) and John Benton, "Individualism and Conformity in Medieval Western Europe". *Individualism and Conformity in Classical Islam*. Ed. A. Banani and S. Vyronis, Jr. (Wiesbaden, 1977), 145–158.

tion of audience within the text and the later reception of the text reflect Vincent Gillespie's view that the release of a text by a medieval author did not necessarily mark the end of his/her involvement with it.[17]

II

Apart from the account given in the *Officium*, our knowledge of Rolle's historical relationship with Margaret Kirkeby is based entirely on the name Margaret appearing in manuscripts that contain Rolle's works. The most notable of all Rolle manuscripts, Longleat MS 29, repeats Margaret Kirkeby's full name and is said to preserve a copy of a collection of English writings made for her by Rolle himself, a presumption that rests on the belief that these works were bestowed upon her when he composed and presented her with the one work that bears her name, *The Form of Living*.[18] On this scant evidence, Margaret's relationship with Rolle and her implied reception of the whole Longleat collection have come to be used as an explanation of Rolle's composition of his vernacular works *in toto*. Margaret herself has even been considered as a key figure in the development of English spirituality and a significant personage in the history of English prose.[19] In many ways the friendship itself provides a plausible psychological profile of Rolle's desire to write in the vernacular, but that explanation does not take into account the potential for a wider audience. In both *Ego Dormio* and *The Commandment* Rolle constructs the reader as the individual soul. The construction both assumes and encourages a wider potential audience than the initial reader, which suggests that the composition of his vernacular works is more than a personal response to a single friendship. Therefore, the Longleat collection could be a copy of an autograph collection personally handed down or dedicated to Margaret by Rolle, but, equally importantly, the alternative function of compiling all Rolle's English works into one dedicatory volume may well have been to ensure further dissemination of his collected vernacular writings.

It is generally accepted that Rolle did write two works with Margaret specifically in mind, *The English Psalter* and *The Form of Living*. In modern crit-

---

[17] V. Gillespie, "Vernacular Books of Religion", 324. Of course, Gillespie also points out that "equally, once released, a text might be developed and changed beyond the author's control, without indication of non-authorial intervention in any one copy. Furthermore, regardless of the original intentions of authors (or compilers), or later editors, the manuscripts of most religious texts are likely to suggest a range of identifiably different uses to which each was put."

[18] N. Watson, *Invention of Authority*, 248.

[19] N. Watson, *Invention of Authority*, 242.

ical terms Margaret's relationship to Rolle has not been considered as specifically relevant to the *English Psalter* because it is thought to be only dedicatory
to her, and blatantly designed for a general audience.[20] Indeed, it is not Rolle
who asserts that the *English Psalter* was written for Margaret; instead, this information is supplied by the anonymous author of the metrical preface to this
work that appears in numerous manuscripts:

> Therefore a worthy holy man: cald Rychard Hampole,
> Whom the lord that all thing can: leryd lely on his scole,
> Glosed the sauter that sues here: in englysch tong sykerly,
> At a worthy recluse prayer: caled dame Merget kyrkby.[21]

The Form of Living, on the other hand, because of its familiar tone and address,
has been most widely recognised as an epistle to Margaret, a letter of friendship. As discussed in relation to *Ego Dormio*, letters of spiritual friendship
constituted an epistolary sub-genre in the Middle Ages.[22] But, like *Ego Dormio*,
The Form of Living is not a conventional epistle. Rolle does not respect the
formal constraints of epistolary exchange noted by Giles Constable, nor does
he even address his reader in terms of the genre; the expected formal salutation is absent from the beginning of the work and a specific addressee is not
mentioned until the end.[23] *The Cloud of Unknowing* and Hilton's *Scale of Perfection* are more typical of epistolary convention in that they address their audiences directly as "goostly freend in God" and "ghostly sister in Jhesu Christ"
respectively.[24] Rolle uses none of these conventions in *The Form of Living*. A
fictional, or for that matter real, sister or friend in God is not explicitly
addressed and Margaret is only mentioned as the intended recipient at the
very end of the work. The intimate nature of the work mainly develops an
implied friendship with the reader that is not purely reliant on either epistolary convention, or on any particular relationship Rolle had in his lifetime.

How then does Rolle's "real" relationship with Margaret impact on the

---

20 Critical appreciation of Rolle's *English Psalter* is at present hampered by the lack of a
definitive edition of the work that adequately separates Rolle's own words from the
extensive Lollard interpolations that occur in many of the manuscripts. H. R.
Bramley's edition does not differentiate between Lollard interpolated manuscripts
and genuine copies of Rolle's original.

21 *English Psalter*, 1.

22 E. L. Conner, " 'Goostly freend in God': Aelred of Rievaulx's *De Spirituali Amicitia* as
a Source for *The Cloud of Unknowing*". *Vox Mystica: Essays for Valerie M. Lagorio*. Eds.
Anne Clark Bartlett, Thomas H. Bestul, Janet Goebel and William F. Pollard (Cambridge, 1995), 135.

23 See C. H. Haskins, *Studies in Mediaeval Culture* cited in G. Constable, *Letters and Letter
Collections*. 16–17.

24 J. A. Burrow describes the *Cloud*-author's singular address as "not merely a token
dedication" but one that consciously reflects epistolary convention. See J. A. Burrow,
*Medieval Writers and Their Work: Middle English Literature and Its Background
1100–1500* (Oxford, 1982), 51.

reader/writer friendship offered in *The Form of Living*? The longing for a spiritual companion Rolle mentions in *Incendium Amoris*, described by Watson as his desire to find a woman to play Clare to his Francis, appears to be fulfilled by Margaret's presence later in his life.[25] But it is not Rolle who tells us that this longing is fulfilled by Margaret. Instead, the *Officium* is the only work that provides us with any information regarding Rolle's "known love for Margaret and his miraculous effect on her person"; the eighth Lesson reads:

Cum itaque sanctus iste ex causis necessariis et multum utilibus se ad morandum in Comitatu Richmundie transtulisset contigit dominam Margaretam olim reclusam apud Anderby ebor. dioces. in ipsa die cene domini graui nimis passione infirmitatis urgeri. ita ut per tredecim dies continuos pentitus priuaretur potestate loquendi. Et propter hoc tot sustinuit cruciatus et puncturas in corpore quod nullicubi ualebat consistere. Quidam igitur paterfamilias eiusdem uille sciens sanctum eremitam ricardum eam perfecta caritatis affeccione diligere: utpote qui ipsam de arte amoris dei consueuit instruere: et in modo uiuendi sua sancta institucione dirigere: ad ipsum qui per duodecim miliaria ab habitacione recluse: tunc temporis morabatur: celeriter properauit in equo. rogans quod ad eam festinanter accederet. et sibi consolacionem in tanta necessitate prestaret. Ueniens itaque ad reclusam inuenit eam mutam. et uexacionibus acerimis perturbatum: Cumque resideret ad fenestram domus eiusdem recluse et simul commederent. contigit ut completo prandio. reclusa desideraret dormire: Opressa itaque sompno capud suum decidit. ad fenestram ad quam se reclinauit sanctus dei ricardus et sic cum modicum dormiuisset. appodiando se aliqualiter super ipsum ricardum. subito cum impetu uehementi: apprehendit eam in ipso sompno tam grauis uexacio ut uideretur uelle uiolenter fenestram domus sue dirimere et in ipsa uexacione tam forti euigilauit de sompno: et cum magna deuocione potestate loquendi sibi concessa in hec uerba prorupit. *Gloria tibi domine.* et beatus ricardus uersam inceptum compleuit dicens *qui natus est de virgine* etc que secuntur.

[When therefore, this holy man, for urgent and most practical reasons had betaken himself to dwell in Richmondshire, it befell that the lady Margaret, who had once been a recluse at Ainderby in the diocese of York, on the very day of the Lord's Supper [Holy Thursday] was so overcome by a grave attack of illness that for thirteen days she was utterly deprived of the power of speech. Moreover, it caused her such pains and prickings in her body that she should not rest in any position. Now a certain good man of that town, knowing that the holy hermit Richard loved her with the perfect affection of charity – since he was wont to instruct her in the art of loving God, and to direct her, by his holy teaching, how to order her life – quickly hastened on horseback to the hermit, who was then living twelve miles from the dwelling of the recluse, and besought him to come to her with all speed and bring her consolation in her great need. And when he came to the recluse he found

---

[25] N. Watson, *Invention of Authority*, n. 2, 327.

her unable to speak and troubled with very grievous pains. And as he sat by the window of her dwelling and they were eating together, it befell at the end of the meal that the recluse desired to sleep, she drooped her head at the window where Richard the Saint of God reclined; and after she had slept thus for a short time, leaning slightly upon Richard, suddenly a violent convulsion seized her in her sleep with fearful vehemence, so that it seemed as if she wished to break the window of her house. And being still in this most terrible convulsion, she awoke from sleep, and the power of speech being granted her with great devotion she burst forth with these words: "Gloria tibi Domine", and blessed Richard finished the verse which she had begun, saying: "Qui natus es de Virgine", with the rest which follows in the compline hymn.][26]

The compilers of the *Officium* seem determined to acknowledge Rolle's and Margaret's close bond of love. In turn, the story itself expresses two key points regarding the assumed relationship of Rolle and his disciple: that he "eam perfecta caritatis affeccione diligere" [loved her with the perfect affection of charity] and that "utpote qui ipsam de arte amoris dei consueuit instruere" [he was wont to instruct her in the art of loving God]. *The Form of Living* itself fulfils both these criteria; it is both an instructional work and one that implies friendship between the author and the reader. Rather than relying on the *Officium* to explain the composition of *The Form of Living*, we might well suspect that the *Officium* narrative has been constructed by means of reference to the earlier text. Hence, it is easy to see how the work has been labelled as a letter *for* Margaret herself, even though she is not directly addressed in the work until the very end. In fact, *The Form of Living*'s construction of audience is not confined to the requirements of a letter of personal friendship. It is a more generic treatise that seeks to guide the reader towards an understanding of the contemplative life through a discourse of Christian friendship. Beyond the biographical speculation, *The Form of Living* principally arises out of a long tradition of medieval texts of spiritual *amicitia*.

The concept of spiritual or chaste friendship that could exist between men and women who had devoted their lives to God preoccupied much medieval religious literature. In the Middle Ages the expression "spiritual friendship" appears to have described the profound affective relationship that could exist between persons through their true emotional union with the divine beloved, their mutual desire for God. Such affection could be called Platonic not only in the modern colloquial sense of the term which uses it to mean non-sexual but also in the sense of deep union Plato described in the *Symposium*.[27] The origins of the concept of chaste, Christian friendship lies in the ideals of pre-Christian writers, and medieval works often show the influence of classical writers such

---

[26] *Officium et Miracula*, 39–40; *The Life of Richard Rolle*, 306–308.
[27] R. Mazo Karras, "Friendship and Love in the Lives of Two Twelfth-Century English Saints", *Journal of Medieval History* 14 (1988), 306.

as Aristotle, Cicero, and Seneca.[28] Aristocratic, Aristotelean-Ciceronian *amicitia vera*, which included the fundamental qualities of virtue, wisdom, and beneficence, was frequently viewed with suspicion in monasteries up to the eleventh century because of its emphasis on individual relationships.[29] Monastic tradition relied instead on the ideal of Christian brotherhood based on the promise Christ made in Matthew 18:20: "Ubi enim sunt duo vel tres congregati in nomine meo, ibi sum in medio eorum" [For where there be two or three gathered in my name, there am I in the midst of them].[30] The primary influence of this ideal lay in the writings of the Apostle Paul where there is much greater emphasis on group solidarity than on individual bonds, the one true friendship being reserved for Christ himself.

For this reason, early Christian writers generally discussed spiritual friendship in terms of the monastic experience, where the collective love of all mankind, *caritas*, was considered superior to singular emotional love, *amor*. Individual relationships between monks or nuns were discouraged because they might disrupt the harmonious concord of the monastery.[31] Individual friendships up until the mid-eleventh century can be understood solely in terms of their integration into community life, which took its textual ideal from the description of the first Christian community's shared heart, spirit, and possessions in Acts 4:32:[32]

> Multitudinis autem credentium erat cor unam, et anima una: nec quisquam eorum quae possidebat aliquid suum esse dicebat, sed erant illis omnia communia.

[28] R. Hyatte, *The Arts of Friendship: The Idealisation of Friendship in Medieval and Early Renaissance Literature* (Leiden, 1994), 48. Christian writers frequently quote in their discussions of Christian *amicitia* Aristotle's *Nichomachean Ethics*, Cicero's *Laelius* and *De officiis*, and Seneca's letters. For example, Aelred of Rievaulx adapts Cicero's *amicitia perfecta*, which aspires to practical goodness and wisdom, to Christian love in his treatise *De spirituali amicitia*, and he is most careful to point out the spiritual shortcomings and limits of truth in his classical source.

[29] Brian P. McGuire, *Friendship and Community: The Monastic Experience 350–1250* (Kalamazoo, 1988), xxix–xl. McGuire argues that the revived interest in ancient models of friendship after the mid-eleventh century "can and must be linked with the new schools and their interest in classical texts". For a brief delineation of McGuire's thought see R. Hyatte, *The Arts of Friendship*, 45–50.

[30] See B. P. McGuire, *Friendship and Community*, xxvii–xxviii.

[31] R. Mazo Karras, "Friendship and Love in the Lives of Two Twelfth-Century English Saints", 308. Karras notes that though Ambrose and Jerome both stressed the intimacy and self-revelation of friendship, they were concerned that such intimacy could detract from the common life of monks. Cassian and Basil are also noted as considering intimacy between individual monks as dangerous to the overall harmony of the monastery.

[32] B. P. McGuire cited in R. Hyatte, *The Arts of Friendship*, 45–46. See B. P. McGuire, *Friendship and Community*, xxvii.

[And the multitude of believers had one heart and one soul: and neither did anyone say that ought was his own of those things which he possessed, but all things were common unto them.]

Jean Leclercq observes that for Augustine the City of God is an ideal of a universal *societas amicalis*, or friendly society, where all are united by Christian charity, of which friendship is the active expression.[33] This monastic ideal allowed individual relationships only within the constraints of what Reginald Hyatte refers to as the double bond between God and the person and between persons brought together in God's love. From this we can only assume that the monastic ideal of early Christian writers left little room for particular friendships, whether they were same-sex or otherwise.[34]

From around the mid-eleventh to the early twelfth century an epistolary tradition emerged in which the concept of close friendship found new ground. Individual monks, often of Benedictine or Cistercian houses, corresponded with each other using what has been described as a language of spiritual friendship.[35] Peter the Venerable, the abbot of Cluny, developed close friendships with both Benedictine and Cistercian monks and even corresponded with Bernard of Clairvaux in a warm and affectionate manner that suggested friendship between the two.[36] The Cistercian abbot Aelred of Rievaulx maintained a number of close friendships throughout his monastic life and wrote two significant works on the subject of friendship itself, *De spirituali amicitia* (an adaptation and elaboration of Cicero's *De amicitia*) and *Speculum caritatis*.[37] In the first of these works he discusses real, personal relationships of his

---

33 J. Leclercq, "L'amitié dans les lettres âu Moyen Age". *Revue du Moyen Age latin* 1 (1945), 401 cited in R. Hyatte, *The Arts of Friendship*, 45.

34 R. Hyatte, *The Arts of Friendship*, 45–46. Hyatte again cites McGuire who notes that Pachomius (c. 290–346) taught the equal love of monastic brothers for one another while he strongly discouraged close friendships among them. Early in the piece, Christian writers converted Cicero's *amicitia perfecta*: writing on the duties of friends in the Christian community, Ambrose (c. 334–397), who considered Christ and his father as model friends, replaced Cicero's Roman *amici veri* with Biblical examples in the concluding chapter of his *De officiis ministrorum*. For Augustine (354–430), who personally placed high value on particular friendships, there is only one sort of *vera amicitia*, of which the source is God, who reaches out through the Holy Spirit to offer humans charity and grace.

35 On the importance of friendship in the epistolary exchange of monks in the twelfth century see Jean Leclercq, *The Love of Learning and the Desire for God*. Trans. C. Misrahi (New York, 1982), esp. 180–182.

36 B. P. McGuire, *Friendship and Community*, 251–255.

37 For an extensive overview of Aelred of Rievaulx's writings on spiritual *amicitia* see the doctoral dissertation by K. Long, "Echoes of Friendship: 'Amicitia' and 'Affectus' in the Writings of Aelred of Rievaulx with Special Reference to his Minor Works and the Monastic Foundations of his Theory" (University of Western Australia, 1993).

own.[38] From these writings we can ascertain that from within the monastic ideal of friendship, particular relationships did arise.

The revival of friendship in the monasteries included mixed-sex relationships where nuns and monks, sometimes of double-monasteries, maintained chaste, personal friendships.[39] A collection of letters from Worms in the eleventh century includes a striking letter of friendship from the Bishop of Worms to an apparently powerful superior of a woman's monastery in which he defends spiritual love among men and women.[40] Hyatte explains that chaste, mixed-sex friendships were permissible in theory because gender is, in principle, relatively unimportant in Christian *amicitia* as long as the partners are chaste; and because women on the path to heavenly glory reject the traditional household and marriage dominated by males, they operate, in practice, outside the social context assumed in classical *amicitia*.[41] In theory at least, the Christian context affords women equal footing with men in sublime friendship. As the "in theory" suggests, mixed-sex friendships were not completely discredited but they were often viewed with suspicion because of the fear of the temptation of carnal relations. Bartlett suggests that well-documented events in the twelfth century such as the English nun of Watton's pregnancy by a young monk, a case investigated by Aelred of Rievaulx, and the scandalous relationship of Abelard and Héloise, testify to the difficulties faced by female and male friends in a celibate and often deeply anti-feminist religious culture.[42] The twelfth-century biography of the English recluse Christina of Markyate, written by an anonymous monk of St. Albans, notes Christina's personal struggle with carnal lust in her friendships with men:

> Et certe in inicio nullum cogitaverunt ad invicem: nisi castum et spiritualem amorem. Sed hoc diu non patiens diabolus castitatis inimicus de ipsorum securitate et domestica conversacione nactus oportunitatem. latenter prius surrepsit et callide. et post paulo heu fortiter illos aggressus est impugnare. Et ignita iacula mittens tanta virtute institit. quod viri fortitudinem penitus

---

38 On Aelred's recollections of personal friends see Aelred of Rievaulx, *Spiritual Friendship*. Trans. M. E. Laker (Kalamazoo, 1974), 126, 3: 119.

39 Michael Sargent has shown that this is certainly true of the Carthusian houses of Syon and Sheen, where devotional literature travelled from one house to another across the Thames River regularly. See M. G. Sargent, "The Transmission by the English Carthusians of Some Late Medieval Spiritual Writings", *Journal of Ecclesiastical History* 27 (1976), 228.

40 B. P. McGuire, *Friendship and Community*, 188. The letter is reproduced in Walther Bulst, ed. *Die ältere Wormser Briefsammlung* (Weimar, 1949).

41 R. Hyatte, *The Arts of Friendship*, 51.

42 A. Clark Bartlett, " 'A Reasonable Affection' ", 135. For the nun of Watton incident see Giles Constable, "Aelred of Rievaulx and the Nun of Watton", *Medieval Women*. Ed. Derek Baker (Oxford, 1978), 205–226. On the relationship between the twelfth-century lovers Abelard and Héloise see Betty Radice, ed. *The Letters of Abelard and Héloise* (Harmondsworth, 1974) esp. Abelard's account of his personal downfall entitled "Historia calamitatum", 57–106.

expugnavit . . . Violenter respuebat desideria sue carnis. ne propria membra exhiberet adversum se arma iniquitatis.

[And certainly at the beginning they had no feelings about each other, except chaste and spiritual affection. But the devil, the enemy of chastity, not brooking this for long, took advantage of their close companionship and feeling of security to insinuate himself stealthily and with guile, then later on, alas, to assault them more openly. And, loosing his fiery darts, he pressed his attacks so vigorously that he completely overcame the man's resistance . . . She violently resisted the desires of her flesh, lest her own members should become the agents of wickedness against her.][43]

Despite the evils of sexual temptation, Christina's earthly and spiritual life was dominated by a number of chaste friendships with male religious, supporting the idea that male/female friendships based on a mutual love for God did exist. Ruth Mazo Karras, who compares the language of friendship in Christina's hagiographical *vita* to Aelred of Rievaulx's writings on the subject, suggests that for twelfth-century religious the vow of chastity did not mean renouncing a rich affective life.[44] She argues that the language used by Aelred, and by Christina's biographer, suggests that both participated in mixed-sex relationships based on a type of emotional love outside the accepted norm of monastic *caritas*. But these intimate friendships were as chaste as they were passionate. Both Aelred and Christina may have influenced Rolle's concept of spiritual friendship; both lived in Yorkshire, as did Rolle a century later, and he may have had access to Aelred's writings and Christina's *vita*. Rolle certainly appears to be familiar with Aelred's ideas on friendship[45] and a story from Christina's *vita* shows marked similarities to one of Rolle's own experiences recounted in *Super Canticum Canticorum*.

Despite the fact that twelfth-century religious culture tolerated, at least in theory, chaste spiritual relationships, late medieval English monastic houses were deeply concerned by mixed-sex friendship and attempted in various ways to regulate contact (innocent or otherwise) between the sexes.[46] This policy of sexual segregation leads Sharon Elkins to contend that, in England, spiritual friendships between female and male religious declined after the end of the expansion of women's monasticism at the end of the twelfth century.[47]

---

43 C. H. Talbot, ed. and trans. *The Life of Christina of Markyate: A Twelfth-Century Recluse* (Oxford, 1959), 114/115.

44 R. Mazo Karras, "Friendship and Love in the Lives of Two Twelfth-Century English Saints", 305.

45 On the possible influence of Aelred's writings on Rolle see M. Moyes, *Richard Rolle's Expositio*, I, 56–68.

46 A. Clark Bartlett, " 'A Reasonable Affection' ", 133. Bartlett provides a comprehensive list of works that discuss relations between medieval English nuns and monks in her notes.

47 For a detailed discussion of female monasticism in twelfth-century England see S. Elkins, *Holy Women of Twelfth-Century England* (London, 1988), 105–161.

But the ideal itself appears to have lived on because the concept of spiritual friendship still had deeply rooted significance for religious writers in the fourteenth century. In fact, close relationships between male and female religious were apparently not uncommon in the late Middle Ages and many authors of Middle English devotional works drew on biblical, patristic, and hagiographic models to praise chaste friendships between women and men, both lay and religious.[48] Bartlett argues that a number of English hagiographical texts openly reject misogynistic fears of friendship between men and women, both by depicting mixed-sex spiritual friendships and by revising their earlier medieval sources to omit warnings against such mixed-sex relationships.[49] The Middle English lives of Christina Mirabilis, Marie d'Oignies, and Elizabeth of Spalbeck found in Bodleian Library, Douce MS 114 represent their subjects as members of a circle of chaste female and male friends. The ideal of friendship in the name of God, or more precisely friendship *in* God, was also prominent throughout continental Europe in the fourteenth century. Henry Suso, a contemporary of Rolle, headed a group of devotees known as the "gottesfriund", the Friends of God, and, like Rolle, Suso is known to have had a specific friendship with a woman, Elspeth Stagel, who entered a convent in the mid-1330s, and who is said to have influenced his devotional writings.[50] From this we might conclude that concepts of *amica Dei* and spiritual *amicitia* had a strong association with devotional and instructional religious writing in this period.

To what extent, then, did the ideals of friendship influence the development of Rolle's thought on the subject before he wrote *The Form of Living*? He openly considers the concept of friendship on a number of occasions in his Latin works. As noted above, in *Incendium Amoris* Rolle longs for a spiritual companion with whom to share his mystical journey, but laments that "uix aut raro inuenitur fidus amicus" [a true friend is seldom or scarcely ever found].[51] He goes on to speak of mixed-sex relationships where men and women see each other freely as putting the "fragilem animam" [weak soul] at risk of succumbing to the "uisa temptacio" [visual temptation] of carnal lust. However, he then implies that although friendship may indeed be difficult to

---

[48] A. Clark Bartlett, " 'A Reasonable Affection' ", 135–136. Bartlett argues that although we might expect late medieval English devotional literature for women to accept and repeat restrictions and suspicions regarding mixed-sex activity, many of the texts for women readers written and compiled in the late fourteenth, fifteenth and sixteenth centuries reject the ideal of sexual segregation implicitly or explicitly, and promote, though with some ambivalence, spiritual friendship between cloistered women and men.

[49] A. Clark Bartlett, *Male Authors, Female Readers*, 107.

[50] See the introduction to F. Tobin, ed. *Henry Suso: The Exemplar with Two German Sermons* (New York, 1989).

[51] *Incendium Amoris*, 263; *The Fire of Love*, 175. See also N. Watson, *Invention of Authority*, 224.

find and is often motivated by self-interest only, the possibility of spiritual friendship between men and women is not out of the question:

> Sicque familiaritas mulierum uiris in detrimentum uirtutis accidere solet. Non tamen est illicita illa amicicia, immo meritoria, si bono animo agatur, et pro Deo diligitur, non pro carnis suauitate.

> [Familiarity between men and women is apt to turn to virtue's disadvantage. And yet that sort of friendship is not improper, but rewarding, if it is practiced with a good intention, and is loved for God's sake, and not for carnal delectation.][52]

The position Rolle adopts here is ambiguous. On one hand his stance is firmly situated in the anti-feminist monastic tradition that distrusts mixed-sex friendship on sexual grounds. On the other hand, he states that mixed-sex friendships are possible. Furthermore, in *Melos Amoris* he intimates that he himself is able to act as a spiritual guide (friend) to women because he has a special gift which shields him from concupiscence:

> Non accipe exemplum ex hoc quod narravi, nescisti namque quod dedit michi Deus: eiecit me in ignem et exuri non permisit.[53]

> [Do not take an example from this story I have told; for you don't know what God gave me: he threw me out into the fire and has not let me be consumed.]

Yet he goes on to warn that actual friendship with women is ultimately delusive:

> Ecce, o homo qui amori anhelas, si videre desideras vim dileccionis quam flagrans sit cum fuerit in corde concepta, noli nodari in amaro amore, experiri non audas mundi dilectam. Nam inde torqueberis dirissimo dolore, tenebisque tristiciam, letus non eris cum mentem involverit viciosa voluptas femine formose, et ignis impiissimus gravedoque grandescens tuum cor corruptum ex consueto consument.[54]

> [Behold, O man that gapes after love, if you long to see the power of pleasure, how it rages once it has been conceived in the heart, refuse to be entwined in bitter love, do not dare to try out worldly pleasures. For if you do you will be tortured with terrible agony, you will have sorrow in your grasp, you will not be happy when the wicked pleasure of a shapely woman snares your mind, and a most impious fire and increasing depression consume your heart, perverted away from its accustomed habits.]

---

[52] *Incendium Amoris*, 263; *The Fire of Love*, 175.
[53] *Melos Amoris*, 133/26–28.
[54] *Melos Amoris*, 135/35–136/5.

This last passage could suggest the influence of Bernard who argues in his *Sermones in cantica* that "it is easier to raise the dead than to be alone with a woman and not to have sex".[55] Yet, when we compare it to the other passages his position on the matter becomes difficult to ascertain. As Watson suggests, Rolle's Latin utterances regarding friendship with women exhibit a kind of verbal shuffling of feet, a peculiar sense of authorial awkwardness.[56] But in *The Form of Living* he is neither ambiguous nor irresolute on the subject of spiritual *amicitia*. In fact, he does not actually discuss friendship at all, with women or men. Although the friendship with Margaret, as described in the *Officium*, does reflect the ideal of spiritual *amicitia* outlined above, the discourse of friendship developed in *The Form of Living*, to promote the contemplative life and incite the reader to love God, does not specifically represent traditional notions of mixed-sex friendship at all. Instead, Rolle follows the logic of collective spiritual *amicitia* by creating a subjective space for any reader to occupy without interposing any given friendship of his own. In the context of this type of implied friendship, Margaret's name, appearing as it does at the very end of the work, can be read as both an initial dedication and as a constructed subject position that subsequent (implied) readers are invited to appropriate for themselves.

Challenging the myth of Rolle's writerly intent brings us to his construction of the implied reader in *The Form of Living*, and his subtle appropriation of certain authorial roles. Throughout the work Rolle constructs the reader as a variety of addressees in order to fulfill the affective purpose of drawing the reader, as his friend and disciple, into his own world – the contemplative life. He does so through hints that imply that friendship with him will provide a bridge to friendship with God. In this he may well have been influenced by Aelred who relies on biblical authority to endorse spiritual friendship as a preparation for *amicitia Dei* itself:

> Friendship is a stage bordering upon that perfection which consists in the love and knowledge of God, so that man from being a friend of his fellow man becomes the friend of God, according to the words of the Saviour in the Gospel: "I will not now call you servants, but my friends."[57]

Even though Rolle does not actually discuss friendship itself in *The Form of Living*, and his reliance on authorities to sanction the discourse of friendship he develops in this work is scant, Aelred's definition of friendship could well be considered as a blueprint for the relationships Rolle constructs throughout

---

55 Bernard of Clairvaux, *Patrologia Latina* 183: 1091 cited in A. Clark Bartlett, *Male Authors, Female Readers*, 89. Bartlett is quick to point out that this remark by Bernard tells us more about medieval misogynistic conventions (or perhaps about Bernard himself) than about medieval gender relations.

56 N. Watson, *Invention of Authority*, 225.

57 Aelred of Rievaulx, *Spiritual Friendship*, 2/14. Here Aelred quotes from John 15:15.

this work. The sinful servant of the first part of the work is purged through spiritual growth in the acceptance of the contemplative life finally emerging as the friend. How Rolle opens his work to each and every reader as both the servant and the friend is the key to understanding the constitution of this text.

III

Initially it is the fluctuating manner of address employed throughout *The Form of Living* that alerts us to the idea that a wider audience may have been envisaged for this text at the time of composition. The opening words appear to encompass all Christians because "euery synful man and womman" (3/1) is addressed. At the end of the opening passage the explicit appeal to "euen-Christians" is affirmed by the inclusion of a warning to all sinners in apocalyptic terms: "Al creatures shal ben stirred in to his vengeance in þe day of dome" (3/17). Even though the work is ostensibly directed to one who is about to enter the exceptional vocation of the solitary life, more general subjects such as sin, the wiles of the devil, and "þe occupaciouns and bisynes of worldly thynges" that plague most people (9/269) are all addressed as important aspects of the spiritual journey. From the beginning the reader is made aware that far from being a work of narrow address, *The Form of Living* is a text that will address its reader in terms of the full gamut of human frailty.

Rolle does not simply dismiss "wordly thynges"; the outside world is never obscured from view, or deemed unworthy of comment in this work. Instead, Rolle acknowledges a range of potential failings in his reader by adopting a variety of relationships towards his supposed disciple. In the first part of the text, when he is treating the subject of diabolic temptation, Rolle directs the reader's attention to the rest of the world as an example by which he/she should learn:

> Thou hast herd nowe a partie how þe deuyl deceyueth with his sutil craftes vnstable and vnwise men and wommen. And if þou wilt do good consaille and folowe holy lernynge as I hope thou wolt, þou shalt destroy his trappes, and brand in þe fire of loue al þe bondes þat he wol bynd þe with.
>
> (5/105–109)

Shortly after this Rolle represents himself and the reader standing, as it were, together in a mutual understanding of the joys of solitary life against the misunderstanding of the rest of the world:

> Men weneth þat we haue peyn and penaunce, bot we haue more ioy and verrey delite in oon day þan þei haue in þe world al har lyfe. (6/130–132)

Yet later in the work Rolle chooses to distance himself from the reader:

Men þat comen to þe, praise þe, for þei see þi gret abstinence, and for þay se þe enclosed. Bot I may nat praise þe so lightly, for oght þat I se þe do withouten, bot if þi wil be confourmed entierly to Goddis wille.

(14/460–463)

The distancing is here in contradistinction to the "men" of the outside world who this time will praise the reader, but in their usual misunderstanding fashion, whereas Rolle himself will only praise the reader for his/her true conformity to Christ. Furthermore, in each of these statements there is an implied message to those in the rest of the world who, though often presented only as onlookers or bad examples, may still read the work and presumably learn from it. Familiarity with the reader is hinted at here because in distancing the "men", Rolle creates a triangling effect that entices the reader to join with him against them. The effect is a subtle invitation to the reader to come closer, participate in what is written, and enjoy the praise proffered by the authorial Rolle. As such, it may also entice those who feel themselves distanced, as non-contemplatives, to approach that life.

Rolle's changeable relationship with the reader is part of the collegiality that permeates the work as a whole. Throughout the first part of the work his utterance cleverly fluctuates between the personal and the impersonal, developing a history of discussion between the writer and the reader. In the early part of the work the general address on the "þre wrechednesse" that supposedly encompasses "euery synful man and womman" (3/1) immediately takes the form of Rolle's own utterance: "These wrechednesse þat *I* of told" (emphasis mine). Similarly, his impersonal assessment of "sum men", those who are taken in by the devil (3/29–54), develops into a collegial discussion: "we begynneth for to haat wrechednesse" (4/54–86). His observations on how the devil deceives "vnstable and vnwise men and wommen" (5/106–110) are detached, but are nonetheless coupled with his confidence in the reader – "if þou wilt do good counsail and folowe holy lernynge as I hope thou wolt" – for the course of the reader's spiritual direction. The authorial concern may well be considered as distant here, a pedagogical tool, but the image of the bonds of the devil being burnt in the fire of love is a powerful and emotive one. In turn, the use of the verb hope here draws the reader into a confidential relationship of trust with the writer. In what is supposedly the laborious, didactic part of the work, Rolle's expectation, his desire, for his reader to experience violent joy is a noteworthy development in the discourse of friendship.

That a friendly relationship is being offered in the first part of the work is particularly apparent when Rolle is discussing the solitary life. As the passage quoted above, beginning "Men weneth . . ." (6/130–132), suggests Rolle seeks to promote the solitary life in *The Form of Living*, by encouraging the reader to join him in his own vocation. His focus on the negative aspects of living in solitude, "peyn" and "penaunce", might be construed as an odd form of exhortation, but Robert Boenig argues that Rolle, who generally leans toward positive mysticism, shows the occasional influence of Pseudo-Dionysian language theory in *The Form of Living* by engaging in what appears to be a favoured activity of English mystics, simultaneously affirming and denying the valency of words.[58] Boenig notes that Rolle uses the words *pain* and *penance* deliberately as words whose meaning is affirmed in one direction only: recluses often live a life of harsh ascetic practices. But the words are denied in another direction, that of the mystic's approach to God, for they then become joy and delight.[59] The affirmation/denial construct is utilised to suggest a secure psychological profile for the recluse: those on the outside looking in may find only pain and suffering, whilst those on the inside find only joy:

> Thei seen our body, bot þei seth nat oure herte wher our solace is. If þei saw þat, many of ham wold forsake al þat þei haue for to folow vs. (6/132–134)

He further enhances the image of the vocation by referring to the exalted position solitude enjoys in the Christian religion:

> The state þat þou art in, þat is solitude, þat is most able of al othre to reuelaciouns of þe Holy Goste. (6/138–139)

He goes on to cite a number of examples, calling on the biblical image of John on the Isle of Patmos who had a vision of God's "pryuetees" (Rev. 1:9) through the solitary nature of his existence (6/139–140).

Rolle's choice of John to elaborate his point here performs a dual role. John provides the reader with both an example of the perfect solitary and an accepted image of *amicitia Dei*. Medieval readers would have been well aware of the tradition that John was a close friend to Christ. In his dialogue with the Jews, John (John 3:29) states that he is not Christ but has been sent before him, describing his role as "amicus autem sponsi" [the friend of the bridegroom]. In the Gospels John (John 13:23) defines himself as the one whom Christ loved – "Erat ergo recumbens unus ex discipulis eius in sinu Iesu, quem diligebat Iesus" [There was therefore one of his disciples leaning on the bosom of Jesus, he whom Jesus loved]. Traditionally, John's vision of the Apocalypse occurs at the very moment he lays his head on Christ's bosom thus elevating the importance of the close bond of friendship in Christian religion. At the end of Book One of *De spirituali amicitia* Aelred labours the point of John's close bond with Christ and even has him describe charity itself as friendship, instead of the traditional definition, love:

---

58 R. Boenig, *Chaucer and the Mystics: The Canterbury Tales and the Genre of Devotional Prose* (Lewisburg, 1995), 24.
59 R. Boenig, *Chaucer and the Mystics*, 24.

Ivo. Shall I say of friendship what John, the friend of Jesus, says of charity: "God is friendship"?
Aelred. That would be unusual, to be sure, nor does it have the sanction of the Scriptures. But still what is true of charity, I surely do not hesitate to grant to friendship, since, "he that abides in friendship, abides in God, and God in him".[60]

An early fifteenth-century English carol, that derives from an earlier Latin tradition, explicitly celebrates John's friendship with Christ, as well as his purity, as permitting him the vision of heaven:

> To thee now, Christes dere derling,
> That were a maiden bothe eld and ying,
> Mine herte is set to thee to sing,
> Amice Christi, Johannes.
> For thou were so clene a may
> The prevites of Hevene forsothe thou say
> Whan on Christes brest thou lay,
> Amice Christi, Johannes.[61]

By proposing John as a model in *The Form of Living*, Rolle is elevating the status of the reader in that he/she is offered an opportunity to join in the company of Rolle and John, ostensibly involving the reader in a celebrated community of solitaries, friends of God. The implied message here, that includes Christ's known love for the solitary John, perhaps influenced by Aelred's subtle reconstruction of "God is love" for "God is friendship", serves to develop the discourse of friendship in *The Form of Living*. The image of John, lying close to Christ's heart, valorises and defines the type of friendship Rolle expounds in *The Form of Living* – not a fleshly friendship, but one of the heart. In turn, John's vision of Revelation, granted to the friend who is close to Christ's heart, links friendship with both visionary experience and love.

Quick to balance the work, Rolle immediately stresses that solitude is as much about physical and mental endurance as it is about a state of spiritual being by asserting that:

> No man cometh to such reuelaciouns and grace þe first day, bot þrogh longe trauaille and bisynesse to loue Ihesu Criste, as þou shalt hire aftreward. (6/148–149)

Trials are a condition of perfection, Rolle warns, and "þe greuouser þei stonden agayne and ouercomen, þe moor shal har ioye be in his loue whan þei ben passed" (7/152–154). In this sense Rolle could be seen as aggrandising his

---

60 Aelred of Rievaulx, *Spiritual Friendship*, 1/69–70. Here Aelred quotes from 1 John 4:16. For further discussion of this passage see K. Long, *Echoes of Friendship*, 191–193.
61 R. T. Davies, *Medieval English Lyrics*, Poem 68, 157.

own spiritual achievement, because it is repeatedly implied that he has already overcome such obstacles, but his English writings generally demonstrate that encouragement, rather than self-promotion, is his primary goal.

In *The Form of Living* Rolle never credits himself or his own good works for his extraordinary sensations, but maintains they are a gift from God: "for þat may no man deserue, bot only hit is gyfen of Goddis godenes to ham þat verrayli yeueth ham to contemplacioun and to quyet for Cristes loue" (24/846–848). Similarly, he never claims to be unique in his experience; on the contrary, he says that all who devote themselves to the contemplative life can experience the joy he has experienced in one way or another. When he considers the fourth question on love in *The Form of Living*, "how þou myght knowe þat þou ware in loue and charite?", he maintains that God grants such gifts to those who enter the contemplative life as a sign that they are succeeding in their quest and are indeed living in "loue and charite": ". . . no man wot in erth þat þai ben in charite, bot if it be þrogh any priuelege or special grace þat God hath geven to any man or womman, þat al oþer may nat take ensample bi" (22/774–776). In other words, God gives the believer, "any man or womman", a sign designed especially for him or her (just as Rolle received his gifts of *calor, dulcor,* and *canor*) to let the believer know that he or she is in charity and thereby at peace in his or her own spiritual journey. In *The Form of Living* Rolle constructs an authorial persona who is able to invite the reader to embrace the solitary life. The subtext of this invitation is a self-reflexive one; Rolle is suggesting that while he can encourage self-knowledge and self-assessment in readers, they must accept the solitary life in their own terms as a means of establishing personal contact with the divine.

To draw the reader towards an acceptance of the solitary life, Rolle again amplifies the negative aspects of solitude in order then to endorse the vocation. He warns that the devil actively "tempteth men and wommen þat ben solitarie, bi ham on" (7/161) because, being alone, they are vulnerable to his suggestion. To amplify the point, he invites the reader to identify with the example of a recluse "that was a good womman" who is tempted by a vision of the devil in the guise of a good angel but whom she proves to be a false image after taking the advice of her "shrift-fadyre" and calling "Aue Maria", causing the apparition to disappear. Rolle claims that he relays the story from a single textual source, "as I fynd of a recluse written" (7/166) but the passage itself bears close resemblance to a passage from Cassian's *Collations*, and the idea of Satan changing himself into an angel of light comes from 2 Corinthians 11:14 ("ipse enim Satanas transfigurat se in angelum lucis"), which is exactly how it appears in *Collations*.[62] In *The Form of Living*, as in Cassian, the devil transfigures himself into an angel of light "and so he deceyueth foles. Bot ham þat ben wise, and wol nat anoon trow to al spirites, bot asketh consaille of

---

[62] See Cassian, *Patrologia Latina*, 49: 1025.

conynge men, he may nat begile ham" (7/164–166). On the surface, the reader/writer relationship here is reminiscent of the teacher/pupil arrangement found in *The Commandment*. Rolle clearly identifies his authorial self with the confessor ("a wise man and quaynt") whilst the reader is expected to assume the role of the taker of counsel ("a good womman"). But the implicit message is one of friendship as well as advice. The recluse is overjoyed to see the good angel but "neuerþelatre" calls on her confessor to endorse her vision. This suggests that an understanding, a friendship, exists between the recluse and her confessor which is confirmed as a good and true relationship when the vision is proven to be false. The implied text invites the reader to engage in such a friendship with Rolle if ever the need should arise:

> This I sei, nat for I hoop þat he shal haue leue to tempt þe in þis maner, bot I wol þat þou be warre, if any such temptacioun befalle þe, slepynge or wakynge, that þou trow nat ouer sone til þou knowe þe soth. (7/178–181)

Friendship in God is implied because the qualities of each character, the wisdom of the "quaynt" adviser (Rolle), and the goodness of the recluse (the reader), are God-given. In a strikingly similar example to the one above, the biographer of Christina of Markyate refers to her as "amicam Jhesu Christi" when the devil tries to defeat her through lustful temptation, evil thoughts, and rumours about unchastity.[63] In fact, she is referred to as "amica Dei" on a number of occasions by her biographer because of her devotion to God. Hyatte notes that such examples are typical of the effect of *amicitia Dei* in saints' lives: God shows His friendship in this world through rewards and aid, beyond the grace granted to all, for those who merit extra gifts because of their proven love or their potential for responding to divine love.[64] The traditional notion of God's friendship derives from the *Song of Songs* where the word *amica /amicus* is used repeatedly to refer to the close relationship between the bride and the spouse. The beloved is explicitly described as friend in the *Song of Songs* 5:16: "Talis est dilectus meus, et ipse est amicus meus" [Such a one is my beloved and he is my friend]. Rolle's example functions as a means of expressing how true devotion in the contemplative life can lead to the reader's achievement of *amica Dei* status.

Of course, it cannot be discounted that the example may be a modified borrowing from Rolle's own personal experience, recounted in *Super Canticum Canticorum*, where a beautiful woman appeared to him in his cell but vanished when he crossed himself and said "O Ihesu, quam preciosus est sanguis tuis".[65] Rosamund Allen suggests that in *The Form of Living* Rolle connects

---

63 *The Life of Christina of Markyate*, 130/131.
64 R. Hyatte, *The Arts of Friendship*, 55.
65 See *Super Canticum Canticorum*, 106–107. The Latin quote is cited in S. Ogilvie-Thomson, *Prose and Verse*, 194 (note to 7/176).

such experiences with the initial stages of conversion, as must have been his own situation.[66] It is even possible that Rolle is citing himself in *The Form of Living* as the written source, keen to display his own *auctoritas*. If this is so, it is interesting that he chooses to re-gender his original image of himself calling upon the blood of Jesus in the Latin work, by having a female recluse call on the Virgin Mary to rid her of the evil spirit in the vernacular work:

> Anoon he broght forth the fairest body of womman þat myght be, and shewed hit to hir, and anon she set hir on hir knees and said "Aue Maria", and al vansshed awey. (7/175–178)

The simplest explanation is that Rolle reworked his own story to accommodate the fact that the explicit audience for his work, Margaret Kirkeby, was female and would probably identify more readily with a female example. But to say this does not imply that Rolle constructs his vernacular audience as always female. His reworking of this story is simply the first in a series of feminised images aimed at drawing the reader of any sex to the acceptance of a feminised role: the bride of Christ.

In *Ego Dormio* and *The Commandment*, Rolle uses gendered tropes not because he considers his audience to be entirely female but because he appears to accept that the soul is inherently feminine. Conversely, the construction of the reader as the individual soul invites the reader to become feminised in this work. Until recently this type of feminised writing has been considered as specific to female writers, but in considering many late medieval mystical writings as "ungendered discourse" Kathleen Garay suggests that male and female mystical writers have much more in common than first thought, particularly in the way in which they show a preference for familiar and sometimes domestic imagery.[67] Similarly, Patricia Fite argues that Rolle's exhortation to "sit and synge of loue langynge" (33/284) in the final lyric in *Ego Dormio* combines both the masculine and feminine dimensions of spirituality as truly as Francis of Assisi and Julian of Norwich.[68] The feminine gendering of a male writer's activity, or in Garay's terms the "ungendering" of his imagery, is interesting in relation to *The Form of Living* because of Rolle's apparent desire for his authorial self to form a relationship of equality with the reader. It is as if he considers that through the subtle feminising of their chosen

---

[66] R. S. Allen, *Richard Rolle: The English Writings*, 17.
[67] K. Garay, " 'A Naked Intent Unto God' ", 44. To illustrate her point Garay notes Julian's uses of the humble hazelnut to develop an elaborate meditation. She also shows how the *Cloud*-author, his language reflecting the simplicity of the actions he recommends, counsels the reader to "lift up your heart to God by a humble impulse of love" by using the image of the father with his child, drying its eyes, and playing with it, "kissing and embracing it".
[68] P. P. Fite, "To 'Sytt and Syng of Luf Langyng': The Feminine Dynamic of Richard Rolle's Mysticism". *Studia Mystica* 14:2–3 (1991), n. 2, 13.

vocation, he and his reader can always be considered equal in their role as contemplatives whatever their gender.

In *The Form of Living* Rolle employs a number of gendered tropes in discussing his audience's relationship to God. Early in the work, when discussing the solitary life, he describes the reader's potential life of solitude in terms of the *sponsa Christi* motif:

> In a few yers þou shalt haue more delite to be by þyn on and spek to þi loue and þi spouse Ihesu, þan if þou were lady of a thousand worldes.
>
> (6/128–130)

This is, of course, the passage in which he goes on to include himself and the reader in the shared experience of the joy of the solitary life (6/130–132) which implies that Rolle is at one with an ostensibly female image. Rolle's feminising of himself in relation to the bridal imagery found in *The Form of Living* supports Anne Astell's conviction that Rolle identifies with the bride of the *Song of Songs* in a kind of "affective integration".[69] Her use of this term refers, of course, to Allen's suggestion that the gift of *canor* had gradually led Rolle to an affective integration that enabled him to have friendships with women without moral danger or spiritual disquiet.[70] As her purpose is to construct a psychological profile of Rolle, Astell expands on Allen's point to see this integration as Rolle's entering into a conscious relationship with his own *anima* by appropriating the words and attitudes of the bride of the *Song of Songs* into the English treatises. She argues that in doing so Rolle comes to relate, in the whole and holy way common to the great mystics, not only to the feminine principle within his own soul and to the women in his life, but also to God himself as the bridegroom and source of song.[71]

Rolle's identification in *The Form of Living* of his authorial self and the reader as the eternal bride is most clearly seen in his appropriation of a domestic image – his depiction of his authorial persona as the sitter. He refers to himself sitting, and to the joy of his own spiritual rest, a number of times in *The Form of Living*. Of course, the issue of sitting still for enlightenment is a difficult one to address in terms of gender. Although is true that the common medieval images of good womanhood suggest that women were supposed to be still and not roam about, the theme of the necessity for a male philosopher to sit in his study and pursue enlightenment was also a very common one. Both Augustine and Jerome have a long iconographic history which depicts them sitting in the study surrounded by books.[72] But I believe that Rolle's

---

[69] A. Astell, "Feminine *Figurae*", 117.
[70] H. E. Allen, *English Writings*, li–lii. See also P. Fite, "To 'Sytt and Syng of Luf Langyng' ", 25.
[71] A. Astell, "Feminine *Figurae*", 117.
[72] For an extensive coverage of iconographic representations of Jerome see E. F. Rice, *St. Jerome in the Renaissance* (Baltimore and London, 1985).

sitting in *The Form of Living* is most closely linked to the medieval concept of contemplation, and the solitary life, as spiritually representative of the passive, domestic life usually associated with women. In this Rolle may well have been influenced by Bernard who, in his twelfth sermon on the *Song of Songs*, considered that monks were like women because they shut themselves away from the world, whereas bishops were men because they engaged in the activities of the world.[73] However, as Caroline Walker Bynum points out, Bernard's image has both positive and negative connotations: "To call monks women, as Bernard does, is to use the feminine as something positive (humility) but also to imply that such is *not* the opinion of society. The wisdom of the world is not the wisdom of God."[74] Rolle's own feminised image would appear to draw on a tradition that reflects both positive and negative views of women through the promotion of the passive feminised role as appropriate for enclosed religious.

The question of the medieval concept of the active and the passive, in relation to the practical life and the contemplative life, is crucial to an understanding of gendered differences in medieval religious discourse. Basing her argument on the medieval acceptance of Aristotelean/Galenic concepts of gender difference Bynum argues that male and female were contrasted and asymmetrically valued as intellect/body, active/passive, rational/irrational, reason/emotion, self control/lust, judgement/mercy and order/disorder.[75] On the question of male authors appropriating the feminine in devotional works she suggests that the set of dichotomous symbols clustering around male/female in Western tradition suggested that men – powerful, clerical, authoritative, rational, "divine" men – needed to become weak and human, yet spiritual, "women" in order to proceed toward God.[76] This is particularly interesting in relation to Rolle's concept of sitting in contemplation. In Chapter Fourteen of *Incendium Amoris* the sitter emerges as the archetypical contemplative who could not achieve the meritorious *calor, dulcor* and *canor* in any other pose:

> Ut si uelim stando uel ambulando contemplari, uel procumbendo, uidebam me multum ab illis deficere, et quasi desolatum me existimare. Unde hac necessitate compulsus ut in summa deuocione quam habere possem et perseuerare, sedere elegi.

> [If I were to stand up when I was engaged in contemplation or to walk about or even to lie prostrate on the ground I found that I failed to attain these

---

73 Bernard of Clairvaux, *On the Song of Songs*. Trans Killian Walsh. *The Works of Bernard of Clairvaux* (Shannon, 1971–80), I, 77–85 cited in C. Walker Bynum, *Fragmentation and Redemption*, 36.

74 C. Walker Bynum, *Jesus as Mother*, 144.

75 C. Walker Bynum, *Fragmentation and Redemption*, 151.

76 C. Walker Bynum, *Holy Feast and Holy Fast: The Religious Significance of Food to Medieval Women* (Berkeley, 1987), 287.

three, and even seemed to be left in dryness. Consequently, if I were to hold on to and retain deep devotion I must sit – which is what I have decided to do.][77]

The phrase "quasi desolatum me existimare", which has been interpreted from the context as referring to being left in dryness, is interesting here, and possibly not a random choice in terms of gender. Following the reference Rolle calls upon Aristotle to authorise his point:

Et non est in sua summa quiete, et per consequens nec in perfeccione, quia secundum philosophum, sedendo et quiescendo fit anima prudens.

[He is not quiet as he can be and so is not in his most perfect state; if the philosopher is right, it is the quiet sitting that makes the soul wise.][78]

Medieval ideas about sex difference relied heavily on Aristotelean/Galenic (and Hippocratean) concepts that considered hot and cold, moist and dry as the critical polar principles in almost every aspect of what could be called physiology.[79] And while the subject of this chapter in *Incendium Amoris* is the idea that quiet is needed for contemplation, Rolle's mention of dryness makes it possible that he is not only deferring to Aristotle's expertise on the subject of quietude but also sought to endorse the Aristotelean view of gender difference. Aristotle, supported by Galen, asserted that men and women were fundamentally different, in the generative sense, because the male is naturally hotter and drier than the female; it was the accepted dogma in the medieval period for suggesting difference between men and women.[80] John of Trevisa's 1398 translation of Bartholomaeus Anglicus' very Aristotelean *De proprietatibus rerum* acknowledges that sex difference arises because men are more hot and dry by nature than women.[81] This would suggest that Rolle's reference here implies that in being active, he is dry and male, and by virtue of opposition, in sitting he would become less dry and female.

Sitting and the reception of divine sanction were obviously associated with Rolle in his own period. A well-preserved portrait of Rolle is extant in a fourteenth-century manuscript, British Library, Faustina MS B VI. It accompanies a northern poem, known as *The Desert of Religion*, on the trees of vices and

---

77 *Incendium Amoris*, 185; *The Fire of Love*, 89.
78 *Incendium Amoris*, 185; *The Fire of Love*, 89.
79 For a comprehensive survey of the meanings of sex difference in the Middle Ages see J. Cadden, *The Meanings of Sex Difference in the Middle Ages*.
80 Aristotle, *Generation of Animals*. Trans. A. L. Peck (London, 1963), esp. 91–93, 101–103, 109, 173–175, 185, 459–461. Galen, *De usu partium*. Trans M. Tallmadge May. *Galen on the Usefulness of the Parts of the Body* (Ithaca, 1968), II, 630–632.
81 Bartholomaeus Anglicus, *De proprietatibus rerum. On the Properties of Things: John Trevisa's Translation of Bartholomaeus Anglicus De proprietatibus rerum*, 371. See also A. Lynch, " 'Now, fye on youre wepynge!': Tears in Medieval English Romance", 44–45.

virtues growing in the wilderness of life (falsely attributed to Walter Hilton), illustrated by figures of hermits and nuns; Rolle is represented sitting, with a book in his lap, in a white habit; "Jhesus" is written in gold letters on his breast, angels above bear a scroll with the words "Sanctus Sanctus Sanctus dominus deus saboath, pleni sunt celi et terra gloria tua". The picture is surrounded by a poetic legend:

> A solitari here heremite life i lede,
> For Jhesu loue so dere all flescli lufe i flede;
> Þat gastli comforthe clere þat my breste brede,
> Might me a thowsand Zeere in heuenly strengthe haue stedd.[82]

The appearance of the word "Jhesus", written in gold on Rolle's breast, also links this image to his advocacy of the power of the Holy Name, which is most prominent in *The Form of Living*. The image was not uncommon in the Middle Ages; the medieval *vita* of the second century martyr Ignatius of Antioch reported an unusual miracle: his heart, cut open after his gruesome death, was said to contain the name of Jesus engraved in letters of pure gold.[83] But the seated image is also strikingly similar to many iconographic representations of the Virgin Mary, and sometimes her mother Anne, from the later Middle Ages, in that the representatives of the female side of the holy family are often depicted sitting, and often with a book. Throughout the later medieval period many images depict Anne, teaching her daughter to read, and the Annunciate Virgin seated with a book in readiness to receive the Word that will be made flesh.[84] Moreover, in representations of the mystical marriage of Christ and his mother, the Virgin Mary sits, enthroned, with her spouse in heaven.[85]

---

82 *The Desert of Religion* cited in C. Horstmann, *Richard Rolle and His Followers*, II, xxxiv.

83 C. A. Carsley, "Devotion to the Holy Name: Late Medieval Piety in England". *Princeton University Library Chronicle* 53/2 (1992), 158–159.

84 See P. Sheingorn, " 'The Wise Mother': The Image of St. Anne Teaching the Virgin Mary". *Gesta* XXXII (1993), 69–80. Sheingorn reproduces a number of images that show the Virgin Mary and her mother Anne with books. Marina Warner also reproduces a number of these representations in *Alone of All Her Sex*. The cover of the book shows Fra Angelica's Virgin Mary (c. 1450) seated in the presence of the Archangel Gabriel. The *Hours of the Virgin* (Bruges?, c. 1515) includes an image of the immaculate conception of Mary where Anne is depicted sitting with a book in hand: a ray from heaven illuminates in Anne's womb the child she conceived without stain of original sin (Plate 8). A polychrome statue of the matrilineal ancestry of Christ by the Urban Master from Hildesheim, Lower Saxony depicts the Virgin, with Christ on her lap, and her mother Anne seated. Anne clutches a book whilst her mother Emerita stands behind reading from a book (Plate 41).

85 See M. Warner, *Alone of All Her Sex*. Warner's book includes a number of images of the Virgin Mary as the spouse of Christ: Mary is seen enthroned by Christ's side as his queen in a twelfth-century mosaic in S. Maria in Trastevere, Rome (Plate 6). The mystical marriage is also the subject of Agnolo Gaddi's *Coronation of the Virgin* (Plate 16) and a fourteenth-century Florentine diptych (Plate 17) where Christ is seen

Rolle's depiction of himself as sitting, as well as his identification with the bride, may also suggest a direct identification with the Virgin Mary in *The Form of Living*, drawn from the *Song of Songs*. According to traditional exegesis of the *Song of Songs*, three spouses are alluded to throughout: the general spouse, which is holy church, the special spouse, which is every particular holy soul, and the singular spouse, which is the Virgin Mary herself. As the bride of Christ the Virgin Mary represents the very image that Rolle both accepts as his own and exhorts his reader to accept. In turn, the language Rolle uses to describe love in *The Form of Living* is also drawn from the *Song of Songs*. The phrase "Amore langueo", which is the dominant signifier of the pinnacle of mystical experience, "syngular loue", in this work, was often linked to the Virgin Mary's love for Christ in the Middle Ages. In the Middle English poem "In a tabernacle of a toure" (c. 1400) the Virgin Mary, speaking as both the mother of God and the mother of mankind, cries out the words "quia amore langueo" at the end of every verse as a means of expressing her devotion.[86] The poem evokes an image of warm, tender family relations in the reader, not dissimilar to Rolle's evocation of a relationship of friendship between the writer and the reader in *The Form of Living*.

The explicit identification with the Virgin Mary makes it clear that Rolle's authorial persona and the reader do become subtly feminised in this work, but this does not necessarily mean that they become, as Bynum suggests, women. Rolle recommends *imitatio* here, the reconstruction of the self using the Virgin Mary as a model, because she is the archetypical bride of Christ, a necessarily feminised role, but one that represents the example for every Christian of his/her future joy. In this sense Rolle is free to accept a feminised role himself, feminise the role of his reader and still open his work to a non gender-specific audience because each and every soul can accept the role of the mystical bride. Rolle draws on traditional notions of the Virgin Mary in both the language he uses to describe love and through his recommendation of *imaginatio* to evoke desirable images of sitting enthroned in heaven. He even subtly acknowledges that his own transition to the exalted state of bride allows him to offer his advice on this matter to his reader – "As I haue grace and connynge, I wil lere þe" (15/488) – and to instruct the reader in the art of sitting. The primary function of Rolle's own transformation, described in *The Form of Living* as his ability to sit in spiritual peace – "For syttynge am I in most reste, and my hert most vpward" (23/832–24/833) – is, then, to provide readers with a model for their own "affective integration" into the feminised role of the bride. Rolle's passivity in sitting, his own feminisation as the bride, and his subtle feminisation of the reader as the bride, are more closely linked to the unitive

clasping the right hand of his mother, the formal and legal gesture of nuptial union, "dextrarum iunctio".

[86] R. T. Davies, *Medieval English Lyrics*, Poem 62, 148–151.

goal, and his desire to construct a shared mutual experience of God for himself and the reader, than they are to gendering the vocation of contemplation itself. It is a complex objective that at once accepts sitting, the contemplative life, as representative of traditional female roles, as well as feminising the contemplative's spirituality by permitting him/her to wed Christ mystically, without specifying the gender of the reader who must learn to accept these roles.

Throughout *The Form of Living* Rolle is also concerned with notions of spiritual action (work) and spiritual passivity (rest) within the contemplative life; not necessarily related to gender, but important to his involvement of the reader in a friendly relationship based on shared vocation. Rolle attempts to reconcile active spirituality, the working or earning of God's love that he recommends in the first part of the work, with the achievement of rest, in the acceptance of the contemplative life in the second part of the work. In this, he is clearly influenced by the writings of Bernard of Clairvaux. In his forty-sixth sermon on the *Song of Songs* Bernard suggests that it is a sign of self-indulgence that one should earnestly desire to rest before earning that rest by labour.[87] In the following sermon he teaches that the reward of contemplation is intrinsically related to the work which earns it. Similarly, Walter Hilton assures his reader that good works in the active life "help mickle and ordain a man in the beginning to come to contemplative life".[88] Good works, spiritual effort, it seems, necessarily precede the reward of spiritual rest.

Towards the end of *The Form of Living* Rolle describes love itself in terms of spiritual work:

> Loue wil nat be ydel: hit is wirchynge sum good euermoor. If it cesse of worchynge, wit þou þat hit keleth and vansheth away. (20/702–4)

Later still rest is described as the end reward of contemplative life: "And namely al þat loueth contemplatif lif, þai seke rest in body and soule" (23/825–826). Rolle's reference to an as yet untraced "gret doctour" in this passage who "seith þat þay ben Goddis trone þat dwellen stille in a stid, and ben nat about rennynge" (23/827–828) may well be to Bernard. Rolle's concern with spiritual work and rest, and with love and sitting, in *The Form of Living* is outlined as a process of active love followed by the stable reward of contemplative rest. The implied message is that Rolle has spiritually worked, he is a lover of the contemplative life. This draws the reader to an understanding of an aspect of their shared vocation, that love is the work that precedes true rest, which promotes the collegial relationship offered in this text; as the lovers of the contemplative life Rolle and the reader sit together. The didactic language used here leaves the text open to let the reader in but with subtle paths and directions for them to follow along the way.

---

87 See Bernard of Clairvaux, *On the Song of Songs*. Trans Killian Walsh, II, 241–247.
88 W. Hilton, *The Scale of Perfection*, Ch. 2, 4.

To highlight the process of working towards the true rest of "syngular loue" the differences between rest (contemplation/soul) and sleep (active/ body) for the solitary are carefully developed throughout the work. The culmination of rest, the superior act of sitting, is only mentioned in the later part of work where the subject of contemplation is more specifically addressed. Bodily sleep and spiritual rest are contrasted in the instructional section of the work where it is implied that "reste" is true contemplation, but "slep" itself is described as dangerous because the devil can become active in dreams:

> Also our enemy wol nat suffre vs to be in reste when we slep, bot þan he is
> about to begile vs in many maneres: orwhiles with grisful ymages for to
> make vs ferd, and mak vs loth with our state . . . (8/203–205)

The collegial term "our state" evokes shared anxiety in the contemplative life which Rolle counters by exhorting shared submission to God's will:

> Bot he þat is ordeynour of al þynge suffreth nat þat oure sleep be without
> meed to vs, if we adresse oure lif at his wille. (8/210–211)

Rolle's and the reader's attainment of rest in their shared vocation not only defeats the devil, it has the potential to align the human will with the will of the divine. In the interesting passage that follows, Rolle pursues the idea that dreams disturb true rest because they denote a state where the devil can be active in deception. Rolle draws on Ecclesiastes 5:2: "Multus curas sequuntur somnia" [For a dream comes with much business], and Ecclesiasticus 34:7: "Multas enim errare fecerant somnia, et exciderunt sperantes in illis" [For dreams have deceived many, and those who have put their hope in them have failed] for the following point:

> Bot many hath þe deuyl desceyuet þrogh dremes . . . Forþi seith the wise
> man that many bisynesse foloweth dremes . . . For wher so many dremes
> ben, þer ben many vanytees, and many þei make to erre, for þei heghen
> vnstable men, and so deceyueth ham. (8/214–232)

The connection between dreaming, falsity and vanity leads conveniently to a discussion of hypocrisy in which Rolle takes up the theme of the "habite of holynesse", how the outer should reflect the inner, begun in *The Command-ment*. In *The Commandment* Rolle was keen to elaborate on the point at length as if it were crucial to the reader's development at this stage. In *The Form of Living* the discussion is short and functions as a reminder to "turne þi þoзt perfitly to God, as hit semeth þat þou hast þi body" (9/235–236), perhaps implying that the reader of this text is more advanced in the spiritual journey, ready to become one who will enjoy suffering "for his loue" and "haue gret confort" in living in solitude (9/258–259). It also implies, just as it did in *The Commandment*, that Rolle's primary concern is not with the reader's body, but with his/her interior life. Sleeping and dreaming are functions of the body, the dangers of which should be guarded against. Turning the body to the solitary life, to rest and sitting, is a further step towards the soul's integration with the divine. Hypocrisy is developed as a theme here because the turning, the redirection of the *affectus*, can only be considered truthful if the motives are pure. In this further development of the theme of hypocrisy, begun in *Ego Dormio* and elaborated on in *The Commandment*, we can discern Rolle's commitment to the perfection of the interior life of his vernacular audience, as well as to friendship with his readers. An explicit warning on the subject of hypocrisy conveniently bears the weight of his own trust in his friend and disciple: "I hope þrogh þe grace of God þat, if men hold þe good, þou shalt be wel bettre" (9/265–266).

At this stage of the journey Rolle exhorts his reader to "turn þe entierly to þi lord Ihesu Criste" (9/266). At a glance this appears to be a strikingly simple didactic statement, one which is usually associated with the very beginning of religious life, rather than with the entry into higher vocations such as religious solitude. But Rolle's emphasis on Christ as "þi lord" and his repetition of the word "turnynge" in the following passage express his preoccupation with how the redirection of the *affectus* can result in perfection; once the will is fully turned to God the role of the bride is there for the taking:

> That turnynge to Ihesu is nat els bot turnynge fro al the couaitise and the lykynge and þe occupaciouns and bisynes of worldly thynges . . . so þat þi þoght, þat was euer downward modelynge in þe erth whil þou was in þe world, now be euer vpward as fyre, sechynge þe heghest place in heuyn, right to þi spouse þere he sitteth in his blisse. (9/267–10/273)

It also engages the reader in a gently persuasive and friendly exchange. The image that is promoted here, Christ as the spouse sitting in heaven, opens the text to the reader because Rolle's own self is manifested as the human friend rather than as the dominant author. The text can become the reader's too if he/she will join with Rolle in the love of God and be seated beside Christ in heaven as the bride. Rolle achieves this by dismissing the turning as "nat els bot turnynge fro al the couaitise . . ." which implies that he has knowledge of such turning from his own experience. This then provides the reader with an exemplary image of Rolle's own reward – his own acceptance of the role of Christ's bride. The effect of this, as with the earlier nuptial image, is that an individual space is created for the reader to occupy, to become the bride with him.

Just as Rolle's sitting represents an implicit reader/writer identification with the bride, his exhortation to endure solitude exhorts the reader to join with him in the company of angels. This is achieved by his description of sitting as the end point of the "wakynges", the "fastynges", and the "heete and cold, hungre and þurste", that a solitary endures, as "trauaille" in which "þou shalt cum to reste þat lesteth euer, and *sit* in a seet of ioy with angels" (22/750–753). A link to another example of Rolle's own affective integration may be discerned here because in *Ego Dormio* he implies that he has achieved an exalted position alongside the angels of heaven as a "messager" of God. Confirmation that Rolle himself is the very model of a successful solitary and the image of seated nuptial bliss comes towards the end of the work when he informs his reader that "he has loued for to sit":

> And I haue loued for to sit, for no penaunce ne for no fantasie þat I wold men spake of me, ne for no such þynge, bot only for I knewe þat I loued God more, and langer lested with me comfort of loue, þan goynge or standynge or knelynge. For syttynge am I in most reste, and my herte most vpward. Bot þerfor peraduenture is hit nat þe best to anoþer to sit as I haue done, and wil do to my deth, bot if he were disposed as I was in his soul. (23/829–832)

Here, at the end of the work, Rolle acknowledges his own sitting as a state of earthly near-perfection that the reader may achieve if similarly disposed. Consequently, the invitation to the reader to sit is linked with a shared disposition of soul and if the reader is similarly disposed it is a special thing that he/she can share with Rolle. The elevation of his own intimate relationships with God in *The Form of Living* is not so much of a self-promoting act as audience-centred, an exhortation to the reader to join with him in the perfection of his own contemplation. In turn, his feminised self in this work, and the subtle feminisation of the reader, do not function as gendered directives for the reader to follow, but as a simple invitation to join in a relationship of equality that transcends gender. His own sitting, whether it be in the company of angels, or as the bride, mirrors the implied friendship he wishes to enjoy with the reader and "the friend in our midst", Christ.

In conjunction with the dual feminisation of the author and audience outlined above, Rolle employs a type of verbal patterning that encourages author-audience familiarity throughout *The Form of Living*. This may not seem as apparent in the first part of the work, where Rolle concentrates on the more penitential aspects of devotion, but it is here that the "turnynge" to Christ takes place and the initial invitation to become his friend and bride occurs. In the second part of the work, Lois Smedick argues, Rolle adopts a rhythmical prose style which is directed to the ear as well as to the understanding and which ostensibly constructs a verbal equivalent of *canor*.[89] Watson agrees that Rolle composes much of this part of the work in a lyrical prose which greatly reinforces both the content of his message concerning love and the reader's sense of his authorial presence.[90] Rolle complements the theme of *amicitia Dei* with the collegial friendship based on his and the reader's shared attainment

[89] L. Smedick, "Parallelism and Pointing in Rolle's Rhythmical Style", *Mediaeval Studies* 41 (1979), 404–405.
[90] N. Watson, *Invention of Authority*, 252.

of *canor* or "syngular loue", in the latter part of the work. The reader's elevation to this shared position is achieved through Rolle's structuring this section
as a dialogue.

As I noted earlier, enlightening literature in dialogue form, often involving
a constructed friend and disciple, was common throughout the medieval
period. Augustine employed the dialogic style in his discourse with his friend
Evodius in *De quantitate animae*.[91] Aelred of Rievaulx's *De spirituali amicitia*,
influenced by the dialogic style of Cicero's *De amicitia*, is a collection of
dialogues between monks about their love toward one another and Christ,
whom Aelred describes as "another friend in our midst".[92] Discussing the collective works of the English mystics Barry Windeatt argues that the writings
of Rolle, Hilton and the *Cloud*-author are often composed as if to inscribe an
intimate exchange that stands in for a confidential conversation, and so represents part of a larger implied dialogue between author and recipient.[93] Before
his translation of the Latin phrase "Amore langueo" (15/489–493) Rolle even
pre-empts the reader's desire for such a dialogue:

> I wot wel þat þou desirest to hyre sum special poynt of þe þe loue of Ihesu
> Criste, and of contemplatif lif þe which þou hast taken þe to at mennys syȝt.
>
> (15/486–488)

The desire to "hyre" Rolle's words could suggest an oral context for the work;
the aural reference implies that the text addresses both reader and hearer or
seeks to indicate that the work will be both read and heard. But the
constructed knowledge of the reader's desire is also the beginning of an
extended implied dialogue between Rolle's authorial self and the reader that
acts as the framework for the more complex and circumspect discussion of
contemplative life in the second part of *The Form of Living*. It also introduces
another affective strategy – the rhythmical prose style that is characteristic of
Rolle's celebration of *canor* in this section.

This section is Rolle's only vernacular discussion of *canor* as the most
singular reward of contemplation. His decision to structure it as a dialogue is
particularly revealing if we consider this work as the culmination of his
thought. Intimacy with the reader is sought in both of Rolle's earlier vernacular treatises, *Ego Dormio* and *The Commandment*, but he does not engage the
reader of either of these texts in any such dialogue; this suggests that the role
of friend is somehow superior to that of lover or pupil, the dominant
reader-identities constructed in the two earlier works. Furthermore, implied
respect for the reader's intelligence permeates this section particularly in his

---

91 See Augustine, *The Greatness of the Soul*. Trans. Joseph. M. Colleran (Westminster,
    1950).
92 Aelred of Rievaulx, *Spiritual Friendship*, 51.
93 See B. Windeatt, *English Mystics of the Middle Ages*, 5–6.

intimation that the reader is the recipient of a "special yift", love, that is awarded to "þo þat ledeth solitary lif". Felicity Riddy also recognises the implied collegiality in this work, suggesting that *The Form of Living* has the easy directness of someone talking to an old friend; she cites the passage:[94]

> Dyuers men in erth haue dyuers yiftes and graces of God, bot þe special yift of þo þat ledeth soltiary life is for to loue Ihesu Criste. Thou saist to me "Al men loueth hym þat holdeth his commaundementȝ". Soth hit is, bot al men þat kepeth his biddynge kepeth nat also his consail, and al þat doth his consail is nat as fulfilled of þe swetnesse of his loue, ne feleth nat þe fyre of loue brennynge in his herte. (15/494–499)

Rolle does not instruct here, he discusses a point of spiritual concern with an intellectually worthy partner. The effect is to place the reader in a position of equal status. The conversational tone could easily be regarded as singularly reflective of Rolle and Margaret's friendship but one would imagine that for an audience beyond the initial reaches of the original work it would serve as a device for engaging the reader in a more open discourse of friendship.

The constructed dialogue offers Rolle's authorial persona a chance to imply personal knowledge of the reader's feelings and desires. He repeats the phrase "I wot wel", at the end of the passage as an affirmation of his knowledge of how he/she will feel when in prayer and meditation:

> If þou be in praier and in meditaciouns al þe day, I wot wel þat þou mow wax gretly in þe loue of Ihesu Criste, and myche fele of delite, and within short tyme. (16/523–524)

Immediately he assumes the role of pedagogical friend and declares "I shal tel þe" of the three degrees of love because "I wold þat þou myȝt wyn to þe heghest" (16/525–526). This one line serves to bolster the reader's confidence in his/her own ability to achieve the third degree of love, and in Rolle's ability to guide him/her to it; the word "wold" here could imply either wish or intend. Either way, a positive affective response is expected from the reader who is now primed to await explication of how the three degrees of love can be achieved.

The three degrees of love are found in all three of Rolle's vernacular treatises and perform a variety of functions. Like the descriptive outline of the three degrees of love found in *The Commandment*, those in *The Form of Living* are drawn from *Emendatio Vitae*. In *The Commandment* they are accorded little more than a brief delineation which appears to reflect the humbler didactic function of the text as a whole. In *Ego Dormio* they provide both the framework and the main subject of the work, reflecting the novitiate nature of the

---

[94] F. Riddy, " 'Women talking about the things of God': a late medieval sub-culture". *Women & Literature in Britain, 1150–1500*. Ed. C. M. Meale (Cambridge, 1993), 107.

intended audience. Here in *The Form of Living* Rolle appears to reiterate the three degrees of love to reinforce to the reader the progressive nature of love, and how it leads to bliss in the contemplative life. Each degree eagerly antici-pates the next until the utterance "I languysshe for loue" (17/563–564), which is itself anticipated by the phrase "Amore langueo" at the beginning of Rolle's discussion of the contemplative life. This is followed by Rolle's further permissive "þan þou may say 'I sleep and my hert waketh' " (17/564), another utterance anticipated in *Ego Dormio*. Rolle, as the author of *Ego Dormio*, is already able to cry out these words. His repetition of these phrases binds together the three treatises as documents on love, while they join Rolle and the reader of *The Form of Living* in one voice of "syngular loue", calling out for Christ.

Having aroused the reader's voice Rolle is now able to introduce his friend and disciple to the rapturous joy of *canor*, his own gift of spiritual "syngynge gostly to Ihesu and in Ihesu" (17/574). But it is not a bodily crying out to Christ the reader will experience:

> And "Ihesu" not bodily crynge with þe mouth: of þat maner of syngynge speke I nat of, for þat songe hath both good and il. (17/574–576)

Earthly song is clearly flawed; it is not a true sign of the heart, but because of the order which it manifests in itself, it is closer to heavenly song than other kinds of speech.[95] As Vincent Gillespie points out, in his recommendation of the *cantus amoris* here Rolle appears to contradict all his statements on the ability of man to describe or capture true song.[96] And because Rolle stresses that the lyric is to be sung "when þou coueiteste his comynge and þi goynge" the song here functions as an affective trigger, to be employed when desirous of achieving the state of *canor*: "In þis þrid degre, if þou may wyn therto . . . þi may in þi longynge synge þis in þyn herte" (18/594–596). Gillespie further suggests that the lyric in *The Form of Living*, which describes the highest grade of love, is at the head of a hierarchy of lyric writing in Rolle's vernacular trea-tises and that the lyrics in Rolle's first vernacular treatise *Ego Dormio* reflect the earliest levels of spiritual awareness.[97] This perhaps supports the view that in *The Form of Living* Rolle accepts friendship as a more advanced spiritual rela-tionship with his reader than he has previously achieved.

---

[95] V. Gillespie, "Mystics Foot", 211. Gillespie suggests that Rolle's use of literary devices such as alliteration, rhythm and verse, then, are an attempt to enact the order which he has perceived to be at the heart of his spiritual experience. He also notes that Rolle's audience would be receptive to these devices because the medi-eval mind was highly conscious of rhythm and structure.

[96] V. Gillespie, "Mystics Foot", 216.

[97] V. Gillespie, "Mystics Foot", 216. Gillespie argues that Rolle's lyric writing can be viewed as a progression because his lyrics appear to provide meditative paradigms appropriate to the level of advancement under discussion.

Rolle's Christocentric hierarchy of love can also be observed here. An experience of love without Christ is rare in Rolle's writings and *The Form of Living* is no exception. For his description of the exalted experience of *canor* in the passage directly following the meditative lyric "When wil þou cum to comfort me?" (18/598–609) Rolle exhorts the reader to fasten the name of Jesus in their heart:

> If þou wil be wel with God, and haue grace to reul þi lif right, and cum to þe ioy of loue, þis name Iesus, fest hit so faste in þi herte þat hit cum neuer out of þi þoght. (18/610–612)

Christocentric devotion had reached a peak in the fourteenth century and is perhaps one of the reasons for *The Form of Living*'s contemporary popularity. Devotion to Christ pervades most of Rolle's major works, which leads Watson to suggest that along with *The Form of Living*, Rolle's authorship of the devotional passage *Encomium Nominis Ihesu* (the fourth section of *Super Canticum Canticorum*) gained him a reputation as the foremost exponent of devotion to the Holy Name of Jesus.[98] The Yorkshire aristocracy, who were among Rolle's first patrons and early readers of his works in the fourteenth century, are known to have been early advocates of the cult of the Holy Name in England.[99] Evidence of Rolle's popularity amongst these Yorkshire book owners, the Scropes of Masham, the Fitzhughs of Tanfield and the Stapletons of Bedale,[100] as well as accurately dating *The Form of Living*, certainly establishes Rolle as one of the most influential early advocates of the cult in late medieval England. Its tradition and Rolle's previous involvement with it are important to understanding his references to it in *The Form of Living*.

The Feast of the Holy Name, unlike some other late medieval liturgical

---

[98] N. Watson, *Invention of Authority*, 55. Watson refers to Allen's listing of all the manuscripts that include this popular passage. See H. E. Allen, *Writings Ascribed.* 66–68. Malcolm Moyes notes that there is a compilation of passages from Rolle's *Emendatio Vitae, Melos Amoris, Incendium Amoris, Super Canticum Canticorum,* and *Expositio Super Novem Lectiones Mortuorum* in the fifteenth-century University Library Cambridge MS Kk.vi.20, ff. 11r–26v, called *Orationes Excerpte de Diversis Tractatibus quos Composuit Beatus Ricardus Heremita ad Honorem Nominis Ihesu.* It is an excellent example of early fifteenth-century devotion to the Holy Name in England and of the association of Rolle with that particular devotion. See M. Moyes, *Richard Rolle's Expositio*, I, 83–84.

[99] For a discussion of how Rolle's advocacy of the Holy Name influenced certain members of the Yorkshire nobility in the late Middle Ages, leading to wider dissemination of the cult itself see J. Hughes, *Pastors and Visionaries*, 90–92. Hughes names the Neville family, Rolle's first patrons, as early devotees of the cult of the Holy Name. He posits that the "Lollard knight", Sir William Neville, may have introduced Rolle's works to his friends at court, Sir John Clanvowe, the author of a devotional tract, and Sir William Beauchamp, who owned the works of Rolle and Clanvowe.

[100] J. Hughes, *Pastors and Visionaries*, 91.

feasts in England, evolved from previous devotional cults.[101] Well before Rolle, the venerable Bede, Anselm, Bernard of Clairvaux, Aelred of Rievaulx, the poet John of Hoveden and the anonymous author of the hymn *Jesu Dulcis Memoria* took an active part in the making of this cult.[102] In the liturgical calender the Feast of the Name of Jesus, which takes place on August 7th, precedes the Feast of the Assumption by a week. The first lesson in the Sarum breviary ascribes papal approval for this office to Alexander IV (Pope 1254–61).[103] The chronology for the two feasts follows a rational course, as the intense concentration on the name of Jesus leads the devotee to consider his incarnation. In fact, the Feast for the Holy Name anticipates in its last *lectio* the following liturgical event, where the role of the Virgin Mary is seen as obliterating the disobedience of Eve, while that of Christ nullifies the role played by Adam.[104] The liturgy for this feast is made up of eight *lectiones* and, as Denis Renevey points out, among the chapters, hymns, responses, anthems and prayers which constitute each *lectio*, the hymn *Jesu Dulcis Memoria*, the response *Osculetur Me Osculo Oris Sui*, the *Oleum Effusum Nomen Tuum* of *Lectio* Four and the homily attributed to Origen are particularly relevant to some of the most important themes developed by Rolle throughout his works.[105]

In *Incendium Amoris* Rolle expounds the importance of participation in liturgical and para-liturgical devotions, particularly the importance of a liturgical celebration for the coming of *canor*.[106] Following a description of the spiritual gifts, Rolle states the importance of the love for the Holy Name:

> Proinde arbitror hoc nulli datum meritis, sed gratis cui uoluerit Christus. Puto tamen neminem illud accepturum, nisi specialiter nomen Ihesum diligat, et eciam in tantum honoret ut ab eius memoria numquam, excepto sompno, recedere permittat.

> [From which I deduce that they are not given for merit, but freely to whosoever Christ wills. All the same I fancy that no one will receive them unless he has a special love for the Name of Jesus, and so honours it that he never lets it out of his mind, except in sleep.][107]

---

101 R. W. Pfaff, *New Liturgical Feasts in Later Medieval England* (Oxford, 1970), 62–83. See also R. Woolf, *The English Religious Lyric*, 172–179.

102 D. Renevey, *The Moving of the Soul*, 193. See also N. Watson, *Invention of Authority*, 55. Watson, in summarising Malcolm Moyes, suggests that Rolle's devotion to the Holy Name can also be traced to his Yorkshire background, in that he was ostensibly heir to a local tradition of Cistercian and Cistercian-inspired spiritual writing, in which affective devotion to Christ featured prominently. For further discussion of Rolle's Cistercian heritage see M. Moyes, *Richard Rolle's Expositio*, esp. I, 27–37.

103 R. W. Pfaff, *New Liturgical Feasts*, 69. See also D. Renevey, *The Moving of the Soul*, 189.

104 *York Breviary*, Col. 776 cited in D. Renevey, *The Moving of the Soul*, 194.

105 D. Renevey, *The Moving of the Soul*, 194.

106 D. Renevey, *The Moving of the Soul*, 191.

107 *Incendium Amoris*, 190; *The Fire of Love*, 93–94.

Denis Renevey suggests that devotions to the Holy Name produced the change of consciousness required from the reception of the gifts of *calor, dulcor* and *canor* allowing Rolle, in this state of grace, to write works that evolve around elements present in the liturgy and which originate from various authorities. The recurrence of the Holy Name and other liturgical practices in the English works attests to the power of those practices for the needs of beginner contemplatives and, at a more pragmatic level, the liturgy also provides patterns of alternative voices which Rolle imitates and shapes in the English writings to move their recipients.[108] Indeed, spiritual formulas, more especially the Holy Name, seem to be regarded favourably by Rolle because of their ability to bring the individual to greater self awareness. Repeated annotations of the name "Ihesu" in the margins of the Longleat versions of *Ego Dormio*, *The Commandment* and *The Form of Living* indicate favourable contemporary reception given to this devotional practice.[109]

Rosamund Allen suggests that Rolle's extensive use of this aid to devotion which all can follow, no matter how little their degree of proficiency, must have influenced the growth of the cult of the Holy Name in England.[110] Having examined Rolle's influence on the rhythmic invocations of the Holy Name of Jesus that characterise three Latin prayers of Princeton MS 126, Catherine Carsley concludes that in medieval England the power of the Holy Name had become intimately coupled with Rolle's much admired mysticism, and that prayers to the Holy Name probably evoked some kind of emulation of the piety of Rolle in the late medieval period.[111] Whether Rolle himself considered his advocacy of devotion to the Holy Name as a defining factor in the popularisation of a medieval cult is difficult to say. His writings on the subject veer, as much of his thought does, towards the affective qualities of the devotional practice. Renevey goes as far as suggesting that the association of the cult of the Holy Name with Rolle's works, in particular the evidence of extensive manuscript marginalia, may be viewed as somehow forcing Rolle within a devotional context about which his own writings contribute only a limited part.[112] And while this may well be the case, what we can ascertain is that the evidence of popular reception of his writings on the cult amongst the

---

[108] D. Renevey, *The Moving of the Soul*, 191.
[109] For line references to the occurrence of the word "Ihesu" in the margins of these texts in Longleat MS 29 see S. Ogilvie-Thomson, *Prose and Verse*, 193, 204 and 207. See also D. Renevey, "The Name Poured Out: Margins, Illuminations and Miniatures as evidence for the practice of devotions to the Name of Jesus in Late Medieval England" *Analecta Cartusiana* 130 (1996), 127–147.
[110] R. S. Allen, *Richard Rolle: The English Writings*, 40. Allen suggests that while Rolle did not initiate this devotion and did not introduce it to England, he must have been instrumental in its steady growth in popularity which actually survived the change of religion in the sixteenth century.
[111] C. A. Carsley, "Devotion to the Holy Name", 166.
[112] D. Renevey, "The Name Poured Out", 134.

Yorkshire aristocracy certainly supports the idea that his advocacy of the cult, as well as his works, had broad appeal.

Returning to the subject of Rolle's appeal to the *affectus* of the reader in *The Form of Living*, we can see that he uses the devotion to the name of Jesus to focus the reader on the affective qualities of devotion to Christ, to explain to the reader how he/she will feel in the third degree of love:

> Bot þe soul þat is in þe þrid degre is as a brennynge fyre, and as þe nyghtgalle, þat loueth songe and melody, and failleth for mykel loue; so þat soul is only conforted in praisynge and louynge of God, and til deth cum is syngynge gostly to Ihesu and in Ihesu ... and þis maner of songe hath none bot if þai be in þis þrid degre of loue, to þe which degree hit is impossibil to cum bot in gret multitude of loue. (17/571–578)

Assigning devotion to the Holy Name to the third degree of love, the most singular reward, has the effect of elevating its importance in devotional practice. Referring to the same passage Malcolm Moyes argues that the Holy Name is not simply associated with pious meditation and devotional exercise, but with the most ineffable religious experiences: an idea not found in the writings of Bernard of Clairvaux or John of Hoveden, but one that was to be taken up by later English spiritual directors.[113] Within the text itself, it has the effect of drawing the reader closer to understanding the power of the Holy Name and to generating a desire to embody it within the heart. The passage, which follows the highly emotive lyric "When wil þou cum to comfort me?" (18/598–609), explicitly exhorts the reader to call on the Holy Name, "þis name Iesus, fest hit so feste in þi herte, þat hit cum neuer out of þi þoght" (18/611), appealing directly to the *affectus* of the reader. It is an adaptation of a passage from Rolle's *Super Canticum Canticorum* which gives a precise account of the transforming power of the name "Jesus":[114]

> This name Jesus, faithfully retained in the mind, eradicates vices, plants virtues, engrafts love, pours out the taste of heavenly things, empties discord, reforms peace, demonstrates internal quiet, destroys utterly the annoyance of carnal desires; converts all earthly things into loathing, fills the lover with spiritual joy, so that worthily it is said, "And all who love your name will be glorified, because you bless the just."[115]

After listing the benefits of calling on the Holy Name and keeping it always in your thoughts Rolle states that "hit openeth heuyn and maketh a contemplatif man" (18/619). The act of calling on the Holy Name then actually constructs the self as a contemplative. This not only focuses the reader on the nature of

---

113 M. Moyes, *Richard Rolle's Expositio*, I, 62.
114 N. Watson, *Invention of Authority*, 252.
115 *Super Canticum Canticorum*, 101–104.

the vocation that is the subject of *The Form of Living* but it invites the reader to join with Rolle in his own mystical experience of "syngular loue". Again Rolle uses the power of friendship to draw the reader towards a shared experience of enlightenment.

The phrase "maketh a contemplatif man" could also suggest that the reader is made or becomes a contemplative through the text itself, which functions as a mediatory presence between the reader and the power of the Holy Name. Echoes of the "messager" function which Rolle assigned his authorial self in *Ego Dormio* are evident here. Interestingly though, after he has apparently granted the text a primary functional role in the process of ascent, he then denounces book learning, as if *The Form of Living* were a self-consuming artifact to be discarded once its affective work had been accomplished. The value of the text is primarily left up to the reader, who alone, except for God, knows his/her own soul.

Rolle's mistrust of book learning may also reflect what has been called his anti-intellectualism, a suspicion of relying on learned texts as opposed to the experience of loving God. In *Desire and Delight* it would seem that Rolle inverts the monastic triad of reading, prayer and meditation to position reading as the inferior part:[116]

> Another is þat þe skyl mekely be vsed in gostly þynges, as in meditation and orisone and lokynge in haly bokes. (40/20–22)

In *The Form of Living* his suspicion of book reading is explicit and he advises: "The dar nat gretly couait many bokes" (18/622–623). Earlier in the work he maintains that "a foul lecherie hit is to haue lykynge and delite in mennes wordes, þat can no more deme whate we bene in our soule þan þei wote whate we thynke" (5/91–93). Anne Clark Bartlett notes that whereas reading was deemed important for the female anchoritic audience of *Ancrene Wisse* Rolle assures his "female" audience that reading is ultimately not very important for them.[117] She sees this as a gendered concern, that Rolle accepted the medieval commonplace that "female" and "well-educated" were terms that were incompatible.[118] Yet here it seems to be more a development of Rolle's commitment to the interior life of his reader. The idea that spiritual truth can not be discovered through "lokynge in haly bokes" alone is clearly seen in his suggestion that internalised devotion, such as prayer and meditation, is superior to the bodily action of reading of "mennes wordes". After all, he explicitly includes himself, an author of books, as among the company of those whose words will become meaningless once the love of God fills the heart: "hold loue in hert and in werke, and þou hast al done þat we may say or

---

116 V. Gillespie, " 'Lukynge in haly bukes' ", 5.
117 A. Clark Bartlett, *Male Authors, Female Readers*, 155.
118 A. Clark Bartlett, *Male Authors, Female Readers*, 155.

write" (18/622–625). The implicit message assures the reader that, like himself, he/she will have no use for earthly words when they are fully immersed in the love of God because "loue is perfeccioun of lettres" (18/649).[119] Words are a stage in the journey; Rolle's utterance is not important in itself, but potentially of huge importance if its spirit is internalised and acted upon. Such an attack on "lettres" may have also been a comfort to the unlearned amongst Rolle's audience, *illiterati* who desired spiritual fulfilment but who lacked advanced religious instruction.

Much of the remainder of the work is taken up with the five questions on love which consolidate the dialogic relationship that now exists between Rolle and the reader:

> Bot now may þou ask me and say: "þou spekest so mych of loue; tel me what loue is, and whare it is, and how I shal loue God verrayly, and how I may knowe þat I loue hym, and in what state I may most loue hym".
>
> (18/626–629)

The same five questions appear in a Wycliffite tract in which God's law is a prominent subject.[120] In some ways Rolle's systematic answering of these questions could be viewed as a return to the didactic style employed in the first part of the work, an establishment of Rolle's law. However, because it is structured as a dialogue, the answer to each question is only quasi-instructional because Rolle's primary concern is with the recapitulation of personal concern for the reader's understanding of love. In answering the first question he assures the reader "we shal afforce vs to cloth vs in loue" (19/670), later he assures the readers that he/she is truly the lover of God, using the familiar "þou":

> Fro þou hast getten þis loue, al þi lif til deth cum is ioy and confort, and þou art verraily Cristis louer, and he resteth in þe, whose stid is maked in pees.
>
> (32/770–772)

The fourth question acknowledges that if the reader "had grace þat he myght wyn to þe þrid degre of loue, þat is cald syngular, he wold knowe þat he ware in loue" (22/783–784). The dialogue builds slowly towards the fifth question, which discusses sitting and the contemplative life as the "state men may moste loue God in" (23/819–835); the text positively resonates with his desire

---

119 See V. Gillespie, "Strange Images of Death", 143. Gillespie defines Rolle's quote as "the word made flesh will remake fleshly words".

120 H. E. Allen, *Writings Ascribed*, n. 1, 265. Allen points out that this section is largely derived from the *Compendium Theologicae Veritatis*, and most of it comes ultimately from the *De Vita Contempliva* ascribed to Prosper of Aquitaine. She further notes that borrowings also occur in this section from Bernard's *De Diligendo Deo*, and from Bonaventure's *De Triplici Via*. See n. 2 and n. 3, 265 for comparative quotations. See also N. Watson, *Invention of Authority*, 63.

for the reader to join with him "syttynge . . . in most reste", to understand true love as he does.

The last passages of the work are curious in that instead of pursuing the friendly relationship he has spent much of the work developing Rolle draws the reader full circle, back to more practical and broad concerns found earlier in the work, by launching into a very general comparison of active and contemplative living:

> Two lives ben þat Cristen men lyuen in. On is cald actif lif, for hit is in more werke bodily. Anoþer, contemplatif, for hit is in more swetnesse gostly.
>
> (24/836–838)

The active life is discussed as more perilous compared to the contemplative life which is praised in glowing terms: it is "lestynger and sykerer, restfuller, delitabeller, louelier and more medeful" (24/840–841). Rolle returns to more general terms of address, comparing "men and wommen þat taketh to actif lif" (24/849) with "a man or a woman þat is ordeynet to contemplatif lif" (25/875). The generality of this final passage could be construed as leading away from the familiarity, the friendship, alluded to and promised throughout the work, but in fact Rolle is still subtly drawing the reader closer to the goal of love here. The final passage reads as a rush of experiential fulfilment: the eye of the soul is finally opened to "loke in to heuen", "þe fire of loue verrailye lighteth in to har hert, and brenneth therin", the contemplative is made "clene of al erthly filth" and "rauist in loue" (25/885–889). The full affective force of this passage culminates in a mutual experience of earthly unworthiness which leads to a mutual desire for the ecstasy of death:

> Bot þou shalt witte þat no man hath perfite sight of heuyn whils þei ben in body lyvynge here, bot as sone as þei dey, þai ben broght bifor God, and seth hym face to face and egh to eigh, and wonneth with hym withouten end, for hym þai soght, and hym þai couaited, and hym þai loued in al har myght.
>
> (25/889–893)

The face to face image, a common scriptural expression of the beatific vision, was widely used by commentators on the *Song of Songs* and mystic writers who appropriated the metaphorical expression to make it the climax of spiritual union.[121] In *The Form of Living* the image signals the culmination of the reader's ascent. United at last in a truly mutual experience with the reader, the desire for eternal life after death, the friendship with the reader Rolle has carefully developed throughout the work is finally acknowledged. Rolle calls upon his friend, Margaret, as a textual endorsement of friendship itself. Far

---

[121] D. Renevey, *The Moving of the Soul*, 40–41. Renevey discusses this image with close reference to the writings of William of St. Thierry who, he argues, applies the nuptial imagery of the *Song of Songs* to the concept and image of the "face to face" in three important works, namely *De Contemplando Deo*, the *Meditationes* and the *Expositio super Canticum Canticorum*.

from limiting the text to a narrow audience, the use of Margaret's name opens the work further by providing every reader of *The Form of Living* an identifiable space to occupy; the friend and disciple of Richard Rolle who will "thanke God and pray for me" (25/896) if this work profits them in any way.

IV

The Form of Living is a text with many pedagogic aspects but is difficult to classify purely as a rule of living due to its innately affective thematics. Rolle shows that his use of the word "fourme" has connotations of shape and mould, as if he is offering the reader agency to form his/her own life by using the guidelines he has provided and that have been gained from his own experience as a contemplative. Perhaps this was also a part of the danger perceived by the author of *The Cloud of Unknowing* and by the conservative canon Walter Hilton, who were quick to condemn what they considered to be dangerous affective content within a didactic model. Self-knowledge as a road to knowledge of God was accepted, but unregulated procedure and such egalitarian instruction to one who is obviously a novice would have gone against the grain of most practice in regard to didactic works. An example is the *Epistle of Discretion of Stirrings*, attributed to the *Cloud*-author, which is addressed to a young contemplative who had apparently inquired as to how far he/she should follow certain promptings to special ascetic practices. In answer, the *Cloud*-author urges the novice to choose his/her own level carefully "for it is ful perilous to streine the kynde to any siche werke of devocion".[122] The work expands on the theme of the gaining of self-knowledge and is much concerned with external behaviour in observing such devotional practices as silence, fasting, and living the solitary life. This concern for proper guidance in the spiritual life is probably to be seen as a response to the tendency to unregulated eremitism best represented by Rolle.[123] It is easy to imagine how Rolle's offer of collegial friendship in guiding the reader to the "fourme of perfect lyvynge" would have been viewed as a rather free mode of religious instructional discourse – it is also probably the very reason why it was so widely read throughout the Middle Ages in that it offered the reader very special, yet very attainable, agency in his/her own spiritual journey.

Evidence that medieval readers did indeed respond to Rolle's invitation to appropriate the role of "Margaret" in his text are extant in a number of manuscripts copies of *The Form of Living* from the fourteenth and fifteenth centuries. These manuscripts acknowledge both the existence of an explicit reader for

---

[122] *Epistle of Discretion of Stirrings. Middle English Religious Prose.* Ed. N. F. Blake (London, 1972), 120.
[123] See *A Manual of the Writings in Middle English*, Vol. IX, 3071–3072.

the work, Margaret Kirkeby, and the implicit reader Rolle constructs in the work. One adapted copy omits Margaret's name and instead addresses itself to "my fulle dere and wel loued frende in god".[124] A contemporary response to Rolle's implicit invitation to occupy Margaret's position in this work can also be seen in a fifteenth-century booklet copy of *The Form of Living* where the name Cicely (probably Cicely, Duchess of York) is written over that of Margaret.[125] Vincent Gillespie suggests that such substitution would seem to illustrate the very literal identification of later audiences with the earlier female spiritual friends to whom treatises were addressed. Anne Clark Bartlett argues that it is an example of male authors offering "idealised gender positions" to female readers.[126] Yet the same book in which Cicely inserted her name over Margaret's was later owned by a "dominus Johannes Marchel", probably a Yorkshire secular priest.[127] The incipit of an extract from *The Form of Living* that occurs in the widely read *Remedy against the Troubles and Temptations* implies an intimate relationship with the recipient of the work but does not supply a name. In both the printed editions of this work by Wynkyn de Worde in 1508 and 1519, as well as in the early manuscripts, the treatise is prefaced by an abridged extract "taken out of þe thyrde chapter of a deuoute tretyse & a fourme of lyuinge that the dyscrete & vertuous Richard hampole wrote a deuoute & holy persone for grete loue".[128] In Magdalene College Cambridge, Pepys MS 2125, an extract from *The Form of Living* is headed "For men and wymmen that beþ enclosed" and "Womman" is substituted for Margaret, making even the dedication less specific.[129] Such evidence supports the idea that in the case of Rolle's *The Form of Living* the text certainly offers an idealised relationship, that of friend, but that this relationship is not necessarily only specific to the initial reader Margaret Kirkeby nor is it always an explicitly gendered relationship that is being offered.

124 Trinity College Cambridge MS 1053 cited in H. E. Allen, *English Writings*, 84. Trinity College Dublin MS 155 also has "dere frend" substituted for Margaret. See S. Ogilvie-Thomson, *Prose and Verse*, xli.
125 V. Gillespie, "Vernacular Books of Religion", 327–328. Gillespie notes that booklet circulation was common for sequences of devotional texts and that *The Form of Living* circulated quite widely in booklet form. The copy of *The Form of Living* in which Cicely's name appears is the second booklet in a four-booklet collection found in Bodleian Library, Rawlinson MS C. 285.
126 A. Clark Bartlett, *Male Authors, Female Readers*, 100.
127 V. Gillespie, "Vernacular Books of Religion", 328.
128 H. E. Allen, *Writings Ascribed*, 263.
129 S. Ogilvie-Thomson, *Prose and Verse*, xl. Ogilvie-Thomson notes a number of other manuscripts where Margaret's name is either omitted or substituted. One manuscript that suggests that *The Form of Living* reached a wide audience is University Library, Cambridge MS Ii iv 9 in which a "translation" of *The Form of Living* occurs where Margaret's name is omitted and an explanatory note takes its place: "Here endith the informacioun of Richard the Ermyte þat he wrote to an Ankyr translate oute of Northern tunge in to Sutherne that it schulde the bettir be vnderstondyn of men that be of the Selve countre Amen."

Internal evidence suggests that Rolle's development of a discourse of friendship in *The Form of Living*, his invitation to the reader to enter into a relationship of personal friendship, and the intimate tone of his prose is designed to draw the reader closer to an understanding, and empowerment, of himself/herself as an individual identity within the text. The construction of his reader as the individual soul therefore permits an audience that could include male and female religious, as well as a lay audience that comprised both male and female readers, to participate in a friendly discourse that brings them closer to an understanding both of themselves and God. In short, Rolle's offer of friendship in this work is not gender, or even recipient, specific because Rolle opens his work to as wide a readership as possible. This is most apparent in that throughout *The Form of Living* Rolle does not discuss the concept of friendship itself nor does he intimate that his authorial relationship with the reader is based on a singular personal experience. Rather, Rolle extends the friendship with Margaret to an indefinite list of potential others. The only way the work could be read as a monument to a single, real spiritual friendship is if we choose to accept Rolle's friendship with Margaret Kirkeby, which is based entirely on the account given in the *Officium*, as the cause of this work. But Rolle develops a discourse of friendship in *The Form of Living* not because, as he states in *Melos Amoris*, that he has a ministry to women, not because of the spiritual companion he longs for in *Incendium Amoris*, but because friendship itself is an exalted spiritual relationship that can be achieved in the contemplative life; a relationship both with and *in* God.

The reader/writer relationships promoted within *The Form of Living* clearly draw on accepted notions of spiritual *amicitia* but are ultimately manifestations of Rolle's own discourse of friendship that seeks to draw the reader into occupying the special place within the text which will lead to a tripartite union with both his authorial self and the divine. He invites the reader to experience bliss at the end of their long "trauaille" as a fellow sitter in contemplation. The exhortation to love God becomes, as it did in *Ego Dormio* and *The Commandment*, an exhortation to love Rolle as well. Through the appropriation of feminised language and images Rolle is able to promote the *sponsa Christi* motif that is prominent in all three vernacular treatises, but here the bride's status seems more established, more settled because sitting in the solitary life is closer to the heavenly reward of being seated in the presence of God. Rolle's three vernacular treatises exhibit a certain hierarchical progression like the three stages in the mystical marriage outlined in *Ancrene Wisse*:

I þe frumðe nis þer buten olhnunge forte drahen in luue. Ah Sone se he eauer understont þat he beo wel acointet. he wule forbeoren ow leasse. Efter þe spreoue on ende. þenne is muchele ioie.[130]

---

[130] *Ancrene Wisse*. Ed. J. R. R. Tolkien, 113/19–23.

Ego Dormio woos the reader to enter the first stages of mystical life, to become the lover of God by accepting the role of the new bride of Christ. *The Commandment* consolidates this marriage, carefully instructing the young spouse in the dangers of worldly love and how to direct their affections more appropriately. And finally, in *The Form of Living*, the reader, having accepted the ideals of the contemplative life, is elevated further to become the well-beloved friend, the *amica Dei* and true spouse, and occupy the collective space of lover, disciple and friend in God to whom Rolle writes "speciali" in the vernacular.

Indeed, throughout Rolle's vernacular treatises it is evident that the turning of the reader to the love of God is primarily achieved through engagement of the reader's *affectus*, the capturing or inflaming of the reader's will. Rolle's plea to the reader in *Ego Dormio* to "gif al þyn entent to vndrestond þis writynge" is a clear indication that his own interest in writing is not primarily to promote his own *auctoritas*, to exercise authorial control over an audience, or even to assert the worth of the speaking persona within the text, but to draw the reader into a set of subject positions and a process which will help them come to an understanding of what is written to them. When we consider this aspect of Rolle's vernacular utterance it appears less self-centred and authoritarian than previously thought; the primary function of the text is seen to be the involvement of the reader and writer in an intimate exchange; the reading process, though opened to many, remains individualised. The articulation of interiority found throughout the works, the continual appeal to the reader to "sek inwardly" and to "þynke" Rolle's words in the heart, further speaks for the importance of empowering the individual within Rolle's religious discourse.

Rolle's achievement in his English writings, I believe, offers a valuable insight into how medieval religious texts could successfully appeal to both actual and potential reading subjects through the individualisation of the reading process. Each and every reader who chooses to occupy the various reader-identities offered within the English treatises is empowered in the role of personal addressee – "þat þou wil gif þi þoght to fulfil in dede þat þou seest is profitable for þi soule" (26/34–35).

BIBLIOGRAPHY

Abelard, Peter, *Ethica. Peter Abelard's Ethics*. Ed. D. E. Luscombe. Oxford: Clarendon Press, 1971.

The Abbey of the Holy Ghost. Yorkshire Writers: Richard Rolle of Hampole and his Followers. Ed. Carl Horstmann. London: Swan Sonnenschein & Co., 1895–1896. Vol. 1. 321–337.

Aelred of Rievaulx, *De institutione inclusarum. Aelred of Rievaulx's "De institutione inclusarum". Two Middle English Versions*. Eds. J. Ayto and A. Barratt. EETS (os) 287. London: Oxford University Press, 1984.

———. *Spiritual Friendship*. Trans. Mary Eugenia Laker. Cistercian Fathers Series, 5. Kalamazoo: Cistercian Publications, 1974.

———. *Aelredi Rievallensis Opera Omnia I: Opera Ascetica*. Eds. Anselm Hoste and C. H. Talbot. Corpus Christianorum, Continuatio Medievalis I. Belgium: Brepols, 1971.

Aers, David, *Community, Gender and Individual Identity: English Writing 1360–1430*. London: Routledge, 1988.

———. *Medieval Literature: Criticism, Ideology, and History*. New York: St. Martin's Press, 1986.

Alford, John A. "Richard Rolle and Related Works". *Middle English Prose: A Critical Guide to Major Authors and Genres*. Ed. A. S. G. Edwards. New Brunswick: Rutgers University Press, 1984. 35–60.

———. "Biblical *Imitatio* in the Writings of Richard Rolle". *Journal of Literary History* 40 (1973): 1–23.

Allen, Hope Emily, "New Manuscripts of Richard Rolle". *The Times Literary Supplement* 31 (1932): 202.

———. "Richard Rolle". *The Times Literary Supplement* 31 (1932): 516.

———. *English Writings of Richard Rolle, Hermit of Hampole*. Oxford: Clarendon Press, 1931.

———. *Writings Ascribed to Richard Rolle, Hermit of Hampole, and Materials for his Biography*. Modern Language Association Monograph Series, 3. New York: Modern Language Association of America, 1927.

———. "The Mystical Lyrics of the *Manual des Péchiez*". *Romantic Review* 9 (1918): 154–193.

———. *The Authorship of "The Prick of Conscience"*. Radcliffe College Monographs, 15. Boston and New York: Ginn and Co., 1910.

Allen, Rosamund, "The Implied Audience of Laȝamon's *Brut*". *The Text and Translation of Laȝamon's Brut*. Ed. Françoise Le Saux. Cambridge, England: D. S. Brewer, 1994. 121–139.

———. trans. *Richard Rolle: The English Works*. The Classics of Western Spirituality. New York: Paulist Press, 1988.

———. "*Singular lufe*: Richard Rolle and the Grammar of Spiritual Ascent". *The Medieval Mystical Tradition in England: Papers Read at Dartington Hall, July, 1984*. Ed. Marion Glasscoe. Cambridge: D. S. Brewer, 1984. 28–54.

Amassian, Margaret G., trans. *Richard Rolle: The English Works*. The Classics of Western Spirituality. New York: Paulist Press, 1988.

Amassian, Margaret G. and Lynch, Denis, "The *Ego Dormio* of Richard Rolle in Gonville and Caius MS. 140/80". *Mediaeval Studies* 43 (1981): 218–249.

———. "The Rolle Material in Bradfer-Lawrence MS 10 and its Relationships to Other Rolle Manuscripts". *Manuscripta* 23 (1979): 67–78.

Ancrene Wisse. The English Text of the Ancrene Riwle/Ancrene Wisse edited from MS Corpus Christi College, Cambridge 402. Ed. J. R. R. Tolkien. EETS no. 249. London: Oxford University Press, 1962.

Il Libro della Beata Angela da Foligno: edizione critica. Eds. L. Thier and A. Calufetti. Spicilegium Bonaventurianum, 25. 2nd edition. Roma: Editiones Collegii S. Bonaventurae ad Claras Quas, 1985.

Aristotle, *Generation of Animals*. Trans. A. L. Peck. London: Heinemann, 1963.

———. *Nichomachaean Ethics*. Trans. J. L. Ackrill. *Aristotle's Ethics*. London: Faber & Faber, 1973.

Arnould, E. J. F. "Richard Rolle of Hampole". *The Month* 23 (1960): 13–25.

———. "Richard Rolle and the Sorbonne". *Bulletin of John Rylands Library* 23 (1939): 68–101.

———. "Richard Rolle and a Bishop: A Vindication". *Bulletin of John Rylands Library* 21 (1937): 55–77.

———. "On Richard Rolle's Patrons: A New Reading". *Medium Aevum* 6 (1937): 122–124.

Arnzt, Mary Luke, *Richard Rolle and The Holy Boke Gratia Dei: An Edition with Commentary*. Salzburg Studies in English Literature: Elizabethan and Renaissance Studies, 92: 2. Salzburg: Institut für Anglistik und Amerikanistik, 1981.

Astell, Ann, *The Song of Songs in the Middle Ages*. Ithaca: Cornell University Press, 1990.

———. "Feminine *Figurae* in the Writings of Richard Rolle: A Register of Growth". *Mystics Quarterly* 15/3 (1989): 117–124.

Aston, Margaret, *Faith and Fire: Popular and Unpopular Religion 1350–1600*. London: Hambledon Press, 1993.

———. *Lollards and Reformers: Images and Literacy in Late Medieval Religion*. London: Hambledon Press, 1984.

Atkinson, Clarissa W. *Mystic and Pilgrim: The Book and World of Margery Kempe*. New York: Cornell University Press, 1983.

———. "*Precious Balsam in a Fragile Glass*: The Ideology of Virginity in the Later Middle Ages". *Journal of Family History* 8 (1983): 131–134.

Audelay, John, *The Poems of John Audelay*. Ed. and intro. Ella Keats Whiting. EETS (os) 184 [1931]. Reprint. New York: Kraus, 1971.

Augustine, *De Doctrina Christiana* (Christian Instruction). Trans. John J. Gavigan. *The Fathers of the Church: A New Translation*. Vol. 2. Washington: The Catholic University Press of America, 1985.

———. *Faith, Hope and Charity*. Trans. Bernard M. Peebles. *The Fathers of the Church: A New Translation*. Vol. 2. Washington: The Catholic University Press of America, 1985.

———. *The Greatness of the Soul*. Trans. Joseph. M. Colleran. Westminster: Newman Press, 1950.

Ayenbite of Inwit. Ed. Richard Morris. Reprinted as *Dan Michel's Ayenbite of Inwit:*

Or Remorse of Conscience. Ed. Pamela Gradon. 2 vols. EETS (os) 23 and 278. London: Oxford University Press, 1965 and 1979.

Baker, Denise N., "The Active and the Contemplative Lives in Rolle, the *Cloud*-Author and Hilton". *The Medieval Mystical Tradition: England, Ireland and Wales*. Ed. Marion Glasscoe. Cambridge: D. S. Brewer, 1999. 85–102.

———. "Julian of Norwich and Anchoritic Literature". *Mystics Quarterly* 19/4 (1993): 148–160.

Baker, Derek, *Medieval Women*. Oxford: Blackwell, 1978.

Bakhtin, Mikhail, *Marxism and the Philosophy of Language*. London: Seminar Press, 1973.

Barratt, Alexandra, *Women's Writings in Middle English*. London: Longman, 1992.

———. "Works of Religious Instruction". *Middle English Prose: A Critical Guide to Major Authors and Genres*. Ed. A. S. G. Edwards. New Brunswick: Rutgers University Press, 1984. 413–432.

Barthes, Roland, "The Death of the Author". *Image-Music-Text*. Trans. Stephen Heath. New York: Hill & Wang, 1977. 142–148.

Bartholomaeus Anglicus, *On the Properties of Things: John Trevisa's Translation of Bartholomaeus Anglicus, De proprietatibus rerum*. Ed. M. C. Seymour. Oxford: Clarendon Press, 1975.

Bartlett, Anne Clark, *Male Authors, Female Readers: Representation and Subjectivity in Medieval Devotional Literature*. Ithaca and London: Cornell University Press, 1995.

———. " 'A Reasonable Affection': Gender and Spiritual Friendship in Middle English Devotional Literature". *Vox Mystica: Essays for Valerie M. Lagorio*. Eds. Anne Clark Bartlett, Thomas H. Bestul, Janet Goebel and William F. Pollard. Cambridge: D. S. Brewer, 1995. 131–145.

Baumgardt, David, "The Concept of Mysticism: Analysis of a Letter Written by Hildegard of Bingen to Guibert of Gembloux". *Review of Religion* 12 (1948): 277–286.

Beckwith, Sarah, *Christ's Body: Identity, Culture and Society in Medieval Writings*. London and New York: Routledge, 1993.

———. "A Very Material Mysticism: The Medieval Mysticism of Margery Kempe". *Medieval Literature: Criticism, Ideology, and History*. Ed. David Aers. New York: St. Martin's Press, 1986. 34–57.

Beer, Frances, *Women and Mystical Experience in the Middle Ages*. Woodbridge: Boydell Press, 1992.

Bell, Susan Groag, "Medieval Women Book Owners: Arbiters of Lay Piety and Ambassadors of Culture". *Women and Power in the Middle Ages*. Eds. M. Erler and M. Kowaleski. Athens: University of Georgia Press, 1988. 149–187.

Bennett, H. S. *English Books and Readers 1475–1557: Being a Study in the History of the Book Trade from Caxton to the Incorporation of the Stationers' Company*. 2nd edition. London: Cambridge University Press, 1969.

Bennett, J. A. W. *Poetry of the Passion: Studies in Twelve Centuries of English Verse*. Oxford: Clarendon Press, 1982.

Benson, R. H. *The History of Richard Raynal, Solitary*. London: Pitman, 1906.

Bernard of Clairvaux, *Bernard of Clairvaux: Selected Works*. Ed. Gillian Rosemary Evans. The Classics of Western Spirituality. New York: Paulist Press, 1987.

———. *On the Song of Songs*. Trans. Killian Walsh. *The Works of Bernard of Clairvaux*.

Cistercian Fathers Series; no. 4, 7, 31, 40. Shannon, Ireland: Irish University Press, 1971–1980.

———. *Sancti Bernardi Opera*. Ed J. Leclerq, C. H. Talbot, H. M. Rochais. Rome: Editiones Cistercienses, 1957–.

Bestul, Thomas H. "Devotional Writing in England Between Anselm and Richard Rolle". *Mysticism: Medieval and Modern*. Ed. Valerie M. Lagorio. Salzburg Studies in English Literature: Elizabethan and Renaissance Studies, 92: 20. Salzburg: Institut für Anglistik und Amerikanistik, 1986. 12–28.

Birrell, T. A. "English Catholic Mystics in Non-Catholic Circles". *Downside Review* 94 (1976): 213–231.

Blake, N. F. "*The Form of Living* in Prose and Poetry". *Archiv für das Studium der Neueren Sprachen und Litteraturan* 211 (1974): 300–308.

———. *Middle English Religious Prose*. York Medieval Texts. London: Edward Arnold, 1972.

———. "Middle English Prose and its Audience". *Anglia: Zeitschrift für Englische Philologie* 90 (1972): 437–435.

Blamires, Alcuin, ed. *Woman Defamed and Woman Defended: An Anthology of Medieval Texts*. Oxford: Clarendon Press, 1992.

Boenig, Robert, *Chaucer and the Mystics: The Canterbury Tales and the Genre of Devotional Prose*. Lewisburg: Bucknell University Press, 1995.

———. "St. Augustine's *Jubilus* and Richard Rolle's *Canor*". *Vox Mystica: Essays for Valerie M. Lagorio*. Eds. Anne Clark Bartlett, Thomas H. Bestul, Janet Goebel and William F. Pollard. Cambridge: D. S. Brewer, 1995. 75–86.

———. "*Contemplations of the Dread and Love of God*, Richard Rolle and Aelred of Rievaulx". *Mystics Quarterly* 16/1 (1990): 27–33.

———. "The Middle English *Contemplations of the Dread and Love of God*". *Studia Mystica* 9/2 (1986): 26–35.

———. "The God-as-Mother Theme in Richard Rolle's Biblical Commentaries". *Mystics Quarterly* 10 (1984): 171–174.

Boenig, Robert, and Pollard, William F., eds. *Mysticism and Spirituality in Medieval England*. Cambridge: D. S. Brewer, 1997.

Bokenham, Osbern, *Bokenham's Legendys of Hooly Wummen*. Ed. Mary S. Serjeantson. EETS (os) 206. London: Oxford University Press, 1938.

Bonaventure, "The Major Life of St. Francis". Trans. B. Fahy. *St. Francis of Assisi, Writing and Earlier Biographies: English Omnibus of the Sources for the Life of St. Francis*. Ed. M. A. Habig. London: Society for Promoting Christian Knowledge, 1979. 629–787.

———. "The Soul's Journey into God". Trans. Ewert Cousins. *Bonaventure: The Soul's Journey into God; The Tree of Life; The Life of St. Francis*. The Classics of Western Spirituality. New York: Paulist Press, 1978.

———. *Opera Omnia Sanctae Bonaventurae*. Ed. A. C. Peltier. 15 vols. Paris: Vives, 1864–1871.

Book of Vices and Virtues. Ed. W. Nelson Francis. EETS (os) 217. London: Oxford University Press, 1942.

Brady, Sister Mary Teresa, "Rolle and the Pattern of Tracts in *The Pore Caitif*". *Traditio* 39 (1983): 456–465.

———. "The Seynt and His Boke: Rolle's *Emendatio Vitae* and *The Pore Caitif*". *Mystics Quarterly* 7 (1981): 20–30.

————. "Rolle's *Form of Living* and *The Pore Caitif*". *Traditio* 36 (1980): 426–435.

Brinton, Thomas, *Sermons 1373–1389*. Ed. Sister Mary Aquinas Devlin. 2 vols. London: Offices of the Royal Historical Society, 1954.

Bridenthal, R. and Koonz, C. *Becoming Visible: Women in European History*. Boston: Houghton Mifflin, 1977.

Brown, Carlton, ed. *Religious Lyrics of the XIVth Century*. 2nd edition. Oxford: Clarendon Press, 1957.

————. ed. *English Lyrics of the XIIIth Century*. Oxford: Clarendon Press, 1932.

Brooke, Odo, "William of St. Thierry's Doctrine of the Ascent to God by Faith". *Studies in Monastic Theology*. Odo Brooke. Kalamazoo: Cistercian Publications, 1980. 134–207.

Bugge, J. *Virginitas: An Essay in the History of a Medieval Ideal*. Archives Internationales d'histoire des Idées. Series minor, 17. The Hague: Martinus Nijhoff, 1975.

Bulst, Walther, ed. *Die ältere Wormser Briefsammlung*. Monumenta Germaniae Historica. Weimar: Hermann Böhlaus Nachfolger, 1949.

Burrow, J. A. *The Ages of Man: A Study in Medieval Writing and Thought*. Oxford: Clarendon Press, 1986.

————. *Medieval Writers and Their Work: Middle English Literature and Its Background 1100–1500*. London: Oxford University Press, 1982.

————. ed. *English Verse 1300–1500*. London and New York: Longman, 1977.

The Hours of Mary of Burgundy. [Codex Vindobonensis 1857 Vienna, Österreichische Nationalbibliothek.] Commentary by Eric Inglis. London: Harvey Miller Publishers, 1995.

Bynum, Caroline Walker, *Fragmentation and Redemption: Essays on Gender and the Human Body in Medieval Religion*. New York: Zone Books, 1991.

————. *Holy Feast and Holy Fast: The Religious Significance of Food to Medieval Women*. The New Historicism: Studies in Cultural Poetics. Berkeley: University of California Press, 1987.

————. *Gender and Religion: On the Complexity of Symbols*. [Other eds. Steven Harrell and Paula Richman.] Boston: Beacon Press, 1986.

————. *Jesus as Mother*. Publications of the Centre for Medieval and Renaissance Studies, UCLA; 16. Berkeley: University of California Press, 1982.

Cadden, Joan, *The Meanings of Sex Difference in the Middle Ages: Medicine, Science and Culture*. Cambridge History of Medicine. Cambridge: Cambridge University Press, 1993.

Caldwell, Ellen, "The Rhetorics of Enthusiasm and of Restraint in *The Form of Living* and the *Cloud of Unknowing*". *Mystics Quarterly* 10 (1987): 9–16.

Carey, Hilary, "Devout Literate Laypeople and the Pursuit of the Mixed Life in Later Medieval England". *Journal of Religious History* 14 (1987): 361–381.

Carsley, Catherine A. "Devotion to the Holy Name: Late Medieval Piety in England". *Princeton University Library Chronicle* 53/2 (1992): 156–172.

Casagrande Carla, "The Protected Woman". Trans. C. Botsford. *A History of Women in the West: Vol. II, Silences of the Middle Ages*. Ed. Christine Klapische-Zuber. Cambridge, Massachusetts and London: Harvard University Press, 1992. 70–104.

Chambers, R. W. "On the Continuity of English Prose from Alfred to More and His School". *The Life and Death of Sir Thomas Moore Knight, Sometymes Lord High*

Chancellor of England: Written in the Tyme of Queene Marie by Nicholas Harpsfield. Eds. E. V. Hitchcock and R. W. Chambers. EETS (os) 186. London: Oxford University Press, 1932. xlv–clxxiv.

The Chastising of God's Children and the Treatise of Perfection of the Sons of God. Eds. Joyce Bazire and Eric Colledge. Oxford: Basil Blackwell, 1957.

Chaucer, Geoffrey, *The Works of Geoffrey Chaucer.* Ed. F. N. Robinson. 2nd edition. Oxford: Oxford University Press, 1985.

Cherewatuk, K. and Wiethaus, U., eds. *Dear Sister, Medieval Women and the Epistolary Genre.* Philadelphia: University of Pennsylvania Press, 1993.

Cigman, Gloria, ed. *Lollard Sermons.* EETS no. 294. London: Oxford University Press, 1989.

Clanchy, M. T. *From Memory to Written Record: England 1066–1307.* London: Edward Arnold, 1987.

Clark, J. P. H. "Richard Rolle, a Theological Reassessment". *Downside Review* 101 (1983): 15–29.

———. "Richard Rolle as Biblical Commentator". *Downside Review* 104 (1983): 165–213.

Clay, Rotha Mary, *The Hermits and Anchorites of England.* London: Methuen, 1914.

Cleve, Gunnel, "Some Remarks on Richard Rolle's Prose Style". *Neuphilologische Mitteilungen* 85 (1984): 115–121.

The Cloud of Unknowing and the Book of Privy Counselling. Ed. Phyllis Hodgson. EETS (os) 218. London: Oxford University Press, 1944.

Coakely, John, "Gender and the Authority of Friars: the Significance of Holy Women for Thirteenth-Century Franciscans and Dominicans". *Church History* 60/4 (1991): 445–460.

Coleman, Janet, *Ancient and Medieval Memories: Studies in the Reconstruction of the Past.* Cambridge: Cambridge University Press, 1992.

———. *English Literature in History 1350–1400, Medieval Writers and Readers.* London: Hutchinson, 1981.

Coleman, Joyce, *Public Reading and the Reading Public in Late Medieval England and France.* Cambridge: Cambridge University Press, 1996.

Coleman, T. W. *English Mystics of the Fourteenth Century.* London: The Epworth Press, 1938.

Colledge, Edmund, "Early English Spirituality". *The Month* 30 (1963): 108–120.

———. ed. *The Medieval Mystics of England.* London: John Murray, 1961.

———. "The Medieval Mystics and their Critics". *Life of the Spirit* xv (1961): 554–559.

———. "*Epistola Solitari ad Reges*: Alphonse of Pecha as Organiser of Brigittine and Urbanist Propaganda". *Mediaeval Studies* 17 (1956): 19–49.

Collins, John E. *Mysticism and New Paradigm Psychology.* Maryland: Rowman & Littlefield, 1991.

Comper, Frances M. M. *The Life of Richard Rolle, Together With an Edition of his English Lyrics.* London: J. M. Dent, 1928.

———. ed. *The Fire of Love or Melody of Love and the Mending of Life or the Rule of Living, with an Introduction by Evelyn Underhill.* London: Methuen, 1914.

Conner, Edward L. " 'Goostly freend in God': Aelred of Rievaulx's *De spirituali amicitia* as a Source of *The Cloud of Unknowing*". *Vox Mystica: Essays for Valerie M.*

Lagorio. Eds. Anne Clark Bartlett, Thomas H. Bestul, Janet Goebel and William F. Pollard. Cambridge: D. S. Brewer, 1995. 87–98.

Constable, Giles, *Letters and Letter Collections*. Typologie des Sources du Moyen Age Occidental. Fasc. 17. Turnhout, Belgium: Brepols, 1976.

———. "Twelfth-Century Spirituality and the Late Middle Ages". *Medieval and Renaissance Studies* 5 (1971): 27–60.

———. "Aelred of Rievaulx and the Nun of Watton: An Episode in the History of the Gilbertine Order". *Medieval Women*. Ed. Derek Baker. Oxford: Blackwell, 1978. 205–226.

Contemplacyons of the Drede and Loue of God. London: Wynkyn de Worde, 1506. Reprinted in *Yorkshire Writers: Richard Rolle of Hampole and his Followers*. Ed. Carl Horstman. London: Swan Sonnenschein & Co., 1895–1896. Vol. 2. 72–105.

Contemplations of the Dread and Love of God. Ed. M. Connolly. EETS no. 303. London: Oxford University Press, 1993.

Copeland, Rita, "Richard Rolle and the Rhetorical Theory of the Levels of Style". *The Medieval Mystical Tradition In England: Papers Read at Dartington Hall, July, 1984*. Ed. Marion Glasscoe. Cambridge: D. S. Brewer, 1984. 55–80.

Cousins, Ewert H., "Francis of Assisi: Christian Mysticism at the Crossroads". *Mysticism and Religious Traditions*. Ed. S. T. Katz. New York: Oxford University Press, 1983. 163–191.

Culler, Jonathon, *On Deconstruction: Theory and Criticism After Structuralism*. Jonathon Culler. Ithaca: Cornell University Press, 1982.

Cursor Mundi: A Northumbrium Poem of the Fourteenth Century. Ed. Richard Norris. Issued in 7 parts, bound into 3 vols. EETS (os) 57, 59 and 62. London: Oxford University Press, 1874–1893.

Curtius, Ernst Robert, *European Literature and the Latin Middle Ages*. [Trans. from the German by Willard R. Trask.] London: Routledge & Keegan Paul, 1953.

Dahood, Roger, "*Ancrene Wisse*, the Katherine Group and the *Wohunge* Group". *Middle English Prose: A Critical Guide to Major Authors and Genres*. Ed. A. S. G. Edwards. New Brunswick: Rutgers University Press, 1984. 1–33.

Darwin, F. F., *The English Mediaeval Recluse*. 2nd edition. London: Society for Promoting Christian Knowledge, 1944.

R. T. Davies, *Medieval English Lyrics: A Critical Anthology*. London: Faber, 1963

Davis, Virginia, "The Rule of St. Paul, the First Hermit in Late-medieval England". *Monks, Hermits and the Ascetic Tradition*. Ed. W. J. Sheils. Ecclesiastical History Society: Studies in Church History, 22. Oxford: Blackwell, 1984/85. 203–214.

Davlin, Mary, "*Kynde Knowyng* as a Middle English Equivalent for 'Wisdom' in *Piers Plowman* B". *Medium Aevum* 50 (1981): 5–17.

Deanesly, Margaret, "Vernacular Books in England in the Fourteenth and Fifteenth Centuries". *Modern Language Review* xv (1920): 348–358.

———. *The Lollard Bible and Other Medieval Biblical Versions*. Cambridge: Cambridge University Press, 1920.

deFord, Sara, "The Use and Function of Alliteration in the *Melos Amoris* of Richard Rolle". *Mystics Quarterly* 12 (1986): 59–66.

———. "Mystical Union in the *Melos Amoris* of Richard Rolle". *The Medieval Mystical Tradition in England: Papers Read at the Exeter Symposium, July, 1980*. Ed. Marion Glasscoe. Exeter: Exeter University Press, 1980. 173–201.

Deonise Hid Diuinite. Ed. Phyllis Hodgson. EETS (os) 231. London: Oxford University Press, 1955.

Depres, Denise Louise, *Ghostly Sights: Visual Meditation in Late Medieval Literature*. Oklahoma: Pilgrim Books, 1989.

Dives and Pauper. Ed. Priscilla Heath Barnum. Oxford: Oxford University Press, 1980.

Doyle, Ian, "Carthusian Participation in the Movements of Works of Richard Rolle Between England and the Other Parts of Europe in the Fourteenth and Fifteenth Centuries". *Analecta Cartusiana* 55/2 (1981): 157–166.

Dronke, Peter, *The Medieval Lyric*. 2nd edition. London: Hutchinson, 1978.

Edmund of Abingdon, *Speculum Religiosorum* and *Speculum Ecclesie*. Ed. H. P. Forshaw. Auctores Britannici Medii Aevi, III. London: Oxford University Press, 1973.

Edwards, A. S. G. *Middle English Prose: A Critical Guide to Major Authors and Genres*. New Brunswick, New Jersey: Rutgers University Press, 1984.

Edwards, A. S. G., Gillespie, Vincent and Hanna, Ralph, *The Medieval Book: Studies in Memory of Jeremy Griffiths*. London: The British Library, 2000.

Elkins, Sharon K. *Holy Women of Twelfth-Century England*. London: Chapel Hill, 1988.

Ellis, Roger, "The Choices of the Translator in the Late Middle English Period". *The Medieval Mystical Tradition in England: Papers Read at Dartington Hall, July, 1982*. Ed. Marion Glasscoe. Exeter: Exeter University Press, 1982. 18–46.

Elwyn, Verier, *Richard Rolle, A Christian Sannyasi*. The Baktas of the World, 3. Madras: Christian Literature Society for India, 1930.

Everett, D. "The Middle-English Prose Psalter of Richard Rolle of Hampole". *Modern Language Review* xvii and xviii (1922–1923): xvii, 217–227, 337–350 and xviii, 381–393.

Exon, Margaret, "The Production and Ownership of Manuscript Books in Late Medieval England". Diss. University of Western Australia, 1994.

Farmer, Hugh, "The Meditations of the Monk of Farne". *Analecta Monastica* 4 (1957): 141–245.

Ferrante, Joan M. *To The Glory of Her Sex: Women's Roles in the Composition of Medieval Texts*. Bloomington, Indiana: Indiana University Press, 1997.

———. *Woman as Image in Medieval Literature from the Twelfth Century to Dante*. Columbia: Columbia University Press, 1975.

Finke, Laurie A. and Shichtman, Martin B. *Medieval Texts & Contemporary Readers*. Ithaca: Cornell University Press, 1987.

Finucane, Ronald C. *Miracles and Pilgrims: Popular Beliefs in Medieval England*. London: J. M. Dent, 1977.

Fite, Patricia, "To 'Sytt and Syng of Luf Langyng': The Feminine Dynamic of Richard Rolle's Mysticism". *Studia Mystica* 14/2–3 (1991): 13–29.

Flynn, Elizabeth A. and Schweickart, Patrocinio P., eds. *Gender and Reading: Essays on Readers, Texts, and Contexts*. Baltimore and London: The Johns Hopkins University Press, 1986.

Foucault, Michel, "What is an Author?". *Language, Counter-Memory, Practice*. Ed. Donald F. Bouchard. New York: Cornell University Press, 1977. 124–127.

Frankis, J. "The Social Context of Vernacular Writing in Thirteenth Century

England: The Evidence of the Manuscripts". *Thirteenth Century England*. Eds. P. R. Cross and S. D. Lloyd. Woodbridge: Boydell Press, 1986. 175–184.

Froomberg, Hilary, "*The Virtue of Our Lord's Passion* by Richard Rolle of Hampole". *Life of the Spirit* 3 (1948): 221–225.

Galen, *De usu partium*. Trans. Margaret Tallmadge May. *Galen on the Usefulness of the Parts of the Body*. Ithaca: Cornell University Press, 1968.

Ganim, John M. *Style and Consciousness in Middle English Narrative*. Princeton: Princeton University Press, 1983.

Garay, Kathleen E. " 'A Naked Intent Unto God': Ungendered Discourse in Some Late Medieval Mystical Texts". *Mystics Quarterly* 23/2 (1997): 36–51.

Gardiner, H. M. *Feeling and Emotion: A History of Theories*. American Psychology Series. New York: American Books, 1937.

Sir Gawain and the Green Knight. Ed. W. R. J. Barron. Manchester Medieval Classics. Manchester: Manchester University Press, 1974.

Georgianna, Linda, *The Solitary Self: Individuality in the Ancrene Wisse*. Cambridge, Massachusetts and London, England: Harvard University Press, 1981.

Gilchrist, Roberta, *Gender and Material Culture: The Archaeology of Religious Women*. London: Routledge, 1994.

Gillespie, Vincent, "Never Look a Gift Horace in the Mouth: Affective Poetics in the Middle Ages". *Litteraria Pragensia: Studies in Literature & Culture* 5/10 (1995): 59–82.

———. "Postcards from the Edge: Interpreting the Ineffable in the Middle English Mystics". *Interpretation: Medieval and Modern*. Ed. Piero Boitani. Cambridge: D. S. Brewer, 1993. 137–165.

———. "Vernacular Books of Religion". *Book Production and Publishing in Britain, 1375–1475*. Eds. J. Griffiths and D. Pearsall. Cambridge: Cambridge University Press, 1989. 317–344.

———. "Strange Images of Death: The Passion in Later Medieval English Devotional and Mystical Writing". *Analecta Cartusiana* 117 (1987): 111–159.

———. " 'Lukynge in haly bukes': *Lectio* in Late Medieval Spiritual Miscellanies". *Analecta Cartusiana* 106 (1984): 1–27.

———. "The *Cibus Anime*, Book 3, a Guide for Contemplatives?" *Analecta Cartusiana* 35/3 (1983): 90–119.

———. "Mystic's Foot: Rolle and Affectivity". *The Medieval Mystical Tradition in England: Papers Read at Dartington Hall, July, 1982*. Ed. Marion Glasscoe. Exeter: Exeter University Press, 1982. 199–230.

Glasscoe, Marion, *English Medieval Mystics: Games of Faith*. London: Longman, 1993.

———. *The Medieval Mystical Tradition in England: Papers Read at Dartington Hall, July, 1984*. Cambridge: D. S. Brewer, 1984.

———. *The Medieval Mystical Tradition in England: Papers Read at Dartington Hall, July, 1982*. Exeter: Exeter University Press, 1982.

———. *The Medieval Mystical Tradition in England: Papers Read at the Exeter Symposium, July, 1980*. Exeter: Exeter University Press, 1980.

Godden, Malcolm, "Plowmen and Hermits in *Piers Plowman*". *Review of English Studies* 35 (1984): 129–163.

Goldberg, P. J. P., ed. *Woman is a Worthy Wight: Women in English Society c.1200–1500*. Gloucestershire, England: Alan Sutton, 1992.

Goodall, John A. "The Invocation of the Name of Jesus in the English XIVth Century Spiritual Writers". *Chrysostom* iii. No. 2 (1972): 113–117.

Goodich, Michael, "The Contours of Medieval Piety in Later Medieval Historiography". *Church History* 50 (1981): 20–32.

Graff, E. S. "A Checklist of Rolle Scholarship 1896–1993". *Mystics Quarterly* 20/2 (1994): 68–75.

Gray, Douglas, ed. *A Selection of Religious Lyrics.* Oxford: Clarendon Press, 1975.

———. *Themes and Images in the Medieval English Religious Lyric.* London and Boston: Routledge & Kegan Paul, 1972.

Griffiths, Jeremy and Pearsall, Derek, eds. *Book Production and Publishing in Britain, 1375–1475.* Cambridge: Cambridge University Press, 1989.

Grundmann, Herbert, *Religiose Bewegungen im Mittelalter.* Hildesheim: Georg Olms Verlagsbuchhandlung, 1961.

Hagen, Susan K. *Allegorical Remembrance: A Study of the Pilgrimage of the Life of Man as a Medieval Treatise on Seeing and Remembering.* Athens and London: University of Georgia Press, 1990.

Hali Meiðhad. Medieval English Prose for Women. Eds. Bella Millett and Jocelyn Wogan-Browne. Oxford: Clarendon Press, 1990. 2–43

Happold, F. C. *Mysticism: A Study and Anthology.* Harmondsworth: Penguin Books, 1963.

Hamburger, Jeffrey, *Nuns As Artists: The Visual Culture of a Medieval Convent.* Berkeley: University of California Press, 1997.

———. "The Visual and the Visionary: The Image in Late Medieval Monastic Devotion". *Viator* 20 (1987): 161–185.

Hardwick, J. C. "A Medieval Anti-Scholastic". *Modern Churchman* 6 (1916–1917): 251–255.

Hargreaves, Henry, "*Lessouns of Dirige*: A Rolle Text Discovered". *Neuphilologische Mitteilungen* 91 (1990): 311–319.

Hartung, Albert E., ed. *A Manual of the Writings in Middle English, 1050–1400.* 9 vols. New Haven: Connecticut Academy of Arts and Sciences, 1967–1993.

Harvey, Barbara, *Living and Dying in England, 1100–1540: The Monastic Experience.* Oxford: Clarendon Press, 1993.

Heseltine, G. C., ed. *Selected Works of Richard Rolle.* London: Longmans, Green & Co., 1930.

Hilton, Walter, *On the Mixed Life.* Ed. Sarah Ogilvie-Thomson. Salzburg Studies in English Literature: Elizabethan and Renaissance Studies, 92: 18. Salzburg: Institut für Anglistik und Amerikanistik, 1986.

———. *The Scale of Perfection.* Ed. Evelyn Underhill. London: John M. Watkins, 1923.

———. "On Angels' Song". *Yorkshire Writers: Richard Rolle of Hampole and his Followers.* Ed. Carl Horstmann. London: Swan Sonnenschein & Co., 1895–1896. Vol. 1. 175–182.

Hodapp, William F. "Sacred Time and Space Within: Drama and Ritual in Late Medieval Affective Passion Meditations". *Downside Review* 115/4 (1997): 235–248.

———. "Richard Rolle's Passion Meditations in the Context of his English Epistles: *Imitatio Christi* and the Three Degrees of Love". *Mystics Quarterly* 20/3 (1994): 96–104.

Hodgson, Geraldine, ed. *Rolle and "Our Daily Work"*. London: Faith Press, 1929.

———. *The Sanity of Mysticism: A Study of Richard Rolle*. London: Faith Press, 1926.

———. *English Mystics*. London, Oxford, Milwaukee: A. R. Mowbray & Co. Ltd., 1922.

———. ed. *The Form of Living and Other Prose Treatises of Richard Rolle of Hampole*. London: Thomas Baker, 1910.

Holdsworth, C. J. "John of Ford and English Cistercian Writings 1167–1214". *Transactions of the Royal Historical Society* 5th series xi (1961): 117–136.

Horstmann, Carl, ed. *Yorkshire Writers: Richard Rolle of Hampole, an English Father of the Church, and His Followers*. 2 vols. London: Swan Sonnenschein & Co., 1895–1896.

Horstmann, Carl and Furnivall, F. J., eds. *Minor Poems of the Vernon MS*. EETS (os) 98. London: Keegan Paul, Trench & Trübner, 1892.

Hudson, Ann, ed. *Two Wycliffite Texts*. EETS (os) 301. London: Oxford University Press, 1993.

von Hügel, Friedrich, *The Mystical Element in Religion*. 2 vols. London: J. M. Dent, 1909.

Hugh of Strasbourg, *Compendium Theologicae Veritatis. Opera Omnia Sancti Bonaventurae*. Ed. A. C. Peltier. Paris: Vives, 1864–1871. Vol. 8. 60–246.

Hughes, Jonathan, *Pastors and Visionaries: Religion and Secular Life in Late-Medieval Yorkshire*. Woodbridge: Boydell Press, 1988.

Hunt, Alan, *Governance of the Consuming Passions: A History of Sumptuary Law*. New York: St. Martin's Press, 1996.

Hussey, S. S. "The Audience for The Middle English Mystics". *De Cella in Seculum: Religious and Secular Life and Devotion in Late Medieval England*. Ed. M. G. Sargent. Cambridge: D. S. Brewer, 1989. 109–122.

———. "The Text of *The Scale of Perfection*". *Neuphilologische Mitteilungen* 65 (1964): 75–92.

Hyatte, Reginald, *The Arts of Friendship: The Idealisation of Friendship in Medieval and Early Renaissance Literature*. Brill's Studies in Intellectual History, 50. Leiden: E. J. Brill, 1994.

Ingram, J. K., ed. *The Earliest Translations of the First Three Books of "De Imitatione Christi"*. EETS (es) 63. London: Kegan Paul, Trench & Trübner, 1893.

Irigaray, Luce, *Speculum of the Other Woman*. Trans. Gillian C. Gill. Ithaca: Cornell University Press, 1985.

Iser, Wolfgang, *The Act of Reading: A Theory of Aesthetic Response*. Baltimore and London: The Johns Hopkins University Press, 1978.

———. *The Implied Reader: Patterns of Communication in Prose Fiction from Bunyan to Beckett*. Baltimore and London: The Johns Hopkins University Press, 1974.

James, S. B. "Richard Rolle, Englishman". *Christian Review* 20 (1941): 31–44.

James, W. *The Varieties of Religious Experience*. Gifford Lectures. London: Longmans, Green & Co., 1902.

Jantzen, Grace Marion, *Power, Gender and Christian Mysticism*. Cambridge: Cambridge University Press, 1995.

———. *Julian of Norwich: Mystic and Theologian*. New York: Paulist Press, 1988.

Jennings, Margaret, "Richard Rolle and the Three Degrees of Love". *Downside Review* 93 (1975): 193–200.

Jolliffe, P. S., ed. "Two Middle English Tracts on the Contemplative Life". *Mediaeval Studies* 37 (1975): 85–121.

———. *A Checklist of Middle-English Prose Writings of Spiritual Guidance*. Toronto: Pontifical Institute of Medieval Studies, 1974.

Jones, E. A. "A Chapter from Richard Rolle in Two Fifteenth-Century Compilations". *Leeds Studies in English* 27 (1996): 139–162.

Julian of Norwich, *A Revelation of Divine Love*. Published as *A Book of Showings to the Anchoress Julian of Norwich*. Eds. Edmund Colledge and James Walsh. 2 vols. Studies and Texts, 35. Toronto: Pontifical Institute of Medieval Studies, 1978.

Karras, Ruth Mazo, "Friendship and Love in the Lives of Two Twelfth-Century English Saints". *Journal of Medieval History* 14 (1988): 305–320.

Keesey, D., ed. *Contexts for Criticism*. California: Mayfield Publishing Company, 1993.

Keiser, G. " 'Noght How Lang Man Lifs; Bot How Wele': The Laity and the Ladder of Perfection". *De Cella in Seculum: Religious and Secular Life and Devotion in Late Medieval England*. Ed. M. G. Sargent. Cambridge: D. S. Brewer, 1989. 145–159.

Kempe, Margery, *The Book of Margery Kempe: The Text from the Unique MS. owned by Colonel W. Butler-Bowden*. Eds. Stanford B. Meech and Hope Emily Allen. EETS (os) 212. London: Milford, 1940.

Ker, Margaret, "Brides of Christ and Poor Mortals: Women in Medieval Society". *Exploring Women's Past*. Ed. Patricia Crawford. Melbourne: Sisters Publications, 1983. 7–47.

Ker, N. R. *Medieval Libraries of Great Britain: A List of Surviving Books*. 2nd edition. London: Office of the Royal Historical Society, 1964.

Kieckhefer, Richard, *Unquiet Souls: Fourteenth Century Saints and their Religious Milieu*. Chicago: University of Chicago Press, 1984.

Knight, Stephen, *Geoffrey Chaucer*. Oxford: Basil Blackwell, 1986.

Knowles, David, *The Religious Orders in England*. 2 vols. Cambridge: Cambridge University Press, 1962.

———. *The English Mystical Tradition*. London: Burns & Oates, 1961.

Knowlton, Sister Mary, *The Influence of Richard Rolle and Julian of Norwich on the Middle English Lyric*. The Hague: Mouton, 1973.

Kohl, Benjamin G. *Renaissance Humanism, 1300–1500: A Bibliography of Materials in English*. New York: Garland, 1985.

Kolve, V. A. *Chaucer and the Imagery of Narrative: The First Five Canterbury Tales*. Stanford: Stanford University Press, 1984.

———. "Chaucer and the Visual Arts". *Geoffrey Chaucer: Writers and their Background*. Ed. D. Brewer. London: G. Bell, 1974. 290–320.

Kuczynski, Michael P. *Prophetic Song: The Psalms as Moral Discourse in Late Medieval England*. Philadelphia: University of Pennsylvania Press, 1995.

Lagorio, Valerie M. "Variations on the Theme of God's Motherhood in Medieval English Mystical Tradition and Devotional Writings". *Studia Mystica* 8 (1985): 15–37.

———. "Problems in Middle English Mystical Prose". *Middle English Prose: Essays on Bibliographical Problems*. Eds. A. S. G. Edwards and D. Pearsall. New York: Garland, 1981. 129–148.

Langland, William, *The Vision of Piers Plowman*. Ed. A. V. C. Schmidt. London: J. M. Dent, 1978.

Latham, R. E. *Revised Medieval Latin Word-list from British and Irish Sources*. Prepared by R. E. Latham, under the direction of a committee appointed by the British Academy. London: Oxford University Press, 1965.

Lay Folk's Catechism. Eds. T. F. Simmons and H. E. Nolloth. EETS (os) 118. London: Oxford University Press, 1901.

Lay Folk's Mass Book. Ed. T. F. Simmons. London: N. Trübner, 1879.

Leff, Gordon, *The Dissolution of the Medieval Outlook: An Essay on the Intellectual and Spiritual Change in the Fourteenth Century*. New York: New York University Press, 1976.

Lerner, Robert E. "The Image of Mixed Liquids in Late Medieval Mystical Thought". *Church History* 40 (1971): 397–441.

Lewis, Gertrud Jaron, *By Women, For Women, About Women: The Sister-Books of Fourteenth-Century Germany*. Toronto: Pontifical Institute of Medieval Studies, 1996.

Liegey, Gabriel, "The Rhetorical Aspects of Richard Rolle's *Melum Contemplativorum*". Diss. Columbia University, 1954.

Lochrie, Karma, "*The Book of Margery Kempe*: The Marginal Woman's Quest for Literary Authority". *Journal of Medieval and Renaissance Studies* 16 (1986): 33–55.

Lomperis, Linda and Stanbury, Sarah, eds. *Feminist Approaches to the Body in Medieval Literature*. Philadelphia: University of Pennsylvania Press, 1993.

Long, Kevin, "Echoes of Friendship: 'Amicitia' and 'Affectus' in the Writings of Aelred of Rievaulx with Special Reference to his Minor Works and the Monastic Foundations of his Theory". Diss. University of Western Australia, 1993.

Louth, A. *The Origins of the Christian Mystical Tradition from Plato to Denys*. Oxford: Clarendon Press, 1981.

———. "Bernard and Affective Mysticism". *The Influence of St. Bernard: Anglican Essays with an Introduction by Jean Leclerq O. S. B*. Ed. B. Ward. Oxford: Sisters of the Love of God Press, 1976. 1–10.

Love, Nicholas, *The Mirror of the Blessed Lyf of Jesu Christ*. Eds. J. Hogg and L. F. Powell. 2 vols. Salzburg: Institut für Anglistik und Amerikanistik, 1989.

———. *Nicholas Love's Mirror of the Blessed Life of Jesus Christ: A Critical Edition Based on Cambridge University Library Additional MSS 6578 and 6686*. Ed. M. G. Sargent. Garland Medieval Texts, 18. New York: Garland, 1992.

Lynch, Andrew, " 'Now, fye on youre wepynge!': Tears in Medieval English Romance". *Parergon: Bulletin of the Australia and New Zealand Association for Medieval and Renaissance Studies*. New Series 9/1 (1991): 43–62.

Machan, Tim William, *Textual Criticism and Middle English Texts*. Charlottesville and London: University Press of Virginia, 1994.

Macro Plays. Ed. Mark Eccles. EETS no. 262. London: Oxford University Press, 1969.

Madigan, Mary F. *The Passio Domini Theme in the Works of Richard Rolle: His Personal Contribution in its Religious, Cultural, and Literary Context*. Salzburg Studies in English Literature: Elizabethan and Renaissance Studies, 79. Salzburg: Institut für Anglistik und Amerikanistik, 1978.

Marguerite d'Oingt, *The Writings of Margaret of Oingt, Medieval Prioress and Mystic*. Trans. Renate Blumenfeld-Kosinski. Newburyport, Massachusetts: Focus Library of Medieval Women, 1990.

Marzac, Nicole, ed. *Richard Rolle de Hampole 1300–1349: Vie et œuvres suivies du Tractatus Super Apocalypsim*. Paris: Librairie Philosophique J. Vrin, 1968.

McGinn, Bernard, *The Presence of God: A History of Western Christian Mysticism*. New York: Crossroad, 1991.

———. "Love, Knowledge, and Mystical Union in Western Christianity: Twelfth to Sixteenth Centuries". *Church History* 56 (1987): 7–24.

McGregor, Graham and White, R. S., eds. *Reception Response: Hearer Creativity and the Analysis of Spoken and Written Texts*. London and New York: Routledge, 1990.

McGuire, Brian Patrick, "Holy Women and Monks in the Thirteenth Century: Friendship or Exploitation?" *Vox Benedictina* 6 (1991): 342–373.

———. *Friendship and Community: The Monastic Experience 350–1250*. Cistercian Studies Series, 95. Kalamazoo: Cistercian Publications, 1988.

Meadows, George D. "The Father of English Mysticism: Richard Rolle of Hampole, 1290–1349". *New Catholic World* 126 (1928): 456–460.

Meale, C. M., ed. *Women & Literature in Britain, 1150–1500*. Cambridge: Cambridge University Press, 1993.

Medcalf, Stephen, ed. *The Later Middle Ages*. London: Methuen, 1981.

Middle English Dictionary. Ed. Hans Kurath. 10 vols. Ann Arbor: University of Michigan Press, 1952–1998.

Migne, J.-P., ed. *Patrologia Latina*. Paris: Lutetiae Parisorum, 1844–1864.

Milosh, J. E. *The Scale of Perfection and the English Mystical Tradition*. Madison, Milwaukee and London: University of Wisconsin Press, 1966.

Millett, Bella, "Women in No Man's Land: English Recluses and the Development of Vernacular Literature in the Twelfth and Thirteenth Centuries". *Women and Literature in Britain 1150–1500*. Ed. C. M. Meale. Cambridge: Cambridge University Press, 1993. 86–103.

Millett, Bella and Wogan-Browne, Jocelyn, eds. *Medieval English Prose for Women*. Oxford: Clarendon Press, 1990.

Minnis, A. J., ed. *Latin and Vernacular: Studies in Late-Medieval Texts and Manuscripts*. Cambridge: D. S. Brewer, 1989.

———. *Medieval Theory of Authorship: Scholastic Literary Attitudes in the Later Middle Ages*. 2nd edition. Aldershot: Scholar Press, 1988.

———. "Affection and Imagination in *The Cloud of Unknowing* and Hilton's *Scale of Perfection*". *Traditio* 39 (1983): 323–366.

———. "Discussions of 'Authorial Role' and 'Literary Form' in Late-Medieval Scriptural Exegesis". *Beiträge zur Geschichte der deutschen Sprache und Literatur* 99 (1977): 37–65.

Minnis, A. J. and Scott, A. B., eds. [With the assistance of David Wallace.] *Medieval Literary Theory and Criticism, c.1100–c.1375: The Commentary Tradition*. Oxford: Clarendon Press, 1988.

Misyn, Richard, trans. *The Fire of Love and the Mending of Life or The Rule of Living of Richard Rolle*. Ed. Ralph Harvey. EETS (os) 106. London: Keegan Paul, Trench, Trübner & Co., 1896.

Moorman, F. W. "Richard Rolle, the Yorkshire Mystic". *Transactions of the Yorkshire Dialect Society* 3 (1914): 89–106.

Morgan, Margery, "Versions of the Meditations on the Passion Ascribed to Richard Rolle". *Medium Aevum* xxii (1953): 93–103.

Moyes, Malcolm, ed. *Richard Rolle's Expositio super Novem Lectiones Mortuorum: An*

Introduction and Contribution Towards a Critical Edition. 2 vols. Salzburg Studies in English Literature: Elizabethan & Renaissance Studies, 92: 12. Salzburg: Institut für Anglistik und Amerikanistik, 1988.

————. "The Manuscripts and Early Printed Books of Richard Rolle's *Expositio Super Novem Lectiones Mortuorum*". *The Medieval Mystical Tradition in England: Papers Read at Dartington Hall, July, 1984*. Ed. Marion Glasscoe. Cambridge: D. S. Brewer, 1984. 81–103.

Mueller, Janel A. "Autobiography of a New 'Creatur': Female Spirituality, Self-hood, and Authorship in the Book of Margery Kempe". *Women in the Middle Ages and the Renaissance: Literary and Historical Perspectives*. Ed. Mary Beth Rose. New York: Syracuse University Press, 1986. 155–171.

Muir, Lawrence, "The Influence of the Rolle and Wycliffite Psalters upon the Psalter of the Authorised Version". *Modern Language Review* 30 (1935): 302–310.

Myers, A. R., ed. *English Historical Documents IV, 1327–1485*. London: Eyre & Spottiswode, 1969.

Myrk, John, *Instructions for Parish Priests*. Ed. E. Peacock. EETS (os) 31 [1902]. Reprint. New York: Kraus, 1975.

————. *Mirk's Festial*. Ed. Theodore Erbe. EETS no. 96 [1905]. Reprint. New York: Kraus, 1973.

Myroure of Oure Ladye. Ed. J. H. Blunt. EETS (es) 19 [1873]. Reprint. New York: Kraus, 1973.

A Myrour to Lewde Men and Wymmen. Ed. V. Nelson. Middle English Texts, 14. Heidelberg: Carl Winter, 1981.

Netherton, William D. " 'Joy Gars Me Jangell': Affective Devotion in the English Writings of Richard Rolle". Diss. Texas Tech University, 1997.

Newman, Barbara, "Flaws in the Golden Bowl: Gender and Spiritual Formation in the Twelfth Century". *Traditio* 65 (1989–90): 111–146.

Nichols, John A. and Shank, Lillian Thomas, *Medieval Religious Women I: Peaceweavers*. Cistercian Studies Series, 72. Kalamazoo: Cistercian Publications Inc., 1987.

————. *Medieval Religious Women II: Distant Echoes*. Cistercian Studies Series, 72. Kalamazoo: Cistercian Publications Inc., 1984.

Noetinger, Maurice, "The Biography of Richard Rolle". *The Month* 147 (1926): 22–30.

————. ed. and trans. *Le Feu d'amour, le modéle de la vie parfaite, le Pater, par Richard Rolle l'ermite de Hampole*. Collection Mystiques Anglais. Tours: Maison Alfred Mâme, 1928.

Ogilvie-Thomson, S. J., ed. *Richard Rolle: Prose and Verse*. EETS (os) 293. London: Oxford University Press, 1988.

Oliger, P. L. "Regulae tres reclusorum et eremitarum angliae saec. xiii–xiv". *Antonianum* 3 (1928): 151–190 and 299–320.

Ong, Walter J. *Orality and Literacy: The Technologizing of the Word*. London and New York: Methuen, 1982.

————. "The Writer's Audience is Always a Fiction". *PMLA: Publications of the Modern Language Association of America* (1975): 9–21.

The Orcherd of Syon. Eds. Phyllis Hodgson and Gabriel Liegey. EETS (os) 258. London: Oxford University Press, 1966.

Pantin, W. A. "Instructions for a Devout and Literate Layman". *Medieval Learning and Literature: Essays Presented to Richard William Hunt.* Eds. J. J. G. Alexander and M. T. Gibson. Oxford: Clarendon Press, 1976. 398–422.

———. *The English Church in the Fourteenth Century.* Cambridge: Cambridge University Press, 1955.

———. "The Monk-Solitary of Farne: A Fourteenth-century English Mystic". *English Historical Review* 59 (1944): 162–186.

Parkes, M. B. "The Influence of the Concepts of *Ordinatio* and *Compilatio* on the Development of the Book". *Medieval Learning and Literature: Essays Presented to Richard William Hunt.* Eds. J. J. G. Alexander and M. T. Gibson. Oxford: Clarendon Press, 1976. 115–141.

Patch, Howard R. "Richard Rolle, Hermit and Mystic". *American Church Monthly* 28 (1928): 32–38, 108–114.

Pearsall, Derek, ed. *Manuscripts and Texts: Editorial Problems in Later Middle English Literature; Essays From the 1983 Conference at the University of York.* Cambridge: D. S. Brewer, 1987.

———. *Manuscripts and Readers in Fifteenth Century England: The Literary Implications of Manuscript Studies.* Cambridge: D. S. Brewer, 1983.

Pepler, Conrad, "English Spiritual Writers III: Richard Rolle". *Christian Review* 44 (1959): 78–89.

Perry, George G., ed. *English Prose Treatises of Richard Rolle de Hampole.* EETS (os) 20 [1866]. Reprint. New York: Kraus, 1974.

———. ed. *Religious Pieces in Prose and Verse.* EETS (os) 26 [1867]. Reprint. London: Kegan-Paul, Trench, Trübner, 1914.

Peters, Brad, "Rolle's Eroticised Language in *The Fire of Love*". *Mystics Quarterly* 21/2 (1995): 51–58.

Petroff, Elizabeth Alvilda, *Body and Soul: Essays on Medieval Women and Mysticism.* New York: Oxford University Press, 1994.

———. *Medieval Women's Visionary Literature.* New York: Oxford University Press, 1986.

Petry, R. C. *Late Medieval Mysticism.* Philadelphia: Westminster Press, 1957.

———. "Social Responsibility and the Late Medieval Mystics". *Church History* 21 (1952): 3–15.

Pezzini, Domenico, "The Theme of Passion in Richard Rolle and Julian of Norwich". *Religion in Poetry and Drama of the Late Middle Ages in England.* Eds. Piero Boitani and Anna Torti. Cambridge: D. S. Brewer, 1990. 29–66.

Pfaff, R. W. *New Liturgical Feasts in Later Medieval England.* Oxford Theological Monographs. Oxford: Clarendon Press, 1970.

Phillips, Stephen H. "Mysticism and Metaphor". *International Journal for the Philosophy of Religion* xxiii (1988): 17–41.

Pollard, William F. "Richard Rolle and the 'Eye of the Heart' ". *Mysticism and Spirituality in Medieval England.* Eds. Robert Boenig and William F. Pollard. Cambridge: D. S. Brewer, 1997. 85–105.

———. "The 'Tone of Heaven': Bonaventuran Melody and the Easter Psalm in Richard Rolle". *The Popular Literature of Medieval England.* Ed. Thomas J. Heffernan. Knoxville: University of Tennessee Press, 1985. 252–276.

Porete, Marguerite, *The Mirror of Simple Souls: A Middle English Translation.* Ed. Marilyn Doiron. Roma: Edizioni di storia e letteratura, 1968.

Power, Eileen Edna, *Medieval English Nunneries c. 1275–1535*. Cambridge Studies in Medieval Life and Thought. Cambridge: The University Press, 1922.

The Pricke of Conscience (Stimulus conscientiae): A Northumbrian Poem. Ed. R. Morris. Berlin: Philological Society, 1863.

Radice, Betty, ed. *The Letters of Abelard and Héloise*. Harmondsworth: Penguin, 1974.

Relihan, Robert, "Richard Rolle and the Tradition of Thirteenth-Century Devotional Literature". *14th Century English Mystics Newsletter* 4/4 (1978): 10–16.

Renevey, Denis, *Language, Self and Love: Hermeneutics in the Writings of Richard Rolle and the Commentaries of the Song of Songs*. Cardiff: University of Wales Press, 2001.

———. "Name above Names: the Devotion to the Name of Jesus from Richard Rolle to Walter Hilton's *Scale of Perfection I*". *The Medieval Mystical Tradition: England, Ireland and Wales*. Ed. Marion Glasscoe. Cambridge: D. S. Brewer, 1999. 103–121.

———. "The Name Poured Out: Margins, Illuminations and Miniatures as Evidence of Practice of Devotions to the Name of Jesus in Late Medieval England". *Analecta Cartusiana* 130 (1996): 127–147.

———. "The Moving of the Soul: The Functions of Metaphors of Love in the Writings of Richard Rolle and Antecedent Texts of the Medieval Mystical Tradition". Diss. Oxford University, 1993.

Renevey, Denis and Whitehead, Christiania, eds. *Writing Religious Women: Female Spiritual and Textual Practices in Late Medieval England*. Toronto: University of Toronto Press, 2000.

Richard of St. Victor, *Benjamin Minor*. Trans. Grover A. Zinn. *The Twelve Patriarchs; The Mystical Ark; Book Three of The Trinity*. The Classics of Western Spirituality. New York: Paulist Press, 1979.

———. *Richard of St. Victor: Selected Writings on Contemplation*. Trans. Clare Kirchberger. London: Faber & Faber Ltd., 1957.

———. *De Quattuor Gradibus Violentae Caritatis*. Textes Philosophiques du Moyen Age, 3. Paris: Librairie Philosophique J. Vrin, 1955.

———. *De Gratia Contemplationis. The Cell of Self-Knowledge: Seven Early English Mystical Treatises Printed by Henry Pepwell in 1521*. Ed. Edmund G. Gardner. London: Chatto and Windus, 1925.

Riehle, Wolfgang, "The Authorship of *The Prick of Conscience* Reconsidered". *Anglia: Zeitschrift für Englische Philologie* 111/1–2 (1993): 1–18.

———. *The Middle English Mystics*. Trans. Bernard Standring. London: Routledge & Kegan Paul, 1981.

Robbins, H. W. "An English Version of St. Edmund's *Speculum* Ascribed to Richard Rolle". *PMLA: Publications of the Modern Language Association of America* 40 (1925): 240–251.

Robertson, Elizabeth, *Early English Devotional Prose and the Female Audience*. Knoxville: University of Tennessee Press, 1990.

Rolle, Richard, "The Bee". *English Writings of Richard Rolle, Hermit of Hampole*. Ed. Hope Emily Allen. Oxford: Clarendon Press, 1931. 54–56.

———. "Canticum Amoris". Ed. Gabriel Liegey. *Traditio* 12 (1956): 369–391.

———. "Carmen Prosaicum". Ed. Gabriel Liegey. *Mediaeval Studies* (1957): 15–36.

———. "The Commandment". *Richard Rolle: Prose and Verse*. Ed. Sarah

Ogilvie-Thomson. EETS (os) 293. London: Oxford University Press, 1988. 34–39.

———. *Contra Amatores Mundi*. Ed. and trans. Paul Theiner. Berkeley: University of California Press, 1968.

———. "Desire and Delight". *Richard Rolle: Prose and Verse*. Ed. Sarah Ogilvie-Thomson. EETS (os) 293. London: Oxford University Press, 1988. 40.

———. "Ego Dormio". *Richard Rolle: Prose and Verse*. Ed. Sarah Ogilvie-Thomson. EETS (os) 293. London: Oxford University Press, 1988. 26–33.

———. *Emendatio vitae*. Ed. Nicholas Watson. *Richard Rolle's Emendatio vitae; Orationes ad honorem nominis Ihesu edited from Cambridge University Library MSS. Dd.v.64 and Kk.vi.20*. Centre for Medieval Studies. Toronto: Pontifical Institute of Medieval Studies, 1995.

———. "Encomium Nominis Ihesu". Part of *Super Canticum Canticorum* in Middle English. *Yorkshire Writers: Richard Rolle of Hampole, an English Father of the Church, and His Followers*. Ed. Carl Horstman. 2 vols. London: Swan Sonnenshein & Co., 1895–1896. Vol. 1. 186–191.

———. *English Psalter*. Ed. H. R. Bramley. *The Psalter Psalms of David and Certain Canticles, with a Translation and Exposition in English by Richard Rolle of Hampole*. Oxford: Clarendon Press, 1884.

———. "The Form of Living". *Richard Rolle: Prose and Verse*. Ed. Sarah Ogilvie-Thomson. EETS (os) 293. London: Oxford University Press, 1988. 1–25.

———. "Ghostly Gladness". *Richard Rolle: Prose and Verse*. Ed. Sarah Ogilvie-Thomson. EETS (os) 293. London: Oxford University Press, 1988. 41.

———. *Incendium Amoris*. Ed. Margaret Deanesly. Manchester: Longmans, Green & Co., 1915.

———. *Incendium Amoris*. Trans. Richard Misyn. *The Fire of Love and the Mending of Life or the Rule of Living of Richard Rolle*. Ed. Ralph Harvey. EETS (os) 106. London: Keegan Paul, Trench, Trübner & Co., 1896.

———. *Judica Me Deus*. Ed. John Philip Daly. Salzburg Studies in English Literature: Elizabethan and Renaissance Studies, 92: 14. Salzburg: Institut für Anglistik und Amerikanistik, 1984.

———. *Latin Psalter*. Ed. M. L. Porter. Ithaca: Cornell University Press, 1929.

———. "Lyrics". *Richard Rolle: Prose and Verse*. Ed. Sarah Ogilvie-Thomson. EETS (os) 293. London: Oxford University Press, 1988. 42–63.

———. "Meditation A". *Richard Rolle: Prose and Verse*. Ed. Sarah Ogilvie-Thomson. EETS (os) 293. London: Oxford University Press, 1988. 64–68.

———. "Meditation B". *Richard Rolle: Prose and Verse*. Ed. Sarah Ogilvie-Thomson. EETS (os) 293. London: Oxford University Press, 1988. 69–83.

———. *Melos Amoris*. *The Melos Amoris of Richard Rolle of Hampole*. Ed. E. J. F. Arnould. Oxford: Basil Blackwell, 1957.

———. *Orationes ad honorem nominis Ihesu*. *Richard Rolle's Emendatio vitae; Orationes ad honorem nominis Ihesu edited from Cambridge University Library MSS. Dd.v.64 and Kk.vi.20*. Ed. Nicholas Watson. Centre for Medieval Studies. Toronto: Pontifical Institute of Medieval Studies, 1995.

———. "The Seven Gifts of the Holy Spirit". *Yorkshire Writers: Richard Rolle of Hampole, an English Father of the Church, and His Followers*. Ed. Carl Horstmann. 2 vols. London: Swan Sonnenschein & Co., 1895–1896. Vol. 1. 196–197.

———. "Super Apocalypsim". *Richard Rolle de Hampole 1300–1349: Vie et œuvres suivies du Tractatus Super Apocalypsim.* Ed. Nicole Marzac. Paris: Librairie Philosophique J. Vrin, 1968. 118–173.

———. *Super Canticum Canticorum. Richard Rolle: Biblical Commentaries: Short Exposition of Ps. 20; Treatise on the Twentieth Psalm; Comment on the First Verses of the Canticle of Canticles; Commentary on the Apocalypse.* Trans. Robert Boenig, Salzburg: Institut für Anglistik und Amerikanistik, 1984.

———. "Super Lectiones Mortuorum". *Richard Rolle's Expositio Super Novem Lectiones Mortuorum.* Ed. Malcolm Moyes. 2 vols. Salzburg Studies in English Literature: Elizabethan and Renaissance Studies, 92: 12. Salzburg: Institut für Anglistik und Amerikanistik, 1988. 124–283.

———. "Ten Commandments". *Yorkshire Writers: Richard Rolle of Hampole, an English Father of the Church, and His Followers.* Ed. Carl Horstmann. 2 vols. London: Swan Sonnenschein & Co., 1895–1896. Vol. 1. 195–196.

Roman de la Rose. The Romance of the Rose/ by Guillaume de Lorris and Jean de Meun. Trans. Charles Dahlberg. Princeton: Princeton University Press, 1971.

Rosenthal, J. T. *The Purchase of Paradise.* London: Routledge & Keegan Paul, 1972.

Ross, Woodburn O. *Middle English Sermons.* EETS (os) 209. London: Oxford University Press, 1960.

Rubin, Miri, *Corpus Christi: The Eucharist in Late Medieval Culture.* Cambridge: Cambridge University Press, 1991.

Russell, Kenneth C. "Reading Richard Rolle". *Spirituality Today* 30 (1978): 65–80.

Russell, G. H. "Vernacular Instruction of the Laity in the Later Middle Ages in England: Some Texts and Notes". *Journal of Religious History* 2 (1962): 98–119.

Rygiel, Dennis, "Structures and Style in Rolle's *The Form of Living*". 14th Century English Mystics Newsletter 4/1 (1978): 6–15.

Saenger, Paul, "Silent Reading: Its Impact on Late Medieval Script and Society". *Viator* 13 (1982): 367–414.

Salter, Elizabeth, *Fourteenth-Century English Poetry: Contexts and Readings.* Oxford: Clarendon Press, 1983.

Sargent, Michael G., ed. *De Cella in Seculum: Religious and Secular Life and Devotion in Late Medieval England.* Cambridge: D. S. Brewer, 1989.

———. "Richard Rolle, Sorbonnard?" *Medium Aevum* 57 (1988): 284–289.

———. "Contemporary Criticism of Richard Rolle". *Analecta Cartusiana* 55 (1981): 160–205.

———. "A Source of the *Pore Caitiff* Tract of Man's Will". *Mediaeval Studies* 41 (1979): 535–539.

Savage, A. and Watson, N. *Anchoritic Spirituality: Ancrene Wisse and Associated Works.* The Classics of Western Spirituality. New York: Paulist Press, 1991.

Schneider, J. P. *The Prose Style of Richard Rolle of Hampole, with Special Reference to its Euphuistic Tendencies.* Baltimore: J. H. Furst, 1906.

Shahar, Shulamith, *The Fourth Estate: A History of Women in the Middle Ages.* London: Methuen Press, 1983.

Sheingorn, Pamela, " 'The Wise Mother': The Image of St. Anne Teaching the Virgin Mary". *Gesta* XXXII (1993): 69–80.

Shepherd, G. "English Versions of the Scriptures before Wyclif". *The Cambridge History of the Bible.* Ed. G. W. H. Lounpe. Cambridge: Cambridge University Press, 1969. 362–387.

———. ed. *Ancrene Wisse Parts 6 and 7.* London: Thomas Nelson, 1959.

Shoreham, William, *The Poems of William of Shoreham*. Ed. M. Konrath. EETS (es) 86. London: Kegan Paul, Trench, Trübner & Co., 1902.

Sisam, Celia and Kenneth, eds. *The Oxford Book of Medieval and English Verse*. Oxford: Clarendon Press, 1970.

Smedick, L. K. "Parallelism and Pointing in Rolle's Rhythmical Style". *Mediaeval Studies* 41 (1979): 404–67.

Smith, Lesley and Taylor, J. M., eds. *Women, The Book, and the Godly: Selected Proceedings of the St. Hilda's Conference, 1993*. Cambridge: D. S. Brewer, 1995.

South English Legendary. Eds. C. D'Evelyn and A. J. Mill. 3 vols. EETS (os) 235–236. London: Oxford University Press, 1956 and 1959.

Speculum Christiani: A Middle English Treatise of the Fourteenth Century. Ed. Gustaf Holmstedt. EETS (os) 182 [1933]. Reprint. New York: Kraus, 1971.

Stanbury, Sarah, " 'The Virgin's Gaze': Spectacle and Transgression in Middle English Lyrics of the Passion". *PMLA: Publications of the Modern Language Association of America* 106 (1991): 1083–1093.

Stevens, John, "*Angelus ad virginem*: the History of a Medieval Song". *Medieval Studies for J. A. W. Bennett: Aetatis Suae LXX*. Ed. P. L. Heyworth. Oxford: Clarendon Press, 1981. 297–328.

Stock, Brian, *The Implications of Literacy: Written Language and Models of Interpretation in the Eleventh and Twelfth Centuries*. Princeton, New Jersey: Princeton University Press, 1983.

Stuard, Susan Mosher, ed. *Women in Medieval History and Historiography*. Philadelphia: University of Philadelphia Press, 1987.

Sturges, Robert S. "Textual Scholarship: Ideologies of Literary Production". *Exemplaria* 3/1 (1991): 109–131.

Taavitsainen, Irma, "*Pater Noster*: A Meditation Connected with Richard Rolle in BL Royal MS. 17. C. XVII". *Neuphilologische Mitteilungen* 92 (1991): 31–41.

———. "*Ave Maria*: A Meditation Connected With Richard Rolle in Uppsala MS. C. 193 and BL Royal MS. 17. C. XVII". *Neuphilologische Mitteilungen* 91 (1990): 57–66.

Talbot, C. H., ed. and trans. *The Life of Christina of Markyate: A Twelfth-Century Recluse*. Oxford: Clarendon Press, 1959.

A Talkynge of the Loue of God. Ed. Sister M. Salvina Westra. The Hague: Martinus Nijhoff, 1950.

Tanner, Norman, *The Church in Late Medieval Norwich*. Toronto: Pontifical Institute of Medieval Studies, 1984.

Tarvers, Josephine Koster, " 'Thys ys my mystrys boke': English Women as Readers and Writers in Late Medieval England". *The Uses of Manuscripts in Literary Studies: Essays in Memory of Judson Boyce Allen*. Eds. Charlotte Cook Morse, Penelope Reed Doob and Margery Curry Woods. Studies in Medieval Culture, 31. Kalamazoo: Western Michigan University, Medieval Institute Publications, 1992. 305–327.

Taylor, Andrew, "Into his Secret Chamber: Reading and Privacy in Late Medieval England". *The Practice and Representation of Reading in England*. Eds. J. Raven, H. Small and N. Tadmar. Cambridge: Cambridge University Press, 1996. 41–61.

Thomas of Celano, "First and Second Life of St. Francis". Trans. P. Hermann. *St. Francis of Assisi, Writing and Earlier Biographies: English Omnibus of the Sources for the Life of St. Francis*. Ed. M. A. Habig. London: Society for Promoting Christian Knowledge, 1979.

Thompson, Sally, *Women Religious: The Foundation of English Nunneries After the Norman Conquest*. Oxford: Clarendon Press, 1991.

Thornton, Martin, *English Spirituality: An Outline of Ascetical Theology According to the English Pastoral Tradition*. London: Society for Promoting Christian Knowledge, 1963.

Tolkien, J. R. R. "*Ancrene Wisse* and *Hali Meiðhad*". *Essays and Studies* 14 (1929): 104–126.

Tompkins, Jane P., ed. *Reader-Response Criticism: From Formalism to Post-Structuralism*. Baltimore and London: The Johns Hopkins University Press, 1980.

A Devout Treatyse called The Tree & XII Frutes of the Holy Goost. Ed. Johannes Joseph Vassier. Groningen: J. B. Wolters, 1960.

Tretyse of Loue. Ed. J. H. Fisher. EETS (os) 223. London: Oxford University Press, 1951.

Tuma, George, *The Fourteenth Century English Mystics: A Comparative Analysis*. Salzburg Studies in English Literature: Elizabethan and Renaissance Studies, 62. 2 vols. Salzburg: Institut für Englische Sprache und Literatur, 1977.

Turville-Petre, Thorlac, *The Alliterative Revival*. Cambridge: D. S. Brewer, 1977.

Underhill, Evelyn, *Mystics of the Church*. New York: Schocken Books, 1964.

———. *Mysticism: A Study in the Nature and Development of Man's Spiritual Consciousness*. London: Methuen, 1911.

de Voragine, Jacobus, *The Golden Legend*. [Englished by William Caxton.] London: J. M. Dent, 1939.

Wakelin, M. F. "Richard Rolle and the Language of Mystical Experience in the Fourteenth Century". *Downside Review* 97 (1979): 192–203.

Warner, Marina, *Alone of All Her Sex: The Myth and the Cult of the Virgin Mary*. New York: Vintage Books, 1976.

Warren, Ann K. *Anchorites and their Patrons in Medieval England*. Berkeley: University of California Press, 1985.

———. "Nun as Anchoress: England 1100–1500". *Distant Echoes: Medieval Religious Women Vol. 1*. Eds. J. A. Nichols and L. T. Shank. Cistercian Studies Series, 71. Kalamazoo: Cistercian Publications, 1984. 197–212.

Watson, Nicholas, *Richard Rolle and the Invention of Authority*. Cambridge Studies in Medieval Literature, 13. Cambridge: Cambridge University Press, 1991.

———. "Translation and Self-Canonisation in Richard Rolle's *Melos Amoris*". *The Medieval Translator: The Theory and Practice of Translation in the Middle Ages*. Ed. Roger Ellis. Cambridge: D. S. Brewer, 1989. 167–180.

———. "Richard Rolle as Elitist and Popularist: the Case of *Judica Me*". *De Cella in Seculum: Religious and Secular Life and Devotion in Late Medieval England*. Ed. Michael G. Sargent. Cambridge: D. S. Brewer, 1989. 123–144.

———. "Methods and Objectives of Thirteenth-Century Anchoritic Devotion". *The Medieval Mystical Tradition in England: Papers Read at Dartington Hall, July, 1987*. Ed. Marion Glasscoe. Cambridge: D. S. Brewer, 1987. 132–154.

Watts, H. G. "Richard Rolle of Hampole". *New Catholic World* 103 (1916): 798–804.

Weinstein, D. and Bell, R. M. *Saints and Society: The Two Worlds of Western Christendom 1000–1700*. Chicago: University of Chicago Press, 1982.

Wilmart, A. *Auteurs spirituels et textes dévots du moyen âge latin*. Paris: Etudes augustiniennes, 1932.

Wilson, R. M. "Three Middle English Mystics". *Essays & Studies* 9 (1956): 87–112.

Wilson, W. Daniel, "Readers in Texts". *PMLA: Publications of the Modern Language Association of America* 96 (1981): 848–863.

Windeatt, Barry A. *English Mystics of the Middle Ages*. Cambridge: Cambridge University Press, 1994.

———. "Julian of Norwich and Her Audience". *Review of English Studies* New Series, 28 (1977): 1–17.

Wisdom. The Macro Plays: The Castle of Perseverance, Wisdom, Mankind. Ed. Mark Eccles. London: Oxford University Press, 1969. 113–152.

Wogan-Browne, Jocelyn, "Saints' Lives and the Female Reader". *Forum for Modern Language Studies* 7 (1991): 314–332.

Wogan-Browne, Jocelyn and Burgess, Glynn, eds. *Virgin Lives and Holy Deaths: Two Exemplary Biographies for Anglo-Norman Women*. London: J. M. Dent, 1996.

Wogan-Browne, Jocelyn, Watson, Nicholas, Taylor, Andrew and Evans, Ruth, eds. *The Idea of the Vernacular: An Anthology of Middle English Literary Theory 1280–1520*. Exeter: Exeter University Press, 1999.

The Wohunge of Ure Lauerd. Ed. W. Meredith Thompson. EETS (os) 241. London: Oxford University Press, 1958.

Wolters, Clifton, trans., *Richard Rolle: The Fire of Love*. London: Penguin Books, 1972.

Woolf, Rosemary, *Art and Doctrine: Essays on Medieval Literature*. Ed. Heather O'Donoghue. London: Hambledon Press, 1986.

———. *The English Religious Lyric in the Middle Ages*. Oxford: Clarendon Press, 1968.

Woolley, Reginald, *The Officium et Miracula of Richard Rolle of Hampole*. London: Society for Promoting Christian Knowledge, 1919.

Wright, Robert E. "The 'Boke Performyd': Affective Technique and Reader Response in the *Showings* of Julian of Norwich". *Christianity and Literature* 36/4 (1987): 13–32.

Zeeman, Elizabeth, "Continuity in Middle-English Devotional Prose". *Journal of English and Germanic Philosophy* lv (1956): 417–422.

INDEX